100 Excel Simulations

Dr. Gerard M. Verschuuren

Holy Macro! Books

PO Box 541731, Merritt Island FL 32953

100 Excel Simulations

(c) 2017 Gerard M. Verschuuren

Author: Dr. Gerard M. Verschuuren

Cover Design: Shannon Travise

Layout: Bill Jelen

Published by: Holy Macro! Holy Macro! Books, PO Box 541731, Merritt Island, FL 32953USA

Printed in USA

ISBN 978-1-61547-048-8 (Print)

978-1-61547-134-8 (Mobi)

978-1-61547-234-5 (PDF)

978-1-61547-357-1 (ePub)

LCCN 2016938256

Contents

Gambling

1. The Die Is Cast

What the simulation does

We start with a very simple case of simulation—casting a die (on sheet "Dice" in 1-Gambling.xlsx). In cell A1 is a formula that generates a random number between 1 and 6. According to that outcome, the colored die shows the appropriate number of eyes at their proper locations. Each time the random number changes, the die adjusts accordingly.

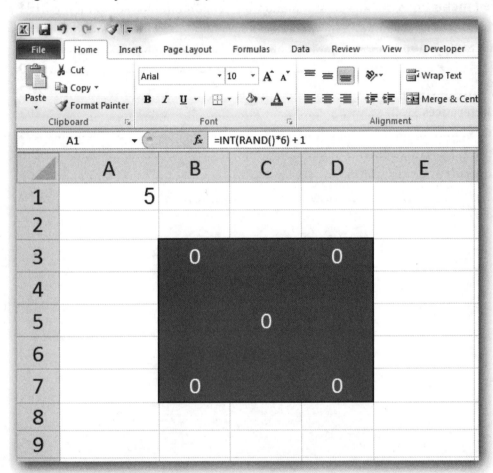

What you need to know

Cell A1 has a formula that uses a volatile function called RAND. On each recalculation, this function generates a new random number between 0 and 1. Because we want numbers between 1 and 6, we need to multiply by 6, round the number down by using the INT function, and then add 1 to the end result. More in general: =INT((high-low+1)*RAND()+low).

Users of Excel 2007 and later can also use the "easier" function RANDBETWEEN which has two arguments for the lower limit (in this case 1) and the upper limit (in this case 6). I decided not to use that function, because in pre-2007 Excel versions this function was only available through the *Analysis Toolpak*.

To generate a new random number, you either hit the key *F9* or the combination of the *Shift* key and the *F9* key. In this file, I would recommend the latter option (*Shift F9*), since that would only recalculate the current sheet—otherwise you would recalculate all sheets in this file, which may take lots of calculating time.

Finally, we need to regulate which eyes should pop up for each new random number. This is done inside some of the die cells by using the IF function. This function is a "decision maker," which determines whether a specific eye should be on or off.

What you need to do

1. Type in cell A1: =INT(RAND()*6) + 1. In this case, the function RAND is "nested" inside the function INT (INT eliminates decimals). Nested functions are very common in Excel; for more information, see Appendix 2.

2. Type in B3: =IF(A1>1,0,""). The two double quotes in the last argument return an empty string, showing up as nothing.

3. Type in D3: =IF(A1>3,0,"").

4. Type in B5: =IF(A1=6,0,"").

5. Type in D5: =IF(A1=6,0,"").

6. Type in B7: =IF(A1>3,0,"").

7. Type in D7: =IF(A1>1,0,"").

8. Type in C5: =IF(OR(A1=1,A1=3,A1=5),0,""). In this case, the function OR is nested inside IF. The function OR returns "true" if any of the enclosed arguments is "true."

9. If you want to see all formulas at once, hit *Ctr* ~ (the tilde can be found below the *Esc* key). This shortcut toggles the sheet, back and forth, between value-view and formula-view.

	A	B	C	D	
1	=INT(RAND()*6) + 1				
2					
3		=IF(A1>1,0,"")		=IF(A1>3,0,"")	
4					
5		=IF(A1=6,0,"")	=IF(OR(A1=1,A1=...	=IF(A1=6,0,"")	
6					
7		=IF(A1>3,0,"")		=IF(A1>1,0,"")	
8					
9					

2. Casting Six Dice

What the simulation does

Open file 1-Gambling.xlsx on sheet "6-Dices." This time we have six different dice. Each die "listens" to a random number above it, to its left.

The settings for each die are similar to what we did in Simulation 1. The number of eyes for each die is plotted in a column chart below the dice.

A die that shows six eyes gets marked with a color. When there are at least 2 dice in a row with six eyes, all dice get marked at the same time.

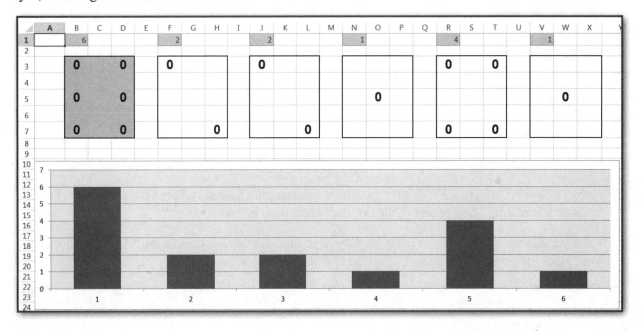

What you need to know

There is not much new on this sheet. The main difference is that we need 6 different cells with a RAND function in order to control the six die displays. Each die has the same structure as the one used in Simulation 1.

In addition, we use conditional formatting to change colors of the dice when they show six eyes, or contain at least two dice with six eyes.

What you need to do

1. Make sure all six dice are set up as was done in Simulation 1, but each die is connected to the random cell just above it.

2. Select range A1:C7 first, then Home | Conditional Format | Formula: =$A$1=6.

3. Do something similar for the other five dice.

4. Finally select A3:W7 (that is all six dice) and format them conditionally:
   =COUNTIF($A$1:$U$1,6)>=2.

5. By using (Sh) F9, you may hit a situation like below where at least two dice have six eyes (F9 recalculates all the sheets of the entire file, whereas Sh F9 only does so for the current sheet and may take less time).

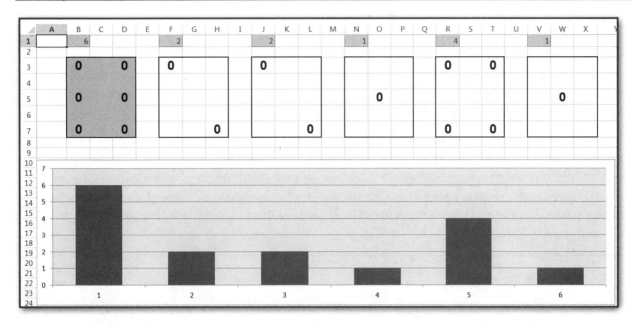

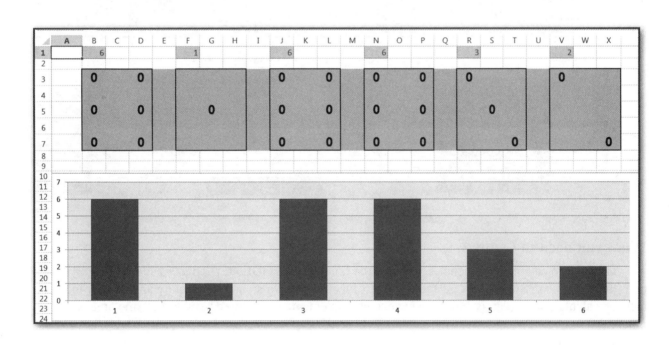

3. Frequencies

What the simulation does

Open file 1-Gambling.xlsx on sheet "Frequencies." This time we cast two dice at once and sum the number of eyes in column C; we repeat this process 9 more times. In column F, we calculate how often we had a hit of 2 eyes in total, 3 eyes, and so on, up to 12 eyes.

The frequencies are plotted in a graph. Cell F14 calculates the average of column C. It turns color for extreme values. The average is also plotted in the graph as a vertical line—based on the two sets of coordinates shown in E16:F17.

The curve keeps changing each time we hit *Shift F9*. Very rarely does it come close to a normal distribution with a mean somewhere in the center. The chance for this to happen would increase if we would have used more dice and more repeats.

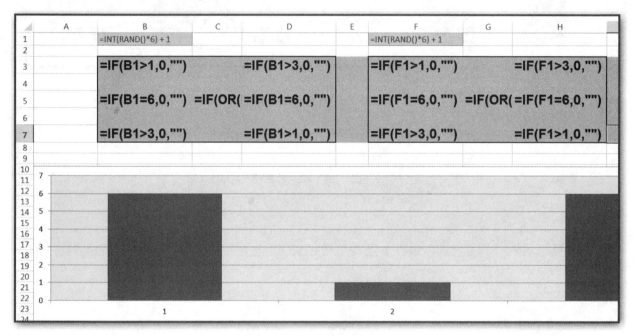

What you need to know

On order to calculate frequencies, we need the function FREQUENCY. This is a so-called *array* function (more on this in Simulations 62 and 63). Such functions return an array or require an array for intermediate calculations. All array functions have to be implemented with three keys at the same time: *Ctr Sh Enter*.

The function FREQUENCY returns an array of multiple answers based on a set of "bins." In this case, the bins are in column E. The function "reads" the bins as follows: 2 covers all cases up to and including 2, 3 covers all cases >2 and <=3, etc. To make this function work, you need to select all the cells that are going to hold the frequency values all at once, before you use the array function. Once the array function has been implemented with *Ctr Sh Enter*, you will see the formula in the formula bar surrounded by braces—like this: {=FREQUENCY(…,…)}. Do not type the braces; they come automatically with *Ctr Sh Enter*.

Changing colors of cells under certain conditions is done with so-called conditional formatting (located under the *Home* tab). When the specified conditions kick in, the cell will be formatted according to certain settings. In our case, we want to flag averages under 5.5 and over 8.5, which requires an OR function.

What you need to do

1. Column C sums the eyes of both dice.

2. Select the entire range F2:F12 first, before you implement =FREQUENCY(C2:C11,E2:E12), and then hit *Ctr Sh Enter*. Notice the braces in the formula bar.

3. Type in cell F14: =AVERAGE(C2:C11).

4. Select cell F14, Home | Conditional Formatting | New Rule | Use a Formula | =OR($F$14<5.5,$F$14>8.5) | Format color.

5. The average line in the graph is based on a new series of values with two sets of coordinates: E16:E17 for the X-values, and F16:F17 for the Y-values.

6. Hit *Sh F9* for new simulations. As they say, "Results may vary" (see below).

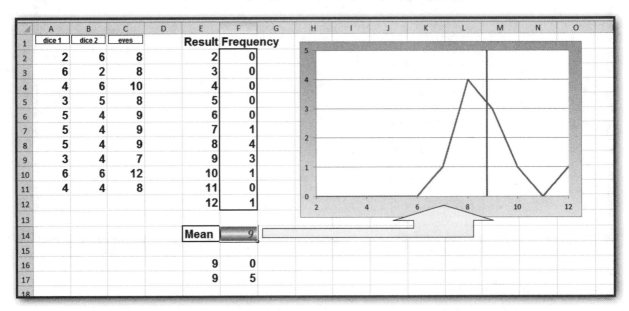

4. Roulette Machine

What the simulation does

Open file 1-Gambling.xlsx on sheet "Roulette." Column A simulates a roulette with 1,000 random numbers between 1 and 36. In column B, you type 1 if you expect the next number to be odd—otherwise 2 for even.

Column E keeps the score: it adds 1, when your prediction was correct—otherwise it subtracts 1. Once you are finished, you can just empty your predictions in B2:B1001—and start all over (you may need *Sh F9*, though).

	A	B	C	D	E	F
1		1 (odd) or 2 (even)		Score:	0	
2	1	1			1	
3	33	1			2	
4	27	1			3	
5	11					
6						
7						
8						

What you need to know

Most people believe that if they keep consistently betting "odd," the ball will most certainly land on an odd number sometime soon. This is called "the law of averages" which says, the longer you wait for a certain random event, the more likely it becomes.

Do not believe it! Try it out in this "real life" simulation and find out how the casino makes money on people who think that way. You may initially gain but eventually lose.

What you need to do

1. Column A has 1,000 random numbers. They were once generated and then changed into values. You will not see all of them because 999 of them are hidden through conditional formatting.

2. Cell E2 has this formula: =IF(MOD(A3,2)=B2,E1+1,E1-1). Copy the formula down to E1001. The MOD function divides a number by 2 and returns the remainder. The remainder is either 0 or 1 here. If what the user had predicted in column B is correct, the score goes up by 1—otherwise down by 1.

3. Select range A3:A1001 and apply the following conditional formatting formula: =$B2="". Notice that B is locked but 2 is not (see Appendix 1 on this issue). Format the entire range to a white font—which means you will not see this number if the cell in the next column of the previous row is still empty, but it will show its value once that cell has been filled with either 1 (odd) or 2 (even).

4. Validate range B2:B1001 with this custom formula: =OR($B2=1,$B2=2). So the cell accepts only 1s or 2s.

5. Now you can make your predictions for every next roulette outcome—either 1 or 2. You may have to hit *Sh F9* each time if the file has been set to manual calculation (or change that).

6. To start all over, just clear the colored cells in column B (and again you may have to manually recalculate the sheet).

7. Notice how easily you can lose by going for the "law of averages" by repeating constantly 1 for "odd" or 2 for "even."

		1 (odd) or 2 (even)		Score:	0	
1						
2	1	1			1	
3	33	1			2	
4	27	1			3	
5	11	1			2	
6	16	1			3	
7	17	1			2	
8	14	1			1	
9	26					
10						

5. Gambler's Ruin

What the simulation does

Open file 1-Gambling.xlsx on sheet "Addiction." This sheet simulates what may happen to people who are addicted to gambling.

The player has 100 chances (in column A) to go for odd or even. We simulate a 50% probability for either choice. If the choice was correct, the count in column A goes up by 1, otherwise it goes down by 1.

Next we simulate that this addicted player repeats the game for some twenty more times. For each game, we calculate average, minimum, maximum, standard deviation, and the final score (in column H). At the end, we calculate how often the player had a positive final score, and how often a negative one. This looks like much more work than it actually is…

	A	B	C	D	E	F	G	H	I
1	0			average	min	max	SD	final	
2	1			-8.7	-16	1	4.790	-13	
3	0			-9.9	-17	0	4.436	-13	
4	-1			-12.6	-20	0	4.667	-17	
5	0			-4.1	-15	6	5.827	-11	
6	1			10.4	-1	23	6.921	23	
7	0			0.8	-8	14	6.043	13	
8	1			-4.8	-10	1	3.113	-9	
9	0			6.5	0	14	2.376	13	
10	-1			5.4	-1	12	3.513	1	
11	-2			-8.2	-16	1	4.460	-11	
12	-1			-7.4	-14	0	3.074	-1	
13	0			-10.5	-18	0	3.852	-13	
14	1			-3.2	-8	3	2.533	1	
15	0			-5.7	-11	0	2.784	-5	
16	-1			-9.1	-16	0	3.851	-9	
17	-2			-1.7	-7	4	2.663	-5	
18	-3			-2.4	-19	8	6.918	-17	
19	-4			7.8	-1	14	3.641	9	
20	-5			-2.0	-9	8	3.801	5	
21	-4			-1.0	-9	6	4.488	5	
22	-5			11.6	0	22	4.972	21	
23	-6								
24	-5						below	12	
25	-4						above	9	
26	-5								

What you need to know

In column A, we use the RAND function for each individual choice the player makes. Then we simulate doing this 20 more times in the right table. To do so, we use Excel's *Data Table* tool (see more details in Appendix 3). I consider this an ideal tool for *what-if* analysis.

How does it work? Usually Data Tables have a formula in the first cell—which would be cell C1 in our case. Based on that formula, a Data Table typically uses a row input of variables and a column input of variables to recalculate the formula placed at its origin. It does so by filling the table cells with a formula that has the following syntax: =TABLE(row-input, col-input).

In this case we use a what-if table merely to trick Excel into simulating 20 (or many more) iterations of column A. We do so by not placing a formula at the origin, by leaving the row-input argument empty, and having the col-input argument refer to an empty cell somewhere outside the table. Yes, that does the trick!

What you need to do

1. Place in cell A2: =IF(RAND()>0.5,A1+1,A1-1).

2. Copy this formula down for 100 rows.

3. Place in cell D2: =AVERAGE(A:A). Do something similar with MAX (in E2), MIN (in F2), and ST-DEV (in G2).

4. Place in cell H2 a reference to the last cell in column A.

5. Now select C2:H22 (yes, the empty cell C2, not D2).

6. Start the table: Data | What-If Analysis | Data Table.

7. Set the row input to nothing and the column input to an empty cell outside the table (say, J2).

8. This automatically places the following formula in the range D2:H22 (yes, D2 this time): {=TABLE(,J2)}. Do not type this formula or the braces—both kick in automatically.

9. # of negative scores in H24: =COUNTIF($H$2:$H$22,"<0").

10. # of positive scores in H25: =COUNTIF($H$2:$H$22,">0").

11. Select H2:H22: Home | Conditional Formatting | Data Bars (the last option is not available in pre-2007).

12. Notice how the Data Table runs 20 x 100 choices each time you hit the keys *Sh F9*. That's what addiction does!

6. Random Walk

What the simulation does

Open file 1-Gambling.xlsx on sheet "RandomWalk." Another way of looking at the situation discussed in Simulation 5 is a *random-walk* approach. As we leave home (position 0), if we flip a coin and get heads, we go one block north (position +1); if we flip tails, we go one block south (position -1). We keep doing this many times and then check how far we end up being from home. (We may also ask what the probability is that we return to where we started—believe it or not, 100% for long, long walks.)

We will simulate first 50 steps for *one* dimension (north-south, in column B, plotted in the top graph as up and down). Then we will do this for *two* dimensions (north-east-south-west, in columns B and C, plotted in the bottom graph). As it turns out, we could make big "gains" and drift far away from where we started.

But not always! In the table to the right, we repeated all 50 steps 14 times. If this random-walk were interpreted as a case of gambling, we could encounter many negative, perhaps even huge outcomes—"losses" in gambling terms.

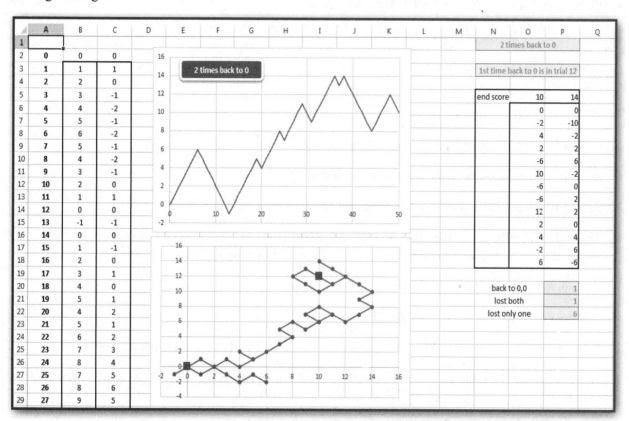

What you need to know

We are going to use a few new functions. First we want to find out in which row position in column B, we did reach position 0 again. To do so, we need the function MATCH to locate in which row the first 0 was found. MATCH has 3 arguments: what to match, in which range, and with which match type (0 for an exact match, 1 for an ascending list, -1 for a descending list).

If MATCH can't find "its match," we get an error. To avoid this, we can use the function IFERROR which allows us to specify in its second argument what to display when there is an error.

In addition to COUNTIF, there is also a function COUNTIFS (missing in pre-2007), which allows for multiple count criteria.

What you need to do

1. Place in cell B3: =IF(RAND()<0.5,B2-1,B2+1). Copy this formula down to cell B1007. RAND determines whether we go one down or one up. This populates the top graph.

2. In cell N1, we display how often the random walk got us back to 0: =COUNTIF(B3:B52,0) & " times back to 0". The ampersand (&) is an operator that "hooks" things together.

3. In cell N3, we display in which row we got back to 0 for the first time: ="1st time back to 0 is in trial " & IFERROR(MATCH(0,B3:B52,0),"-"). Be aware that this is not Excel's row number, but the run number (in column A).

4. Now we make the random walk *two*-dimensional by placing in cell C3: =IF(RAND()<0.5,C2-1,C2+1). Copy this down.

5. Now the bottom graph populates with 2-D random walks. (The start and end positions are marked differently).

6. Select range N5:P18 for a Data Table with no row input and an empty cell (e.g. cell M5) for the column input. This creates the following array formula: =TABLE(,M5).

7. In cell P20: =COUNTIFS(O5:O18,0,P5:P18,0). This counts how often the coordinates 0, 0 popped up in the Data Table.

8. In cell P21: =COUNTIFS(O5:O18,"<0",P5:P18,"<0"). This counts how often we ended up losing in both columns.

9. In P22, we count how often we lost in one column: =SUM(COUNTIFS(O5:O18,"<0",P5:P18,">0"),COUNTIFS(O5:O18,">0",P5:P18,"<0")).

10. Apply Conditional Formatting to B2:B52: =$B$52<0. A loss.

11. And to B2:C52: =AND($B$52=0,$C$52=0). Back to 0,0.

7. Gambling Strategy

What the simulation does

Open file 1-Gambling.xlsx on sheet "Strategy." Let's pretend you are a persistent, but very systematic, gambler. You decide ahead of time how to spend your different kinds of banknotes, which is specified in range D1:E5. The left columns in the chart display these settings as well.

Then we let the machine determine one hundred times, in column A, when and which kind of banknotes to use and in which order. This is a random process, but within the margins set in D1:E5. The results are shown in the right columns of the chart.

Although the process is random, it follows a discrete distribution which comes always very close to what you would expect.

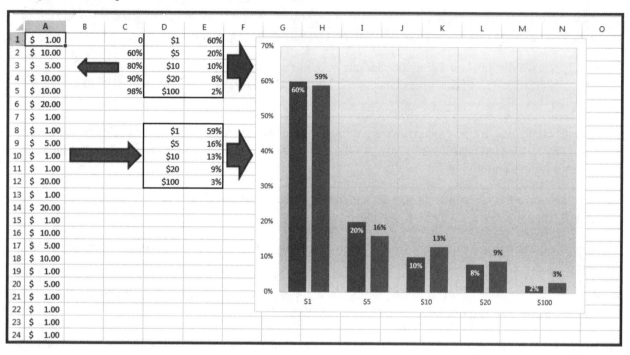

What you need to know

In order to let column A determine which banknote to choose, we call the function RAND to create a random percentage between 0 and 1 (0% and 100%). Then the function VLOOKUP uses this percentage to find the corresponding type of banknote.

However, VLOOKUP always searches *vertically*, from top to bottom, in the *first* column of a table and then finds a corresponding value in a column to the right, specified by a *number*. So we need a lookup column before D1:D5 in order to determine the type of banknote to use. Besides, VLOOKUP looks for the previous value in an *ascending* order, so it would find $1 for all percentages between 0% and 60%, $5 between 60% and 80%, and $100 for percentages greater than or equal to 98%.

So, we need cumulative totals in the first column shown below, starting at 0%. The third column is now redundant, but is still needed for the chart to the right in order to show the expected frequencies—versus the randomly generated frequencies.

0	$1	60%
60%	$5	20%
80%	$10	10%
90%	$20	8%
98%	$100	2%

What you need to do

1. Place in cell C1 the number 0 (or 0%).

2. Place in cell C2: =SUM($E$1:E1). This is a combination of an absolute ("locked") and a relative ("unlocked") cell reference. (See Appendix 1 for more information.)

3. Copy this formula down to E5. This creates cumulative totals.

4. Place in cell A1: =VLOOKUP(RAND(),$C$1:$D$5,2). Copy this formula down to cell A100. This formula does the random work in accordance with a frequency table (C1:D5), where it finds the corresponding type of banknote in column 2 (specified by the last argument in the function).

5. In order to calculate the actual frequencies for the various banknotes, we use the *array* function FREQUENCY in cells E8:E12: =FREQUENCY(A1:A100,D8:D12)/100. Make sure you select E8:E12 ahead of time, place the formula, and then accept this formula with *Ctr Sh Enter*. (For more info on array formulas see Simulation 65).

6. Each time you hit (*Sh*) *F9*, column A updates, as do the right columns in the chart. Notice how close you stay to your preset expectations—but "results may vary," as the saying goes.

8. Cracking a Password

What the simulation does

Open file 1-Gambling.xlsx on sheet "Password." This is not a real password cracker, of course—that would at least require VBA code. But we can still mimic part of the process. Let us assume that the password is "pass." This is a 4-letter word, so if we only use the characters a-z (no capitals), then we would still have 26^4 possible combinations—which amounts to 456,976.

Since Excel 2003 has only 65536 rows, we will limit ourselves to that number of rows. This means of course that we may not hit the right combination in one run. Increasing the number of rows would increase our chances but also our calculation time.

In the example below, we were "lucky enough" to find one matching combination in row 33596.

	A	B	C	D	E	F	G
1	nudi						
2	ngde						
3	kous						
4	bonr		Password:	pass			
5	tjkk						
6	huoe		Combinations:	456,976			
7	uhjg						
8	bddb						
9	pdvk						
10	fzba						
11	goxx		Count:	1			
12	ffru		Found in row:	33596	Type A33596 in the Name Box and hit Enter		
13	byil						
14	mddo						
15	iici						
16	tjif						
17	ohjt						
18	qpow						

What you need to know

There is a function called CHAR which returns the character that comes with a certain *asci* number. The numbers 97 through 122 represent the characters a through z. (To find out what the *asci* number of a certain key is, you could use the function CODE; for instance, CODE("a") would give you the number 97.)

Now we should be able to generate random numbers between 97 and 122 by using either RANDBETWEEN(97,122) or ROUND(RAND()*(122-97)+97,0).

In addition, we need the ampersand operator (&) which hooks characters together—four in a row, this time. Instead you could use the function CONCATENATE.

We also need the function MATCH again to locate in which row the match was found. MATCH has 3 arguments: what to match, in which range, and with which match type (0 for an exact match, 1 for an ascending list, -1 for a descending list).

What you need to do

1. The cells A1:A65536 hold the following formula:
    =CHAR(RANDBETWEEN(97,122))&CHAR(RANDBETWEEN(97,122))&CHAR(RANDBE
    TWEEN(97,122))&CHAR(RANDBETWEEN(97,122)).

2. Cell D11 counts the number of matches: =COUNTIF(A:A,D4).

3. Cell D12 finds the row position of the match: =MATCH(D4,A:A,0).

4. Place in cell E12: =”Type A” & D12 & “ in the Name Box and hit Enter”.

5. Very often no match will be found (see below); very seldom you may get two, or even more, matches.

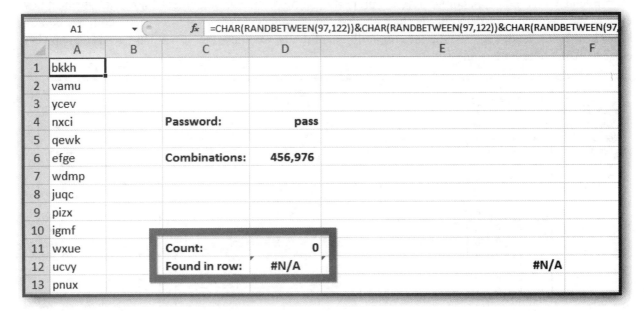

9. A Fair Coin?

What the simulation does

Open file 2-Statistics.xlsx on sheet "FairCoin." It is about flipping a coin six times, calculating how often we hit six times "tails" (0), five times, and so on (column A). The most likely outcome is 3x "heads" (X) and 3x "tails" (0)—actually 31% of all cases (column F); the center curve in the graph is a "bell-shaped" curve that represents this situation. Going more to the left or to the right under the bell-shaped curve, the chances decrease dramatically, but they will not become 0.000000000000.

Events with random outcomes have the property that no particular outcome is known in advance; however, in the aggregate, the outcomes occur with a specific frequency. When we flip a "fair" coin, we do not know how it will land, but if we flip the coin millions of times, we know that it will land heads (X) up very close to 50% of the time—unless...

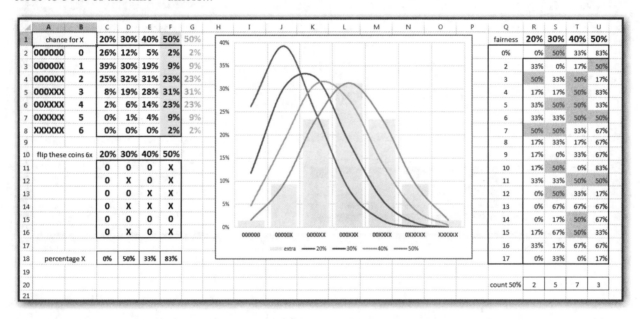

Unless... the coin is not "fair" and has a "preference" for lower X percentages (columns C:E and the other curves in the graph). To determine whether a coin is fair or not, we would need to flip a coin millions of times. In this simulation we only simulated some 100 coin tosses. In the situation shown above, we would probably declare the fair coin unfair (column U). They call this a *Type I error*—a false alarm. And we probably would declare the unfair coins (in columns S and T) fair—which would be a *Type II error* (more on this in Simulation 16). It is clear we need many more flips for a reliable verdict.

What you need to know

The bell-shaped curve is very common in statistics. It is also called a "normal distribution." In order to create this curve for a binary situation—such as yes/no, correct/defect, heads/tails, success/failure—we need the function BINOMDIST. All –DIST functions in Excel are statistical functions that return a probability or percentage, in this case for a binomial situation.

What you need to do

1. Place in cell C2 the following statistical formula: =BINOMDIST($B2,6,C$1,0). This specifies the number of successes (from 0-6 in B2:B8), out of 6 trials (6 coin tosses), with 50% probability of success, in a non-cumulative way.

2. Notice how certain references are "locked" (see Appendix 1 for more details), so you can copy the formula to cell G8.

3. In column F, the highest percentage should be for 3 times "heads" (equal to 3 times "tails"), because this is a "fair" coin. In the other columns, the coins are not fair.

4. In cell C11, we simulate a random flip of the first coin:
   =IF(RAND()<=C$10,"X","0"). Copy this formula to cell F16.

5. In C18, we count the percentage of heads (X) or tails:
   =COUNTIF(C11:C16,"X")/6. Copy the formula to cell F18.

6. We expect cell F18, the fair coin, to be 50%, but because we flip the coin only 6x, chance kicks in—so "results may vary."

7. To repeat each session of 6 flips some 16 more times, we use a Data Table. Place in Q2:
   =C18. In R2: =C18. In S2: = D18. In T2: =E18. In U2: =F18.

8. Select range Q2:U18 and start a Data Table with no row input and an empty cell (e.g. P2) for column input: =TABLE(,P2).

9. Conditional format in R3:U18: Cell Value | Equal to | =0.5.

10. Notice how hard it is to decide whether a coin is fair or not.

10. The Mean of Means

What the simulation does

Open file 2-Statistics.xlsx on the sheet called "MeanOfMeans." Each row represents a sample of 10 random numbers between 0 and 10 with an average in column L.

At the bottom of column L is the average of all 20 averages—the mean-of-the-means, so to speak.

In columns N and O is a frequency table for all the means found in column L. This table is plotted in the graph. The *mean*-of-the-means is shown as a vertical line in the graph.

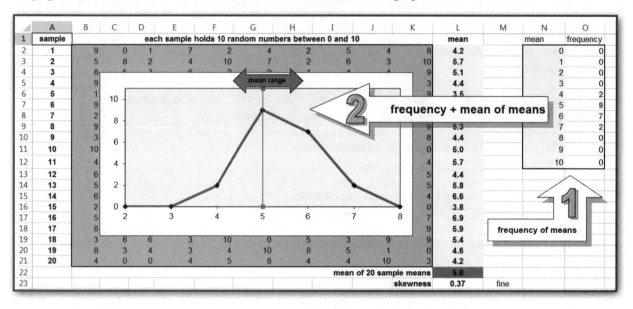

What you need to know

Each time you hit *Sh F9*, Excel recalculates all random numbers plus their averages, etc.

Notice how the means in column L can change dramatically, because each one is based on a sample of only 10 random numbers.

The mean-of-means, on the other hand, does not change that much, as it represents 10 x 20 = 200 random numbers—so it varies within a rather narrow range. This is called the "law of the large numbers" in statistics. Notice also how the curve resembles a normal distribution most of the time, but not always.

To get an idea of the symmetry of the curve, we could use the function SKEW, which finds a numeric value for the skewness of the curve. For more information on this issue, see Simulation 17.

What you need to do

1. Each cell in the range B2:K20 holds the formula =INT(RAND()*11). The INT function eliminates decimals.

2. Cell L2 calculates the average: =AVERAGE(B2:K2), and copy that formula down to cell L21 (not L22).

3. Cell L22 finds the *mean of the means*: =AVERAGE(L2:L21).

4. Cell L23 calculates the skewness: =SKEW(L2:L20).

5. Cell M23 judges the skewness based on this thumb rule:
    =IF(ABS(L23)>1,"highly",IF(ABS(L23)>0.5,"moderate","fine")). The outcome will be "fine" most of the time.

6. The range O2:O12 creates a frequency distribution and holds the following formula:
    =FREQUENCY(L2:L21,N2:N12). Remember, it needs to be applied to the entire range at once, followed by *Ctr Sh Enter*.

7. The curve in the graph is based on the frequency table.

8. The vertical line in the graph represents the mean of the means and is based on two sets of coordinates, hidden in cells N5:O6. The first set is in cell N5 (0) and O5 (=L22). The second set is in cell N6 (11) and O6 (=L22).

9. Hit *Sh F9* repeatedly to watch the results of this simulation.

10. The shape of the curve will obviously vary, but the mean stays within a rather narrow range (see below).

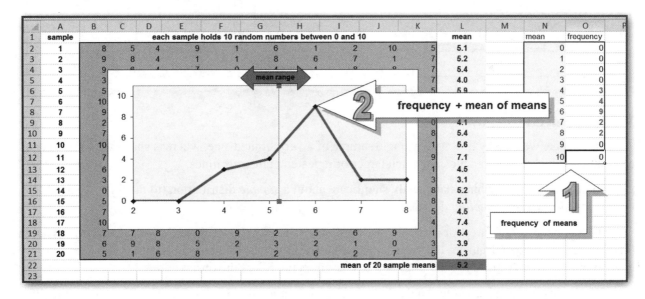

11. Sampling

What the simulation does

Open file 2-Statistics.xlsx on the sheet called "Sampling." The center part is the same as in Simulation 10, but the frequency tables on both sides differ from each other.

The left one calculates frequencies for one specific sample—in this case, the sample of 10 cases in row 6. The right one calculates frequencies for the means of all 20 samples.

Notice how the graph to the right displays a curve that usually comes close to a normal distribution, whereas the one to the left does not at all. The left one shows a *sample* distribution, but the right one a *sampling* distribution.

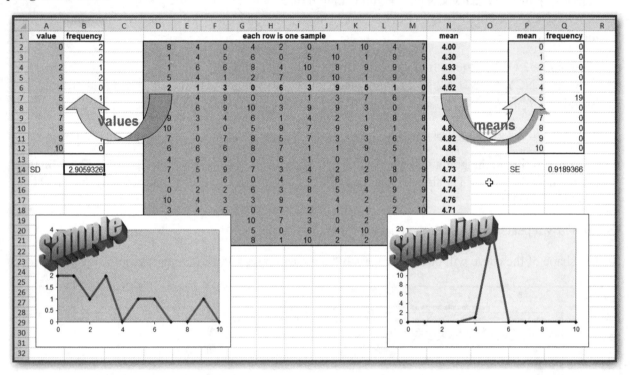

What you need to know

In science, we usually deal with a single sample of a very limited size, whereas statistics wants to deal with situations where the samples are much larger or repeated numerous times.

In order to say something statistically significant about a *sample* distribution (to the left), we need a way to assess what the *sampling* distribution (to the right) would be like.

Two important measures for a sample distribution are the average (or mean) and the standard deviation (or SD). All we have on hand are the mean and standard deviation as found in the sample (to the left). So we have to obtain an *estimate* of the SD of the means based on the SD of the observations.

We do this by calculating the standard error (SE), also called the relative SD. The formula for the SE is as follows: $=SD / \sqrt{n}$. As you can gather from this formula, SE decreases when the sample size increases—and, of course, when SD decreases.

What you need to do

1. The center part is the same as in Simulation 10.

2. Range B2:B12: =FREQUENCY(D6:M6,A2:A12).

3. Range Q2:Q12: =FREQUENCY(N2:N21,P2:P12).

4. Cell B14: =STDEV(D6:M6). There is also a function STDEVP, which is appropriate when dealing with the entire population, not one of its samples.

5. Cell Q14: =B14/SQRT(10). This calculates the *sampling* SE based on the *sample* SD divided by the square root of 10 cases.

6. Hit *Sh F9* to see new simulations. The left graph may vary wildly, but the right one remains more or less stable, staying close to a normal distribution (see below).

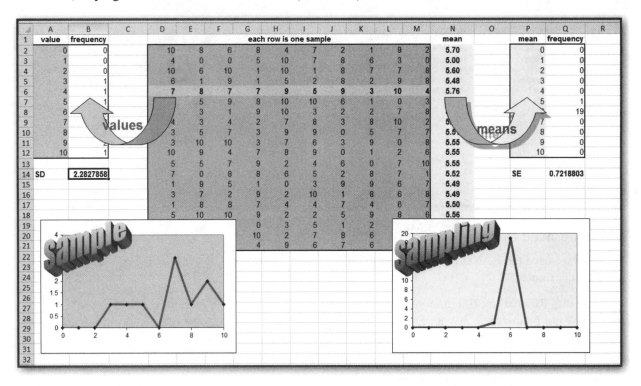

12. The Normal Distribution

What the simulation does

Open file 2-Statistics.xlsx on the sheet called "SimulNorm." This is a "dead" simulation—it will never update, because the 100 random numbers in column A are fixed values created with a special Excel tool that generates these random number according to a specific distribution pattern (in this cas,e the "bell shape" of a normal distribution).

We calculated the frequencies for these 100 random numbers in column E, and then calculated what the probabilities would be for the values in column D, if we were dealing with an *ideal* normal distribution.

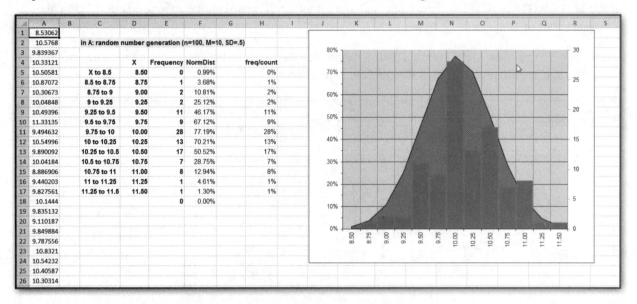

What you need to know

Had we used the RAND function, the random numbers would be "all over the place"—*equally* but not *normally* distributed.

The tool for creating 100 random numbers with a normal distribution pattern is Excel's *Analysis Tool-pak*. It may not be installed on your Excel machine until you go to File | Excel Options | Add-Ins | Excel Add-Ins (at the bottom) | Go | ☑ Analysis Toolpak. From now on, you can find this tool under Data | Data Analysis.

We also need the function NORMDIST. Being a DIST function, it finds the probability of finding a certain value (X) in a population with a specific mean and a specific standard deviation, either in a cumulative (true) or non-cumulative way (false).

What you need to do

1. Select cell A1, then Data| Data Analysis | Random Number Generation | OK | Number of variables: 1 | Number of random numbers: 100 | Distribution: Normal | Mean: 10 | Standard Deviation: 0.5 | (Random Seed is optional; perhaps 5) | Output Range: A1 | OK.

2. Notice that all numbers are hard-coded and will not change until you run the *Analysis Toolpak* again.

3. Place in E5:E18 all at once: =FREQUENCY(A:A,D5:D17). Notice we included one more cell (E18), which acts like a garbage can—if that value is not 0, we must have overlooked a value higher than 11.50.

4. To show how FREQUENCY reads each bin, place in C6: =D5+0.01 & " to " & D6. Copy this formula down.

5. Starting in cell F5, place in F5:F17 the following:
    =NORMDIST(D5,AVERAGE(A:A),STDEV(A:A),FALSE).

6. In H5:H17: =FREQUENCY(A:A,D5:D17)/COUNT(A:A) with *Ctr Sh Enter*. These numbers match the frequency values perfectly, because the sample count happens to be 100.

7. If you repeat the Random Number Generator again, you may get some slightly different results, of course (see below). It is a rule of statistics that "results may vary."

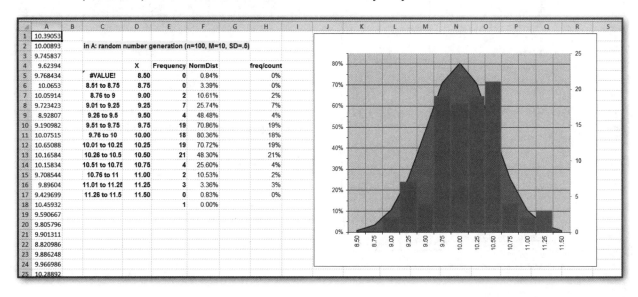

13. Normalizing

What the simulation does

Open file 2-Statistics.xlsx on the sheet called "Normalize." This simulation shows first how the RAND() function creates random numbers with each one having *equal*, or *uniform*, probability (column B)—in other words, variables are drawn with equal probability from all values in the range.

In column C, on the other hand, we use a formula that creates random numbers according to a *normal* distribution (without using the *Analysis Toolpak*), so we get formulas that can update.

Notice how the top graph has dots scattered all over the place, whereas the bottom graph shows a bell-shaped pattern close to a normal distribution.

The two frequency tables in the center show very different frequency patterns as well.

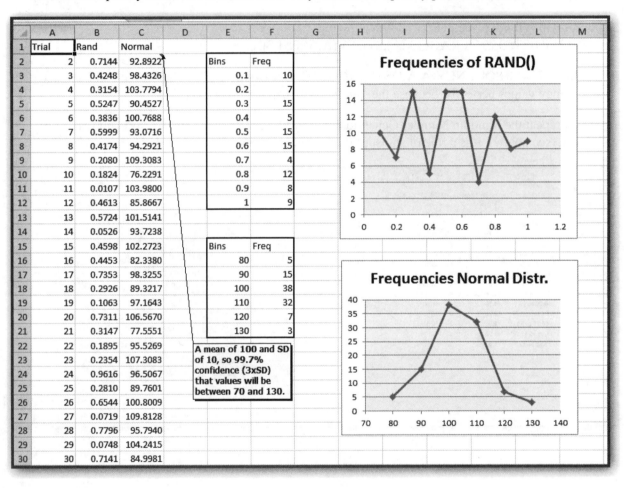

What you need to know

A normal distribution is characterized by a bell-shaped curve that is symmetrical on both sides of the mean. The spread around the mean is expressed in standard *error* units (SE-units, also called *z*-values in a normal distribution, or *t*-values in a Students' *t*-distribution).

You probably know that 1.96 times the SE on both sides of the mean covers a curve surface of 95%—which means that 95% of the values are located in that section of the curve. The units of SE around the mean determine how much of the curve's surface has been covered: 70% for 1 SE on both sides; 90% for 1.65 SE; 95% for 1.96 SE; 97.5% for 2.25 SE, and 99.7% for 3 SE.

Let me word this differently by using the concept of *confidence*. If we have a mean of 100 and a SD of 10, we have 99.7% confidence (3xSD) that values will be between 70 and 130, and 70% confidence (1xSD) that values will be between 90 and 110.

How do we "normalize" a series of random numbers? The answer is by using the RAND function nested inside a NORMINV function. Whereas –DIST functions return probabilities, -INV function return values (that come with probabilities). So the formula =NORMINV(RAND(),100,10) would return a series of random numbers with a mean of 100 and a SD of 10. If RAND would generate 0.7, then NORMINV would generate the 70th percentile of a normal random variable with a mean of 100 and a standard deviation of 10.

What you need to do

1. Column B has in all its top 100 cells: =RAND().

2. The range F3:F12 shows all the RAND frequencies: =FREQUENCY(B:B,E3:E12)

3. Column C has in each of its 100 cells the following formula: =NORMINV(RAND(),100,10).

4. The range F16:F21 shows all the NORMINV frequencies: =FREQUENCY(C:C,E16:E21).

5. *Sh F9* will run new simulations.

14. Repeats

What the simulation does

Open file 2-Statistics.xlsx on the sheet called "Repeats." This time we are going to simulate several repeats of the previous case, Simulation 13, in order to check as to whether the normal distribution we tried to simulate earlier did come out the way we would expect.

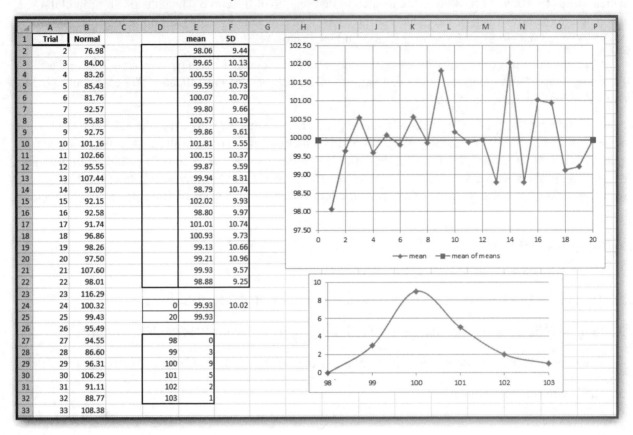

What you need to know

The 100 sequential numbers in column A were calculated by using the ROW function. This function returns the row number of the cell it happens to be in—so ROW() in A10 would return 10. If you provide a cell reference as an argument, it returns the row number of that specific cell reference—so ROW(B25) in cell A10 (or in cell B1) would always return 25.

In column B we simulate again a series of 100 random numbers, as we did in the previous simulation—that is, not equally but *normally* distributed, with a mean of 100 and a SD of 10.

In the range D2:F22, we simulate 20 repeats of this random number generation, so we end up with 20 x 100 = 2,000 trials (which is still a very modest number for statistical standards).

As it turns out, the mean of means oscillates around 100 (cell E24) and the mean of SDs stays more or less around 10 (cell F24). The top graph plots the mean values found in E2:E22.

Even the frequency distribution of all the means, calculated in range D27:E32, creates a rather *normal* distribution with a bell shape in the right lower graph, although the number of cases is still very modest in statistical terms.

What you need to do

1. In cell A2: =ROW() or =ROW(A1). Copy down to A101.

2. Place in cell B2: =NORMINV(RAND(),100,10). Copy this formula down to cell B101.

3. Place in cell E2: =AVERAGE(B:B).

4. Place in cell F2: =STDEV(B:B).

5. Select D2 through F22 and start a Data Table with no row input and an empty cell, say C1, for the column input.

6. This automatically creates the following array formula: {=TABLE(,C1)}.

7. Place in E24 and E25: =AVERAGE($E$2:$E$22). To the left of these two cells are the beginning and the end of the X-axis range (0 and 20). These four cells together are the two sets of coordinates to create a line for the mean of means in the graph.

8. In cells E27:E32, we place this multi-cell array function, but all at once: =FREQUENCY(E3:E22,D27:D31). Use *Ctr Sh Enter*.

9. By using *Sh F9*, you will simulate more and more drawings of random numbers—each time 2,000 trials. Notice how the *means of the means* for each simulation are clustered around 100 (in the top graph).

10. Notice also how the frequency distribution of *the means of the means* (in the lower graph) stays close to your expectations—a normal distribution. Imagine how much work Excel is doing for you in the meantime!

15. Confidence Margins

What the simulation does

Open file 2-Statistics.xlsx on the sheet called "Confidence." This simulation shows for a specific sample or population—with a mean of 4.5 (cell B1), a SD of 0.7 (cell B2), and a size of 35 (cell B3)—that we can have 95% confidence that the mean is going to be between 4.27 and 4.73 (cell B6).

Because we accept a 95% confidence level, we also accept a 5% error chance (cell B4). This allows us to calculate a confidence margin of 0.23 (cell B5). So the lower confidence limit is 4.5 – 0.23 = 4.27 and the upper confidence level is 4.5 + 0.23 = 4.73.

Next the simulation shows us in a table what the two confidence limits would be if either the sample size or the SD were different. This is a case of *what-if analysis* with a simulation based on the input of fixed values. You could then change the fixed values in B1:B3 and see what the new outcome would be.

	A	B	C	D	E	F	G	H
1	Mean	4.5						
2	SD	0.7						
3	Size	35						
4	2-tailed error level	5%						
5	Confidence margin	0.23						
6	95% conf. margin	4.27 to 4.73	30	35	40	45	50	Size
7		0.2	4.43 to 4.57	4.43 to 4.57	4.44 to 4.56	4.44 to 4.56	4.44 to 4.56	
8		0.3	4.39 to 4.61	4.4 to 4.6	4.41 to 4.59	4.41 to 4.59	4.42 to 4.58	
9		0.4	4.36 to 4.64	4.37 to 4.63	4.38 to 4.62	4.38 to 4.62	4.39 to 4.61	
10		0.5	4.32 to 4.68	4.33 to 4.67	4.35 to 4.65	4.35 to 4.65	4.36 to 4.64	
11		0.6	4.29 to 4.71	4.3 to 4.7	4.31 to 4.69	4.32 to 4.68	4.33 to 4.67	
12		0.7	4.25 to 4.75	4.27 to 4.73	4.28 to 4.72	4.3 to 4.7	4.31 to 4.69	
13		0.8	4.21 to 4.79	4.23 to 4.77	4.25 to 4.75	4.27 to 4.73	4.28 to 4.72	
14		0.9	4.18 to 4.82	4.2 to 4.8	4.22 to 4.78	4.24 to 4.76	4.25 to 4.75	
15		1.0	4.14 to 4.86	4.17 to 4.83	4.19 to 4.81	4.21 to 4.79	4.22 to 4.78	
16		SD						
17								

What you need to know

Cell B5 uses the CONFIDENCE function. This function has 3 arguments—the alpha error (in this case 5% error chance, so 95% confidence), the SD (which Excel transforms into SE-units), and the size of the sample. It returns the margin on both sides of the mean, if we accept a 5% error chance.

The ROUND function rounds scientifically (unlike INT which always rounds down) and it rounds to a number of decimals specified in its 2nd argument (which INT cannot do, of course).

The table used in this simulation is probably different from the tables you are used to; I call them "what-if tables" (for more information see Appendix 3). The formula used here is located at the origin of the table.

The cells to the right show various inputs for the variable size, and the cells below show various inputs for the variable SD. The table is made by selecting the entire boxed area (starting at the formula cell), then selecting Data | What-If Analysis | Data Table. In the dialog box set, the row input to B3 and the column input to B2.

Once you hit OK, the table holds an array function: {=TABLE(B3,B2)}. You cannot type the formula or the braces, so you must go through the menu.

What you need to do

1. Place in cell B5: =CONFIDENCE(B4,B2,B3).

2. Place in cell B6 a formula that subtracts and adds the confidence margin around the mean: =ROUND(B1-B5,2) & " to " & ROUND(B1+B5,2). The ampersand (&) acts like a "hook" operator again to join 3 components in this case.

3. Select B6:G15, then Data | What-If Analysis | Data Table.

4. Enter B3 for row input and B2 for column input.

5. Notice the array function for any cell inside the table. In arrays, you are prohibited from deleting or changing any individual cell in the array. They all belong together.

6. Whenever you change any values in the cells B1:B3, all the information will update (perhaps after hitting *Sh F9*).

7. Notice how confidence margins depend heavily on sample size and standard deviation.

16. Power Curves

What the simulation does

Open file 2-Statistics.xlsx on the sheet called "PowerCurves." This simulation allows you to change the alpha error in B2 in order to see how this affects the beta curve and the power curve. To do so, cell B3 calculates a z-value, which represents the number of SE-units around the mean in a normal distribution. All z-values are SE-units. So the critical z-value, or number of SE-units, is 1.96 for an error chance of 2.5% on one end and 2.5% on the other end of the curve—which gives us a confidence of 95%.

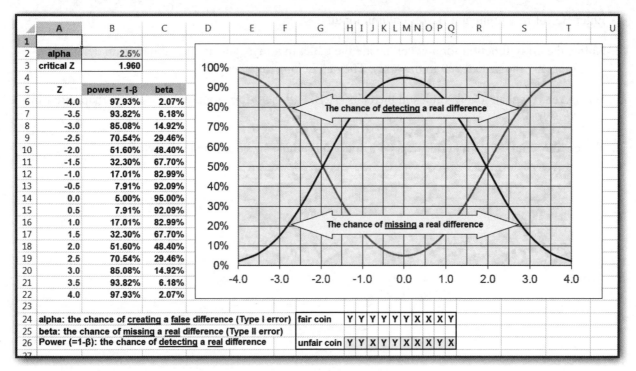

What you need to know

Here is some statistical terminology. *Alpha* stands for the chance of creating a false difference (Type I error). *Beta* represents the chance of missing a real difference (Type II error). Power (=1-β) stands for the chance of detecting a real difference. The up-curve represents *beta*, the down-curve is the *power* curve.

A Type I error represents the situation where the coin was actually fair, but your data led you to conclude it was not, just by chance (H24:Q24). To reduce this chance, lower *alpha*. A Type II error represents the situation where the coin was actually unfair, but your data did not have enough evidence to catch it, just by chance (H26:Q26). To lower this chance raise the sample size.

In cell B3, the function NORMSINV (notice the S in the center) returns a z-value for a specific probability as shown in B2. The z-value is -1.96 at the 2.5% end (left of the mean); it is +1.96 at the 97.5% end (right of the mean).

Something similar holds for NORMSDIST. It return the probability for a specific z-value (which is a SE unit).

What you need to do

1. Select cell B2, then Data | Data Validation | List | in Source: 1%, 2.5%, 5%, 10% | OK.

2. Place in cell B3: =ABS(NORMSINV(B2)). The ABS function eliminates the minus sign for *z*-values left of the mean.

3. Place in cell C6 (and then copy down to cell C22):
   =(NORMSDIST($A6+B$3)-NORMSDIST($A6-B$3)).

4. In cell B6 (and down to cell B22): =1-C6.

5. Changing *alpha* to 10% should have quite an impact; see below how the curves change.

6. H24:Q24 simulates a *fair* coin: =IF(RAND()>0.5,"X","Y").

7. Format for unlikely cases such as <= 1*X* or >= 9*X*s:
   =OR(COUNTIF($H$24:$Q$24,"X")>=9,COUNTIF($H$24:$Q$24,"X")<=1). See also Simulation 9.

8. H26:Q26 is for an *unfair* coin: =IF(RAND()>0.3,"X","Y").

9. Conditional format: =COUNTIF($H$26:$Q$26,"X")=5.

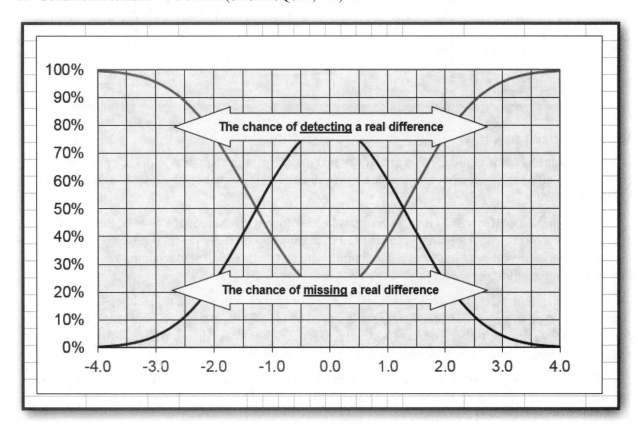

17. Hidden Peaks

What the simulation does

Open file 2-Statistics.xlsx on the sheet called "Peaks." Here we are dealing with a population that is composed of two sub-populations.

As long as the two subpopulations have the same mean, even with different standard deviations, the entire population may look nicely symmetrical. But when the mean of one subpopulation changes, the symmetrical curve may easily lose its symmetry. You can simulate this by changing G2 and G3.

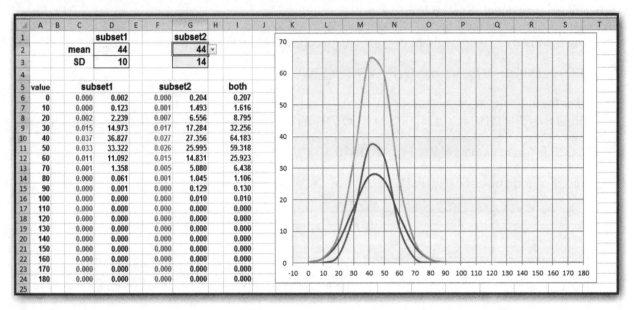

What you need to know

Populations usually include hidden subgroups that may affect the composition of the entire population enormously. Once populations have no longer a symmetrical curve, standard statistical procedures may no longer be valid.

Testing for the degree of the curve's symmetry can be done with the function SKEW. Positive skewness indicates a distribution with an asymmetric tail extending toward more positive values (to the right of the mean). Negative skewness indicates a distribution with an asymmetric tail extending toward more negative values (to the left of the mean).

The rule of thumb is that if skewness is less than −1 or greater than +1, the distribution is highly skewed. However, this is an interpretation of the data you actually have. When you have data for the whole population, that's fine. But when you have a sample, the sample skewness does not necessarily apply to the whole population. A crude way to correct for this is: Divide by $\sqrt{(6/n)}$.

The symmetry of a curve is an important condition for many statistical tests such as the Students t-test and the analysis-of-variance test (ANOVA). Although there are techniques to "normalize" skewed data sets, that issue is beyond the scope of this book.

What you need to do

1. Cells G2 and G3 have been validated with a list.

2. Place in cell C6: =NORMDIST(A6,$D$2,$D$3,FALSE), and copy down to C24.

3. Place in cell D6: =C6*1000. Copy down to D24.

4. Place in cell F6: =NORMDIST(A6,$G$2,$G$3,FALSE), and copy down to F24.

5. Place in cell G6 (down to G24): =F6*1000.

6. Place cell I6 (down to I24): =D6+G6. This represent the value for the total population based on its two subgroups.

7. The figure below simulates what happens to the curve of the total population when the mean of a sub-population changes from 44 to 70 (in cell G2).

8. Be aware: Since the main population does no longer have a normal distribution, standard statistical techniques for significance, etc., may no longer be valid.

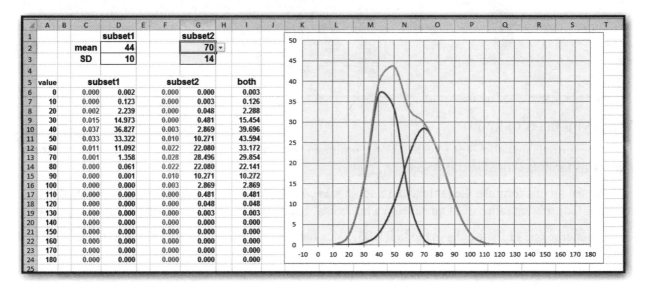

		subset1				subset2			
1			subset1			subset2			
2		mean	44			70			
3		SD	10			14			
4									
5	value	subset1			subset2		both		
6	0	0.000	0.002	0.000	0.000		0.003		
7	10	0.000	0.123	0.000	0.003		0.126		
8	20	0.002	2.239	0.000	0.048		2.288		
9	30	0.015	14.973	0.000	0.481		15.454		
10	40	0.037	36.827	0.003	2.869		39.696		
11	50	0.033	33.322	0.010	10.271		43.594		
12	60	0.011	11.092	0.022	22.080		33.172		
13	70	0.001	1.358	0.028	28.496		29.854		
14	80	0.000	0.061	0.022	22.080		22.141		
15	90	0.000	0.001	0.010	10.271		10.272		
16	100	0.000	0.000	0.003	2.869		2.869		
17	110	0.000	0.000	0.000	0.481		0.481		
18	120	0.000	0.000	0.000	0.048		0.048		
19	130	0.000	0.000	0.000	0.003		0.003		
20	140	0.000	0.000	0.000	0.000		0.000		
21	150	0.000	0.000	0.000	0.000		0.000		
22	160	0.000	0.000	0.000	0.000		0.000		
23	170	0.000	0.000	0.000	0.000		0.000		
24	180	0.000	0.000	0.000	0.000		0.000		

18. Sampling Sizes

What the simulation does

Open file 2-Statistics.xlsx on sheet "SamplingSize." In a sample taken from a certain population, defined by a certain mean (cell B1) and a certain SD (cell B2), we want to detect whether a specific treatment has created a difference or not.

We determine first which margin of error we would accept (cell B3). The simulation sheet uses a certain formula, shown to the right, to determine that the sample should have a size of at least 61 cases (cell B8 and cell I8) in order to discover a certain difference based on a margin of error set to 0.5 (B3).

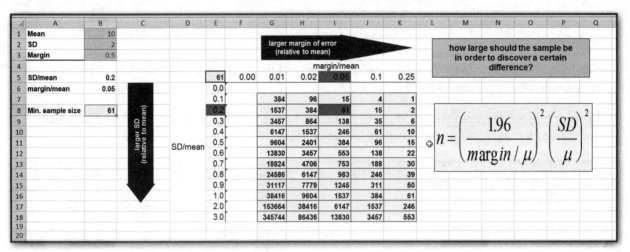

What you need to know

The formula that allows us to calculate the minimum sample size is shown in the figure above to the right. This formula is used in cell B8 and E8.

Based on this formula, the table in the middle was constructed with two dimensions—a vertical dimension for different ratios of SD/mean and a horizontal one for different ratios of margin/mean.

Changing one or more cells in range B1:B3, calculates a new minimum sample size and highlights that value in the table.

What you need to do

1. Cell B5: =B2/B1.

2. Cell B6: =B3/B1.

3. Cell B8: =B5^2*(1.96/B6)^2. The value 1.96 is based on 95% confidence.

4. Cell E5: =B8.

5. Highlight E5:K18, Data | What-If Analysis | Data Table with B6 for row input and B5 for column input. Be aware that column F and row 6 in the table do have formula results, but they are useless and were hidden with a white font.

6. There is conditional formatting for range $E$7:$E$18: =AND($B$5>$E6,$B$5<=$E7). This highlights the chosen SD/mean value.

7. There is conditional formatting for range $G$5:$K$5: =AND($B$6>F$5,$B$6<=G$5). This highlights the chosen margin/mean value.

8. And there is conditional formatting for cells $G$7:$K$18: =AND(AND($B$5>$E6,$B$5<=$E7),AND($B$6>F$5,$B$6<=G$5)). This highlights the minimum sample size.

9. Change any of the cells B1:B3 and watch the results. A smaller error margin and a larger SD (in relation to the mean) would require a much larger sample size (see below).

	A	B	C	D	E	F	G	H	I	J	K
1	Mean	10									
2	SD	7					larger margin of error (relative to mean)				
3	Margin	0.2									
4								margin/mean			
5	SD/mean	0.7			4706	0.00	0.01	0.02	0.05	0.1	0.25
6	margin/mean	0.02			0.0						
7					0.1		384	96	15	4	1
8	Min. sample size	4706			0.2		1537	384	61	15	2
9					0.3		3457	864	138	35	6
10					0.4		6147	1537	246	61	10
11				SD/mean	0.5		9604	2401	384	96	15
12					0.6		13830	3457	553	138	22
13					0.7		18824	4706	753	188	30
14					0.8		24586	6147	983	246	39
15					0.9		31117	7779	1245	311	50
16					1.0		38416	9604	1537	384	61
17					2.0		153664	38416	6147	1537	246
18					3.0		345744	86436	13830	3457	553
19											

larger SD (relative to mean)

19. Quality Control

What the simulation does

Open file 2-Statistics.xlsx on sheet "QualityControl." Here we have an assembly line that creates between 100 and 1000 products (B1) per period of time. One particular value is supposed to be 15 (B2) but varies with a SD of 2 (B3), as shown in column A.

To ensure quality, we take a certain percentage of samples (E1) in which we accept 2% defects (E2). Based on such a sample we decide, with 95% confidence (E3), to accept or reject the entire production lot.

This process is far from certain but depends heavily on probabilities. Therefore, we repeat this process a number of times in the table to the right.

	A	B	C	D	E	F	G	H	I	J	K	L	M	N	O	P
1	Production	100		Sample	10%						mean	mean	count	count	max	verdict
2	Mean	15		Accept defect	2%						products	sample	samples	rejects	rejects	
3	SD	2		Confidence	95%					15.2342	15.2342	15.6181	8	1	1	+
4											14.9107	14.9891	6	0	1	+
5					samples	rejects	max rejects	verdict			14.7704	15.3636	9	1	1	+
6	15.2342			15.6181	8	1	1	+			14.9731	14.5269	10	0	1	+
7											15.1768	14.9959	8	0	1	+
8	15.1073										15.0033	13.9969	10	3	1	reject
9	13.8945			13.8945	OK						15.1059	14.8416	8	0	1	+
10	15.0583										15.0970	15.7888	10	1	1	+
11	17.7839										15.0858	15.2743	10	0	1	+
12	15.6216										14.6425	14.4637	10	0	1	+
13	14.4719										14.7512	13.6824	10	1	1	+
14	13.7799										15.0916	14.7627	10	0	1	+
15	15.1357			15.1357	OK						15.1120	15.1777	7	1	1	+
16	15.5696										14.6925	14.3193	10	0	1	+
17	13.9105										15.1527	15.0951	10	0	1	+
18	16.0605										14.8366	15.1479	9	0	1	+
19	15.6168										15.0632	15.2091	7	0	1	+
20	14.3549										15.0532	13.9896	10	0	1	+
21	13.7264										14.7169	15.2864	10	1	1	+
22	11.7402			11.7402	OK						14.9820	15.1917	9	1	1	+
23	15.5617										15.2489	15.4477	10	0	1	+
24	14.7685										14.9644	14.8263	8	0	1	+
25	17.9009															
26	15.9156									mean	14.9848	14.9088	9.0455			
27	13.5971															
28	14.8332															
29	18.3853			18.3853	OK											
30	14.8378															
31	18.6562															
32	21.9156			21.9156	reject											
33	16.2325															

What you need to know

Column A has 1000 records, but in order to allow for smaller production numbers we need the function OFFSET (see Simulation 37 for more information on this function).

Another new function is CRITBINOM in cell G6. It can be used to determine the greatest number of defective parts that are allowed to come off an assembly line sample without rejecting the entire lot. It has 3 arguments: The number of trials, the probability of a success on each trial, and the criterion value (alpha). Recently, this function has been replaced with BINOM.INV.

What you need to do

1. Place in cells A8:A1007: =NORMINV(RAND(),$B$2,$B$3). This creates normally distributed random values.

2. Place in A6: =AVERAGE($A$8:OFFSET($A$8,$B$1-1,0)). This averages the normally distributed values for the number of products chosen in cell B1—that is, the range from A8 to A8-offset-by-B1-rows. The mean should be around 15 (B2).

3. In column D, we create samples—X% of the total number of products (e.g., 10%). This is a random process, so the number of samples can be lower than 10%, but should not be higher, and cannot go past the maximum number of products.

4. So place in cell D8 a heavily nested function:
   =IF(AND(ROW(D7)+1<=($B$1+7),COUNT($D$7:D7)<($B$1*$E$1)),IF(RAND()
   <=$E$1\,A8,""),""). We use D7 instead of D8 to avoid circular reference. I assume you accept smaller random sample sizes but not larger; if not, change AND.

5. Place in D6: =AVERAGE($D$8:OFFSET($D$8,$B$1-1,0)).

6. In cell E8, we decide that, if the sample value (D8) is more than 1.96 SD-units away from the population mean (B2), the sample should be rejected:
   =IF(D8<>"",IF((ABS($B$2-D8)/$B$3)>1.96,"reject","OK"),"").

7. Place in E6: =COUNT($D$8:OFFSET($D$8,$B$1-1,0)). This counts the number of samples; it should be <=(B1*E1).

8. In cell F6, we count how many rejects we found:
   =COUNTIF($E$8:OFFSET($E$8,$B$1-1,0),"reject").

9. Place in cell G6: =IFERROR(CRITBINOM(E6,E2,E3),"?").

10. Place in cell H6 a verdict: =IF(F6>G6,"reject","+").

11. In J3: = A6. In K3: =A6. In L3: =D6. In M3: =E6. In N3: = F6. In O3: =G6. In P3: =H6.

12. Select range J3:P24 and start a Data Table with no row input and an empty cell (e.g. I3) for column input: =TABLE(,I3).

13. In K26:M26, calculate the mean of the columns above.

14. Test for various entries in B1:B3 and E1:E3.

Genetics

20. Chromosomes

What the simulation does

Open file 3-Genetics.xlsx on sheet "Chromosomes." This simulation just shows what the probability is that an individual still has chromosomes derived from one particular grandparent. Since we have 23 pairs of chromosomes, it is most likely that we have 11 or 12 chromosomes that were handed down to us from one particular grandparent, two generations ago—actually a 16% chance. But the outcome can vary between no chromosomes at all or all 23 chromosomes together—but the extremes are very unlikely (see columns M and N).

The basic idea is that parents randomly contribute part of their genetic material—chromosomes, genes, and DNA—to their children (and grandchildren, etc.). As a consequence, genetics, the science of inheritance of traits and characteristics, is modeled probabilistically.

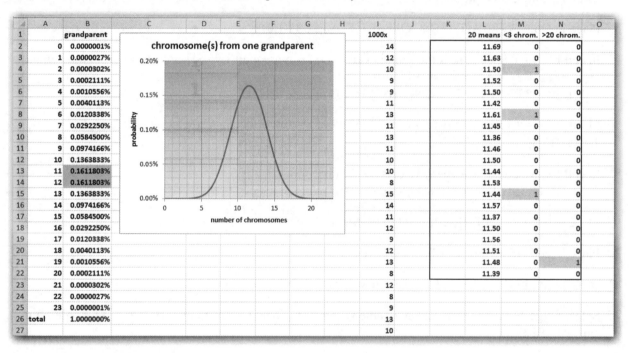

What you need to know

Humans have a double set of 23 chromosomes. Their egg cells or sperm cells contain only a single set of 23 chromosomes. After fertilization and conception, the new human being has 23 double sets again—one set from one parent and one set from the other parent.

From these 23 pairs, one set goes to the next generation again, but it is undetermined whether individual chromosomes are from grandfather's side or grandmother's side. So the new generation could have as little as 0 chromosomes or as many as 23 chromosomes from one of the four grandparents.

As an aside, the situation is much more complicated. One problem is that chromosomes do not remain identical during the formation of reproductive cells, but they can exchange parts between the two of a pair—which is called crossing-over or recombination. On this sheet, we stay clear of that issue.

In addition to the function BINOMDIST (see Simulation 9), we will also use the new function BINOM.INV in this simulation. There is no pre-2010 version of this function, so if you use a file with this function in 2007, you will get an error message. In Excel 2007, an alternative would be CRITBINOM (see Simulation 19).

What you need to do

1. Place in cell B2:B1001: =BINOMDIST(A2,23,0.5,0)/100. BINOMDIST needs to know the number of "successes" (running from 0 to 23 in column A), out of 23 trials (23 chromosomes), with a 50% probability of "success" in each trial, and with a non-cumulative setting in our case. Divide by 100.

2. Place in cells I2:I1001: =BINOM.INV(23,0.5,RAND()). The last argument is a criterion value (alpha) between 0 and 1.

3. Place in cell L2: =AVERAGE(I:I).

4. Place in cell M2: =COUNTIF(I:I,"<3").

5. Place in cell N2: =COUNTIF(I:I,">20").

6. Select K2:N22 and start a Data Table with no row input and an empty cell (say, K1) as column input: {=TABLE(,K1)}.

7. Give range M2:N22 conditional formatting: Cell Value > 0.

8. When the sheet recalculates (*Sh F9*), notice how rare it is that descendants have received less-than-3 or more-than-20 chromosomes from a grandparent (in columns M and N).

21. Sex Determination

What the simulation does

Open file 3-Genetics.xlsx on sheet "SexDetermination." This sheet simulates what happens when a father (XY) and a mother (XX) have one descendant, who has in turn another descendant, and so forth. It is like a family tree.

If the descendant is a female (XX), that cell gets marked with a color. If the descendant still has the original Y-chromosome (Y') from the (great-great-grand-) father, that chromosome is marked with an apostrophe and flagged on the left side of each descendant. In the figure below, there happen to be two female descendants, and the ancestral Y-chromosome got "lost" by chance after two generations.

What you need to know

One of the 23 pairs of chromosomes is called the sex-chromosome pair. It either holds two similar chromosomes (XX) or two unalike chromosomes (XY; Y is actually very short). The presence of the Y-chromosome determines maleness.

The father (XY) produces sperm cells with either an X-chromosome (50% chance) or a Y-chromosome (50% chance). If the egg cell—which has always one X-chromosome—is fertilized by a sperm cell with a Y-chromosome, the descendant will be a male. So there is a 50% chance for either a male or a female descendant (in reality, there is a slight difference, though).

What you need to do

1. Place in cell D3 the following formula:
   =IF(RAND()>0.5,"XX",IF(C1="XY'","XY'","XY")). Do not forget some single apostrophes (') inside the double quotes.

2. This formula creates a 50% chance for either a male or a female. If it is a male, we check whether the father had an ancestral Y-chromosome; if so, this male inherits it.

3. Copy this formula into the cells E5, F7, G9, H11, and I13.

4. Place in cell F3 the following formula: =IF(D3="","",IF(OR(D3="XY",D3="XY'"),"XX","XY")).

5. This formula checks whether there is a descendant (D3), and if so, it determines whether the partner (F3) of this descendant must be a female (XX) or a male (XY).

6. Copy this formula into the cells G5, H7, I9, J11, and K13.

7. Place in cell C3: =IF(D3="XY'","Y'",""). If this person carries the Y' marker, display that Y', for then we are dealing with a Y-chromosome that came from the original male ancestor of this family tree. Otherwise leave the cell empty.

8. Copy this into the cells D5, E7, F9, G11, and H13.

9. Apply conditional formatting to the cells $D$3, $E$5, $F$7, $G$9, $H$11, and $I$13. Choose "Format only cells that contain": Specific Text | Containing | XX (no quotes).

10. Apply conditional formatting to the cells $C$3, $D$5, $E$7, $F$9, $G$11, and $H$13. Choose "Format only cells that contain": Specific Text | Containing | Y'.

11. After hitting *Sh F9*, the ancestral Y-chromosome may disappear immediately, or after one or more generations. It is very unlikely, but not impossible, that the ancestral Y-chromosome remains present all the way down (see below).

22. Radiation and Mutation

What the simulation does

Open file 3-Genetics.xlsx on the sheet called "Radiation." Changes in genes are called mutations. The mutation rate is strongly correlated with the amount of ionizing radiation. This sheet shows the relationship between the two for fruit flies.

Since this looks like a linear relationship, we can calculate in column C what the mutation rate would be if the relationship is indeed linear. Notice how all observation points lie very close to the linear trend line.

Based on this linear relationship, we can also calculate the mutation rate (B17) for a certain amount of radiation that was not observed or measured (A17). The insert in the graph shows the result. A simulation control in the lower left corner allows us to test for different mutation rates.

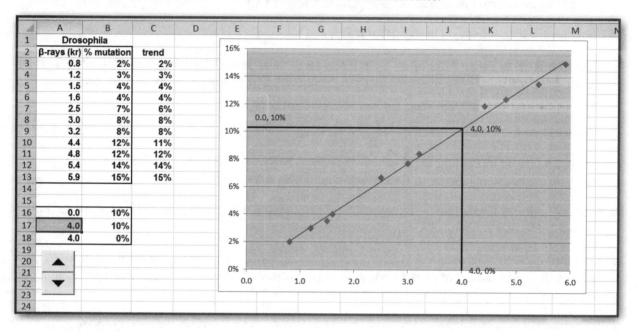

What you need to know

To predict the outcome of a linear relationship, we could use the function TREND. It is a multi-cell array function, so it returns multiple values at the same time; therefore you must select multiple cells first and finish the formula with *Ctr Sh Enter* at once. The function only needs to know the observed X-values (in column A) and the observed Y-values (in column B).

TREND can also be used for new, unobserved X-values and then predicts what the corresponding (un-observed) Y-value would be, given certain observed X-values and Y-values. This is done in range A17:B17. It is called interpolation. In another range, A16:B18, we calculate 3 sets of coordinates that can be used for the insert displayed in the graph.

Finally, the sheet uses a so-called simulation control—in this case a spin button that goes up or down by a specific integer. Since we need one decimal, we run the button from 5 to 60, store that number in a hidden cell (say, A20), and use that number in A17, after dividing it again by 10, so it actually runs from 0.5 to 6. (More details on simulation controls are given in Appendix 5.)

What you need to do

1. To calculate the linear relationship, select the entire range C3:C13 at once and implement this formula: =TREND(B3:B13,A3:A13). Accept the array function with *Ctr Sh Enter*.

2. In cell B17 we use TREND again, but this time for interpolation, so it requires also the new value in cell A17: =TREND(B3:B13,A3:A13,A17). Don't forget *Ctr Sh Enter.*

3. The cells surrounding B17 have simple settings. A16=0 | B16=B17 | A17=4.0 | A18=A17 | B18=0%. These are the three sets of coordinates for the graphical insert.

4. Now the simulation control: Developer | Design Mode ON | Insert Spin-button from ActiveX-Controls | Draw the control. (See Appendix 5 for more details.)

5. Click on the *Properties* option next to *Design Mode*. Set the following properties: Min: 5 | Max: 60 | Linked Cell: A20.

6. Do not forget to click the Design Mode button OFF before using the spin button.

7. Replace A17 with: =A20/10.

8. Clicking the spin button will automatically simulate new interpolation points. The insert nicely follows the linear trend line, of course. If you need to use *Sh F9*, you must activate the sheet first (after clicking the button) before using *Sh F9*.

23. Mendel

What the simulation does

Open file 3-Genetics.xlsx on the sheet called "Mendel." Certain diseases, such as a particular form of dwarfism, are based on a *dominant* allele (say, *A*). Anyone who carries such an allele (*Aa*) is a heterozygote and has the disease.

Other diseases, such as cystic fibrosis, are based on a *recessive* allele (say, *a*). Only people with two of those alleles (*aa*) show the disease; so someone can be a carrier (*Aa*) of the disease without showing its symptoms.

Then there are also diseases, such as a known form of hemophilia, that are called sex-linked because they are based on a recessive allele (say, *h*) located on the X-chromosome; such alleles come always to expression in males (XY)—because there is no second chromosome to counteract it—but in females (XX) only when both X-chromosomes have that recessive allele.

This sheet simulates the chances for passing on such an allele to the next generation. When the allele does come to expression, it is marked with conditional formatting.

	A	B	C	D	E	F	G	H	I	J	K	L	M	N	O
1	dominant A					recessive a					X-linked, recess. H				
2	Aa	x	aa			Aa	x	Aa			Hh	x	H-		
3		⊥					⊥					⊥			
4	aa	aa	'Aa	aa		'aa	Aa	Aa	AA		HH	'h-	HH	Hh	
5															

What you need to know

All of this is based on simple Mendelian rules. All the work is done with (nested) IF functions and the RAND function.

The first case: Parents with *Aa* and *aa* have 50% *Aa* children and 50% *aa* children. The chance that a dominant allele (*A*) from such parents comes to expression in the next generation is 50%.

The second case: The offspring of parents who are both *Aa* is *AA* (25%), *Aa* (50%), and *aa* (25%). The chance that a recessive allele (*a*) comes to expression in the next generation is 25% (*aa*).

The third case: The offspring of a mother with *Hh* and a father with *H-* would be *HH* (25%), *Hh* (25%), *H-* (25%), and *h-* (25%). The chance that a recessive, X-linked allele (*h*) comes to expression in the next generation is therefore 25% (*h-*).

What you need to do

1. Because conditional formatting cannot distinguish between lowercase and uppercase characters, we will mark the diseased genotypes with an apostrophe (').

2. Place in cell A4: =IF(RAND()<0.5,"'Aa","aa"). Notice the single apostrophe in front of *Aa*.

3. Copy this formula to cell D4 to simulate four descendants.

4. Place in cell F4 the following nested formula: =IF(RAND()<0.5,"Aa",IF(RAND()<0.25,"AA","'aa")). Again notice the single apostrophe in front of the diseased genotype *aa*.

5. Copy this formula to the right to cell I4.

6. Place in cell K4 an even more heavily nested formula:
=IF(RAND()<0.25,"HH",IF(RAND()<0.25,"Hh",IF(RAND()<0.25,"H-","'h-"))). This time genotype *h-* is diseased (').

7. Copy this formula to the right to cell N4

8. Format the cells A4:D4, F4:I4, and K4:N4 as follows: Specific Text | Beginning With | an apostrophe (').

9. Hitting *Sh F9* shows you when the abnormal allele kicks is.

10. In the example below, this happened to occur extremely often, which is highly improbable. You may have to try many times before you reach the same result.

	A	B	C	D	E	F	G	H	I	J	K	L	M	N	O
1	dominant A					recessive a					X-linked, recess. H				
2	Aa	x	aa			Aa	x	Aa			Hh	x	H-		
3		⊥					⊥					⊥			
4	'Aa	aa	'Aa	'Aa		'aa	'aa	'aa	'aa		'h-	Hh	'h-	'h-	
5															

24. Hardy-Weinberg Law

What the simulation does

Open file 3-Genetics.xlsx on sheet "Hardy." This sheet is not really a simulation, but more of an explanation of what is coming. A gene can carry various alleles. Let us assume there are only two alleles, *A* and *a*. People who have two of the same alleles are homozygotes (*AA* or *aa*). Those who carry both alleles are heterozygotes (*Aa*). If there are no other alleles in the population, the frequency *p* of allele *A* plus the frequency *q* of allele *a* should be: *p+q=1*.

From this we can deduce that the frequency would be p^2 for the homozygotes *AA* (cell A3), q^2 for the homozygotes *aa* (cell D4), and *2pq* for the heterozygotes (*pq* for *Aa* in cell C4 and *qp* for *aA* in cell D3).

If these genotypes would randomly mate again, the frequencies would stay the same in the next generation (row 5 and column E). This is called the Hardy-Weinberg law or theorem. I will not explain this further, but the sheet shows you the calculations in the top table.

	A	B	C	D	E	F	G	H	I	J	K
1	Parents		A	a							
2			60%	40%	next						
3	A	60%	36.00%	24.00%	60.00%						
4	a	40%	24.00%	16.00%	40.00%						
5	next generation		60.00%	40.00%							
6											
15											
16	phenotype:		normal		albino		0	A	B	AB	
17	genotype:		AA	Aa	aa		OO	AA + AO	BB+BO	AB	
18	occurrence:		99.9951%		0.0049%		45%	43%	9%	3%	100%
19	1 in n individuals:		1 in 1.000049		1 in 20,408		1 in 2.22	1 in 2.33	1 in 11.11	1 in 33.33	
20											
21			p2	2pq	q2		q2	2pq+p2	2rq+r2	2pr	
22	allele frequency:		0.993		0.007		0.6708	0.2673	0.0619		
23			p		q		q	p	r		
24											
25	phenotype freq.		98.6049%	1.3902%	0.0049%		45%	43%	9%	3%	
26											

What you need to know

Once we know what the frequencies of certain allele combinations are, we can calculate the frequency of each allele in the population. This is done in the lower half of the above figure—the dark cells are for input, whereas the lighter shaded cells contain formulas.

Let us take the example of an allele for albinism (*a*). It is recessive, so albinos must be *aa*, whereas the genotypes *AA* and *Aa* are not albinos, but the heterozygote *Aa* does carry a "hidden" allele for albinism that can be passed on to the next generation, but will not come to expression unless is gets combined with a second *a* allele. So if we know the percentage (q^2) of albinos (*aa*), we can calculate the frequency *q* of allele *a*, as well as the frequency *p* of allele *A* if there are no other alleles, since *p=1-q*. See the bottom-left table.

The second example is about a gene with at least three alleles. The alleles for blood type A and B are dominant over the recessive allele for blood type O. But when the alleles for type A and type B are combined, we have an intermediate situation—both come to expression. In this case, we are dealing with 3 frequencies for the types A, B, and O: *p+q+r=1*. See bottom-right table.

What you need to do

1. In cell C18 (merged): =1-E18.

2. In cell C19 (merged): =100/(C18*100). If you wonder where the text "1 in" comes from, go to: Format Cells | Custom | type: *"1 in "0.000000* (no &; the number of zeros after the decimal point determines how many decimals will be shown).

3. In cell E19: =100/(E18*100).

4. In cell G19: =100/(G18*100). Copy this to the right to J19.

5. In cell E22: =ROUND(SQRT(E18),3).

6. In cell C22: =1-E22. In cell C25: =C22^2.

7. In cell D25: =2*C22*E22. In cell E25: =E22^2.

8. In cell G22: = SQRT(G18).

9. In cell H22: = SQRT(G18+H18)-SQRT(G18).

10. In cell I22: =1-G22-H22.

11. In cell G25: =G22^2.

12. In cell H25: =2*G22*H22+H22^2.

13. In cell I25: =2*I22*G22+I22^2.

14. In cell J25: =2*H22*I22.

25. Genetic Drift

What the simulation does

Open file 3-Genetics.xlsx on sheet "GeneticDrift." The Hardy-Weinberg law states that allele frequencies remain the same over the next generations (row 8 in the top left table). Even if you have a recessive allele, it will not disappear.

However, by random chance, the percentage of alleles may, and usually does, change in the next generations. This is called *genetic drift*. The effect is more prominent when the population is smaller.

In the lower left table, we simulate the effect of genetic drift during 50 generations assuming that the frequencies randomly fluctuate by 2% every next generation. During this ongoing process, recessive homozygotes (*aa*) may eventually, by mere chance, disappear from stage, as is shown in the situation below, to the advantage of the dominant homozygotes (*AA*).

When we run the left table 20 times in the Data Table to the right, we see how much the outcome of genetic drift can vary. In column U, we flag situations in which a certain genotype disappears completely ("out") or had disappeared already ("#N/A").

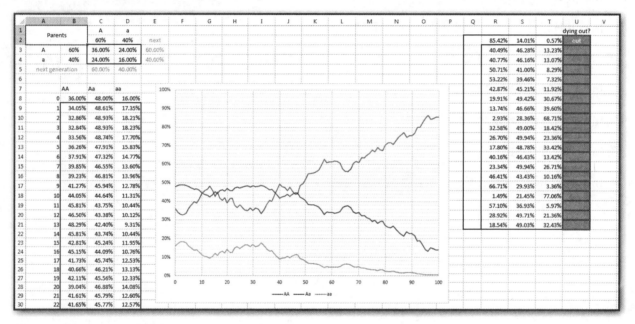

What you need to know

The only functions we need for this simulation are NORMINV, RAND, SQRT, and IFERROR. All of these were used before already. New is the function NA(); it creates "#N/A".

What you need to do

1. Place in cell B9: =NORMINV(RAND(),B8,0.02). It uses the frequency of the previous generation and makes it fluctuate with a SD of 2%. That is going to be the new frequency of genotype AA $(=p^2)$ in the next generation.

2. The frequency of genotype Aa $(2pq)$ would be $2 * \sqrt{p^2} * (1 - \sqrt{p^2})$. So place in cell C9: =IFERROR(2*SQRT(B9)*(1-SQRT(B9)),NA()). If there is an error (e.g., because the allele had already disappeared), IFERROR places "#N/A" in that cell.

3. Place in cell D9: =IFERROR((1-SQRT(B9))^2,NA()). This calculates the new frequency of genotype aa (q^2).

4. Copy the formulas of B9:D9 down to row 108.

5. In cells R2:T2, place a link to the cells B109:D109.

6. Select range Q2:T21 (not U21), and start a Data Table with no row input and an empty cell (e. g., cell P2) as column input: =TABLE(,P2).

7. Place in cell U2: =IF(T2<1%,"out","").

8. Notice how significant—and unpredictable—genetic drift can be. In the situation below, the recessive homozygote disappeared almost completely in three (or actually four) of the 20 simulations, but that is by mere coincidence. This is basically another example of random walk (see Simulation 6).

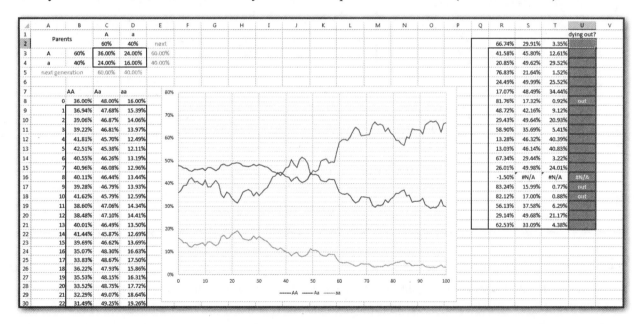

26. Lethal Homozygote

What the simulation does

Open file 3-Genetics.xlsx on sheet "GenePool (1)." This sheet simulates the situation of a gene-pool composed of allele A, with a frequency p of 0.7, and a second, recessive allele a, with a frequency q of 0.3.

The Hardy-Weinberg law (see Simulation 24) states that these frequencies remain stable in future generations, if—yes, the grand if—if mating is random. However, that is usually not the case.

We saw already in Simulation 27, that genetic drift may interfere with the stability of frequencies. Another, and probably more important, factor is natural selection—the fact that certain genotypes have a selective advantage or disadvantage over others, so they have a larger or smaller number of offspring in the next generations.

In this case, the homozygote aa has a lethal disease, which means that its survival rate (f) is 0, so the selection factor (s) against this allele is $1 - f = 1$. As a consequence, we see a gradual decline of aa—and indirectly of Aa—in favor of AA.

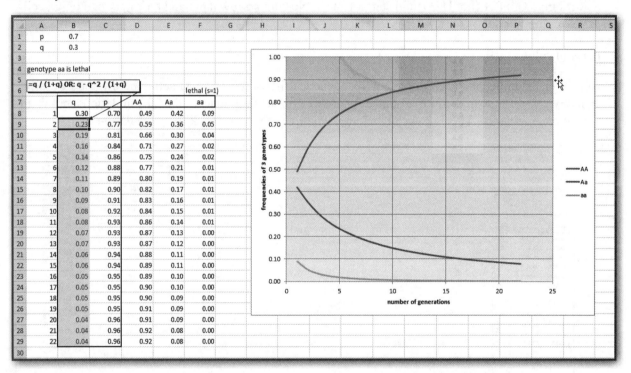

What you need to know

After some mathematical manipulation (which is beyond the scope of this book), we can deduce that the change in q (dq or Δq) would be as follows: $-q^2 / (1+q)$.

By using this equation, we can simulate what the frequencies of the genotypes AA, Aa, and aa would be after N generations. In this case the survival factor f of the recessive homozygote aa is 0, so the selection factor s against this genotype is $(1 - f) = 1$. Put differently, $f = 1 - s$.

What you need to do

1. In cell B2: =1-B1. There are only two alleles, so $p + q = 1$.

2. In cell B9: =B8-B8^2/(1+B8). Copy this formula down to B29.

3. In cell C9: =1-B9. Copy this formula down to C29.

4. In cell D9: =C9*C9. Copy this formula down to D29.

5. In cell E9: =2*B9*C9. Copy this formula down to E29.

6. In cell F9: =B9*B9. Copy this formula down to F29.

7. When you change cell B1, e.g. to 0.5, the rest will update.

8. The frequency of *aa* individuals declines to almost 0, but the allele *a* may stay in the population through *Aa* individuals who seem to go down almost asymptotically.

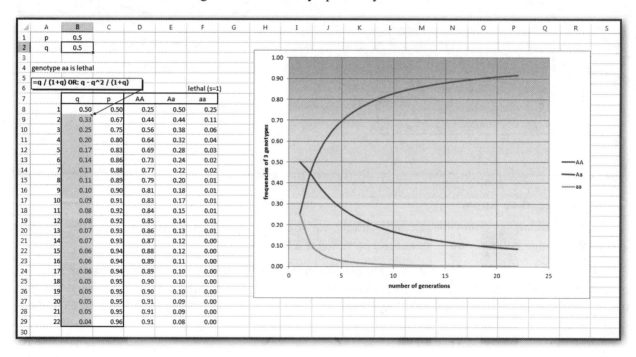

27. Reduced Vitality

What the simulation does

Open file 3-Genetics.xlsx on sheet "GenePool (2)." Instead of assuming that the recessive homozygote (*aa*) has a survival value (*f*) of 0 and a selection factor (*s*) of 1, we make factor *s* this time a variable between 0 and 1 which can be manipulated with a scroll-bar control.

We simulate its effect with a Data Table that uses different values for the selection factor *s* of allele *a* as a row input and different starting values for the frequency *q* of allele *a* as a column input.

The scroll bar regulates where the horizontal row input scale starts: It can start at 0.0 and run to 0.5, or run from 0.1 to 0.6, and so on.

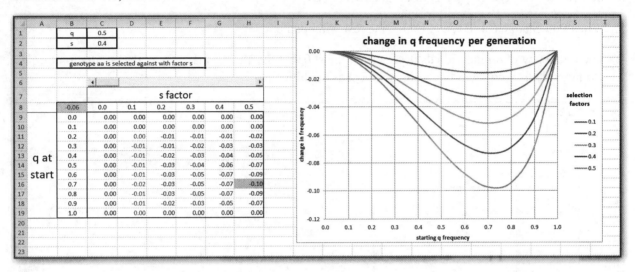

What you need to know

The equation works this time not only with the variables *p* and *q*, but also with *s*, running between 0 and 1. The change in frequency *q* after each generation is a follows: $\Delta q = -spq^2 / (1 - sq^2)$.

In a Data Table we simulate how much *q* would change per generation for various starting values of frequency *q* (in column B) and various selection factors *s* (in row 7). It turns out that the change is the biggest (-0.10 in cell H16) when the starting frequency is 0.7 and the selection factor 0.5 (if limited to the range running from 0.0 to 0.5).

What you need to do

1. Place a scroll-bar control on the sheet (see Appendix 5 for more details). Set Min to 0, Max to 5, and LinkedCell to C6.

2. In cell C8: =$C$6/10. In D8: =$C$6/10+0.1. In E8: =$C$6/10+0.2. And so on to cell H8.

3. From now on, when the scroll bar goes up, the row entries go up. A scroll bar value of 3 would start the row entries at 0.3.

4. In cell B8: =-($C$2*(1-$C$1)*$C$1^2)/(1-$C$2*$C$1^2). This is the formula for Δq, as mentioned above.

5. Select range B8:H19, and start a Data Table with C2 for the row input and C1 for column input. This creates the formula {=TABLE(C2,C1)}.

6. Select range C9:H19 and apply conditional formatting: =C9=MIN($C$9:$H$19). Make sure you lock the proper references (see Appendix 1). This highlights the largest change in frequency q (which is actually the lowest numeric value and the lowest point in the graph).

7. When you move the scroll bar up or down, the table may not recalculate, unless you set the sheet (back) to automatic calculation. If you do not, and you do change the scroll bar, you must activate the sheet first before you hit *Sh F9*.

8. Below is the situation for the selection factor range 0.4 to 0.9. The largest change in frequency q (-0.27) is reached when q starts at 0.8 and s is 0.9.

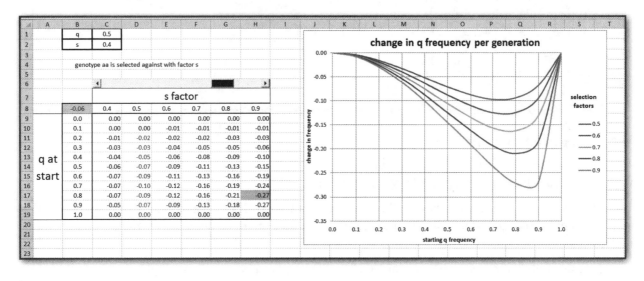

28. Two Selective Forces

What the simulation does

Open file 3-Genetics.xlsx on sheet "GenePool (3)." It is rather common that *both* alleles have a selection factor working against them; let's designate them with the symbols *s* and *t*.

The most well-known case is sickle-cell anemia, which is a genetic blood disorder, characterized by red blood cells that assume an abnormal, rigid, sickle shape, which can cause various complications such as anemia.

The sickling occurs because of an "abnormal" allele for the formation of the oxygen-carrying protein hemoglobin in red blood cells. It is caused by a recessive allele—let us label it *a*.

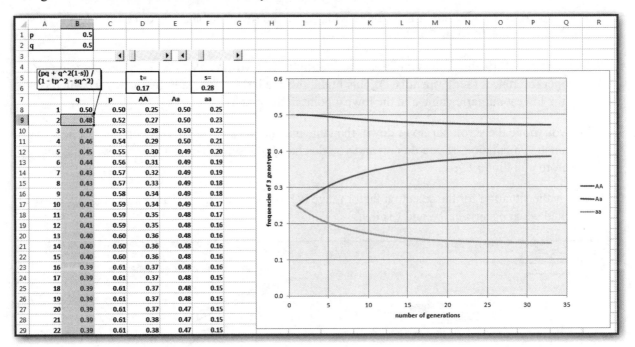

What you need to know

Because there is strong selection pressure (*s*) against the homozygote (*aa*), who suffers from anemia, we would expect allele *a* to disappear from the population.

However, in malaria areas it has a rather stable frequency (*q*). The explanation is that there is also a selection pressure (*t*) against the other homozygote (*AA*), who is more vulnerable to malaria than the other individuals.

It turned out that in areas where malaria occurs, the heterozygote (*Aa*) has a higher level of fitness to resist both malaria and anemia. This leads to new frequencies according to the following formula: *(pq + q^2(1-s)) / (1 - tp^2 - sq^2)*.

With the help of some mathematical manipulations, we are able to deduce that the frequency of alleles will become stable as soon as *tp = sq*. This is a form of balanced polymorphism—an equilibrium mixture of homozygotes and heterozygotes maintained by negative selection against both homozygotes.

What you need to do

1. B9: =(C8*B8+B8^2*(1-$F$6))/(1-$D$6*C8^2-$F$6*B8^2). Copy this formula down to cell B33.

2. In C9: =1-B9. Copy this formula down to C33.

3. In D9: =C9^2. In E9: =2*C9*B9. In F9: =B9^2. Copy all three cells down to row 33.

4. Add two scroll-bar controls (see Appendix 5). Both have Min set to 0 and Max to 100. The left one is linked to D3, the right one to F3.

5. The formulas in D6 and F6 divide the settings of D3 and F3 respectively by 100.

6. Test the outcome for different settings. Below is the situation where t=0.72 and s=0.32. After some 15 generations, equilibrium seems to have set in.

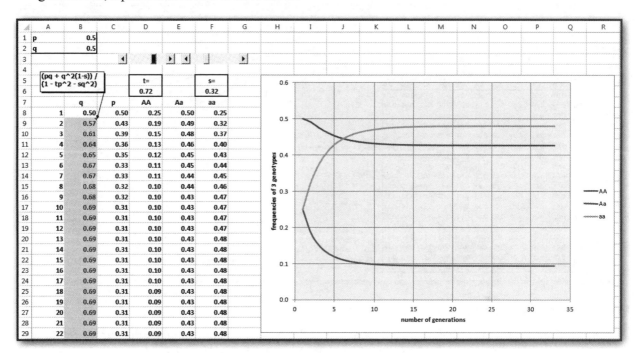

29. Balanced Equilibrium

What the simulation does

Open file 3-Genetics.xlsx on sheet "Equilibrium." In the previous simulation we discussed how, with the help of some mathematical manipulations, we are able to deduce that the frequencies of two alleles, p and q, with each a different selection factor, s and t, will become stable in a population as soon as $tp = sq$.

This phenomenon is called balanced polymorphism—an equilibrium mixture of homozygotes and heterozygotes maintained by negative selection against both homozygotes.

The formula for Δq is: $(tp^2q - spq^2) / (1 - tp^2 - sq^2)$.

With the help of a Data Table, we can find out when we reach equilibrium, given a certain value for q (in column B; $p = 1 - q$), a certain value for s (in row 7), and a certain value for t (cell E4).

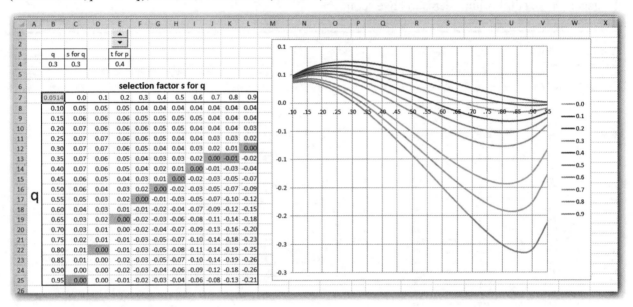

What you need to know

Since Data Tables can only hold two dimensions at the most, we could simulate the third variable with a spin-button control (see Appendix 5 for more details). This control regulates the value of variable t in cell E4.

Notice how the curves in the graph intersect with the X-axis at some point. Until it reaches that point, the frequency q will either increase (to the right) or decrease (to the left) for each generation.

What you need to do

1. Place in cell B7 the formula for Δq:
   =($E$4*(1-$B$4)^2*$B$4-$C$4*(1-$B$4)*$B$4^2)/(1-$E$4*(1-$B$4)^2-$C$4*$B$4^2).

2. Select the range B7:L25 and start a Data Table with cell C4 as row input and B4 for column input.

3. Apply conditional formatting to range C8:L25 with a formula that looks for the lowest value in the positive range (which is very close to 0): =ABS(C8)=MIN(ABS(C$8:C$25))).

4. Place a spin-button control over cells E1:E2 (see Appendix 5 for more details). Set Min to 0, Max to 10, and LinkedCell to E1.

5. Place in cell E4: =E1/10. Now this cell listens to the spin-button control.

6. Whenever a cell shows 0 or whenever the curve reaches the X-axis, a balanced state of equilibrium has been reached.

7. If calculation is set to automatic, you can click the spin button and watch the changes in the table and the graph. Otherwise, you must hit each time *Sh F9* after each button change—but only after you have activated the sheet again.

8. In the case below, *t* has been set to 0.9. Equilibrium can only be reached when *q* is greater than 0.50 for any value of *s*.

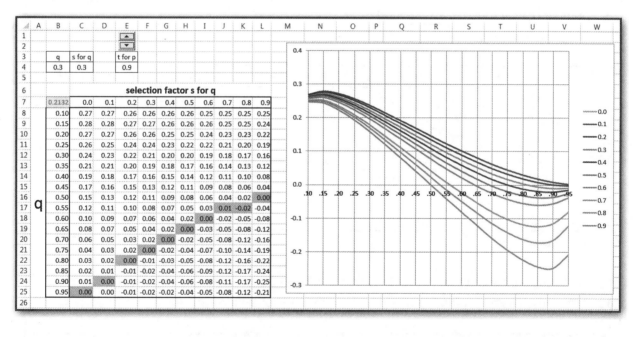

30. Molecular Clock

What the simulation does

Open file 3-Genetics.xlsx on the sheet called "Ancestry." We saw in Simulation 22 that genes may undergo changes, called mutations.

Mutations to non-essential portions of the DNA are useful for measuring time—the so-called molecular clock. It is assumed that such mutations occur with a uniform probability per unit of time in a particular portion of DNA. If P is the percentage of *no*-mutations in a year, then P^N is the probability of *no*-mutations over N years.

On average, given two individuals who had a common ancestor many generations ago, you would expect—assuming that mutations are so rare that it is very unlikely that a mutation in the same segment has occurred in two individuals—that the percentage of segments that are mutated in one or the other is, on average, $2(1 - P^N)$. This is an estimate of the percentage of segments that would be found different when comparing two individuals with a common ancestor N years ago.

	A	B	C	D	E	F	G	H
1	Comparing two individuals with a common ancestor							
2	individuals		2					
3	mutation rate/yr		0.0000001					
4	unchanged		0.9999999					
5	number of years		50000					
6	mutation percentage		1%					
7								
8	1%	0.9999999	0.9999998	0.9999997	0.9999996	0.9999995	1 - mutation rate	
9	50000	1%	2%	3%	4%	5%		
10	100000	2%	4%	6%	8%	10%		
11	150000	3%	6%	9%	12%	14%		
12	200000	4%	8%	12%	15%	19%		
13	250000	5%	10%	14%	19%	24%		
14	300000	6%	12%	17%	23%	28%		
15	350000	7%	14%	20%	26%	32%		
16	years ago							
17								
18	10% could be 100,000 years ago if the rate is 0.9999995							
19	10% could also be 250,000 years ago if the rate is 0.9999998							
20								

What you need to know

This is a simplified version of the technique that has been used to locate the first common ancestors of all human beings in evolution—the first female and the first male, so to speak. Non-essential DNA sections can be tested for single-nucleotide-polymorphisms (SNPs, pronounced "snips"), which are single base pair changes in DNA that occur throughout the genome, including its "silent" DNA sections.

Any specific inherited SNP is known as a haplotype. It is called haplotype because it is only present in one chromosome of the pair, that is, in a haploid state. Haplotypes can be in any of the 46 chromosomes, but in genealogical ancestry research, the term usually refers to "silent" sections of the Y-chromosome and of mitochondrial DNA, because they remain intact from generation to generation.

Thus there are Y-chromosome haplotypes, which trace patrilineal ancestry back to a so-called "Y-chromosomal Adam," and mitochondrial haplotypes, which trace matrilineal ancestry back to a "mitochondrial Eve."

What you need to do

1. Place in cell C4: =1-C3.

2. Place in cell C6: =2*(1-C4^C5). This is the mutation percentage after a certain numbers of years (in this case 50,000 years as shown in cell C4).

3. Cell A8 is linked to cell C6.

4. Select range A8:F15 and start a Data Table with cell C4 as row input and cell C5 for column input: =TABLE(C4,C5).

5. Notice the following: If two individuals have a 10% difference, their most recent common ancestor lived 100,000 years ago if the mutation rate for those DNA segments is 0,9999995, but 250,000 years ago based on a rate of 0,9999998. So small differences in mutation rate can have an enormous impact. Apparently, the accuracy of the molecular clock depends heavily on the accuracy of the mutation rate.

31. DNA Sequencing

What the simulation does

Open file 3-Genetics.xlsx on the sheet called "DNAsequencing." This is a very simple simulation of what was done in the Human Genome Project, and what is still being done. DNA is composed of 4 different nucleotides—A, C, G, and T. The composition of a DNA section is randomly generated in column A. It is clear that this composition is not known yet until we use a technique in the middle section that we are going to describe soon. The end result is shown in the columns AQ and AR.

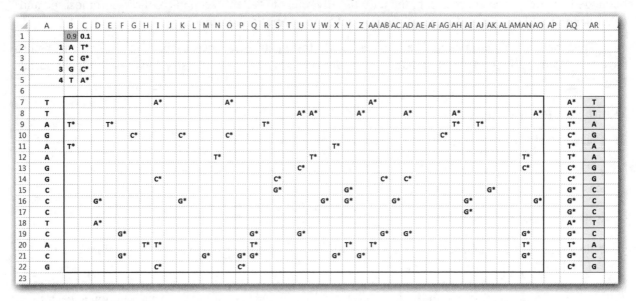

What you need to know

Today, "dideoxy sequencing" (also called the Sanger method) is the method of choice to sequence very long strands of DNA. To determine the unknown sequence of nucleotides in a DNA section of interest, the double-stranded DNA is separated into single strands (denaturation). In the next step, a new DNA strand is made, complementary to the template strand, by using the bacterial enzyme DNA polymerase. During this step A-nucleotides will be "paired" with T-nucleotides, and C-nucleotides with G-nucleotides—they are called complementary.

Then follows the key step. In addition to the four regular single nucleotides, the reaction mixture also contains small amounts of four dideoxy-nucleotides, which lack a group necessary for chain extension. Once in a while—by chance, because of its much lower concentration—a dideoxy-nucleotide will be incorporated into the growing DNA strand instead of the regular nucleotide. This will prevent the DNA chain from growing further. Since each of these four special nucleotides is labeled with a different fluorescent dye, a certain kind of laser can later detect them. We marked them with an asterix (*) in our simulation.

Since an actual sequencing reaction mixture contains thousands of DNA template strands, which are all being sequenced simultaneously, DNA chains end up being very short, very long, and of every possible length in between. The newly synthesized DNA strands are then passed through a laser beam that excites the fluorescent dye attached to the dideoxy-nucleotide at the end of each strand. This color is then detected by a photocell, which feeds the information to a computer. Finally, the computer does the rest of the work by piecing the short sequences together like a puzzle. This is not part of our simulation here.

What you need to do

1. The following formula in A7 generates A, C, G, or T:
   =VLOOKUP(RANDBETWEEN(1,4),$A$2:$B$5,2,0). Copy the formula down. VLOOKUP is explained in Simulation 32.

2. Assuming that 90% (B1) is not dyed, we simulate in B7 the chance that a dyed nucleotide is inserted and stops the chain:
   =IF(RAND()>$B$1,VLOOKUP($A7,$B$2:$C$5,2,0),"").

3. Copy this formula all the way down and right to cell AO22. Each column simulates a new chance for creating strands of different lengths, terminated by a dyed nucleotide (*).

4. In AQ7 we locate the first dyed nucleotide in that row:
   =INDEX(B7:AO7,0,MATCH(TRUE,(B7:AO7)<>"",0)). This is a single-cell *array* formula (*Ctr Sh Enter*). Copy the formula down. The function INDEX is explained in Simulation 79.

5. In cell AR7, we display what the complementary code for the nucleotide is at a specific position in the chain:
   =INDEX($B$2:$C$5,MATCH(AQ7,$C$2:$C$5,0),1). Copy.

6. The values found in column AR should match the values in column A, which were unknown and had to be determined!

7. Setting B1 to a slightly lower value creates shorter strands.

Financial

32. Fluctuating APR

What the simulation does

Open file 4-Financial.xlsx on sheet "APR." Let's say we are trying to predict what our total return would be over a period of years if our initial deposit is fixed and our APR is fluctuating. This sheet calculates how a fixed deposit compounds over a specific number of years with a fluctuating APR.

We use three tables to set up this calculation. In the left table, we set up our parameters and use a simple calculation of return without considering any volatility. In the middle table, we simulate how APR could fluctuate during the time period—in this case 30 years—if the volatility is 0.3%. Since this middle table represents only one of the many possible outcomes, we need to run additional scenarios to model fluctuations in return. In the right table, we run these additional scenarios of the middle table some 25 times. We can call this a "what-if table".

	A	B	C	D	E	F	G	H	I	J	K	L
1	Deposit	$ 60,000.00		Year	APR	Savings		Trials	$ 191,623.16		25%	$191,494.73
2	Number of yrs.	30		1	3.93%	$ 62,355.25			$ 193,639.88		50%	$195,130.42
3	APR	4%		2	3.77%	$ 64,707.35			$ 190,435.31		75%	$197,354.84
4	Volatility	0.3%		3	3.99%	$ 67,290.69			$ 191,451.92		100%	$200,349.24
5	Savings	$194,603.85		4	4.51%	$ 70,327.43			$ 195,949.75			
6				5	3.74%	$ 72,956.18			$ 195,411.60			
7				6	4.17%	$ 75,996.71			$ 199,876.73			
8									$ 197,433.57			
9									$ 191,926.28			
10									$ 199,362.85			
11									$ 190,763.49			
12									$ 196,075.62			
13									$ 188,811.52			
14									$ 200,349.24			
15									$ 189,600.07			
16									$ 188,918.67			
17									$ 196,635.10			
18									$ 200,001.27			
19									$ 190,514.29			
20									$ 194,724.19			
21									$ 195,934.37			
22									$ 200,042.39			
23									$ 194,631.26			
24									$ 197,118.66			
25				24	3.67%	$ 151,623.74			$ 199,939.96			
26				25	4.40%	$ 158,289.81			$ 194,849.23			

In K1:L4, we use percentile categories to estimate what we might expect to have saved after 30 years, starting with $60,000. The end result might cure you from ever doing this with your money, especially when inflation becomes part of the picture.

What you need to know

For the percentile scores, we used the function PERCENTILE in column L. This function works in all Excel versions. In version 2010 and later, it can be replaced with PERCENTILE.EXC or PERCENTILE. INC. The former function does not include k=1, whereas the latter one does. So the latter one is equivalent to the older function PERCENTILE.

Compounding a certain amount of money is based on a very simple formula: the starting amount multiplied by (1+APR) raised to the power of the number of years—or: $X*(1+APR)^{yrs}$. This is the formula used in the left table.

The middle table uses the function NORMINV to simulate fluctuations in the annual percentage rate each year (see Simulation 13 for this function).

The "what-if table" on the right runs the end result of the middle table at least 25 times by using the array formula {=TABLE(,G1)}—pointing to any empty cell outside the table (e.g., cell G1). For more information on this kind of table, see Appendix 3. The more runs, the more reliable the outcome is.

What you need to do

1. In cell B5: =B1*(1+B3)^B2. The savings are: $194,603.85.

2. In cell E2: =NORMINV(RAND(),$B$3,$B$4). Copy down.

3. In cell F2: =B1*(1+E2)^D2. In F3: =F2*(1+E3). Copy this 2nd formula down to cell F31.

4. In cell I1: =F31 (this refers to the final savings amount after 30 years in the center table, based on a volatile APR).

5. Select range H1:I26 and implement a Data Table with no row input but any empty cell as column input (e.g. cell G1). This creates the array formula =TABLE(,G1) in range I2:I26.

6. Place in cell L1: =PERCENTILE($I$1:$I$26,K1). Copy down to cell L4 for a set of confidence margins as to the expected saving amounts.

7. Using *Sh F9* recalculates the sheet and shows us some minor fluctuations in these predictions based on 25 runs.

33. Risk Analysis

What the simulation does

Open file 4-Financial.xlsx on sheet "Risks." Let's say we are trying to the figure out the optimal amount of production needed in order to maximize our profits. If the demand for this product is regulated by a range of probabilities, then we can determine our optimal production by simulating demand within that range of probabilities and calculating profit for each level of demand.

We use three tables to set up this calculation. The table on the right (G:H) sets up the assumed probability of various demand levels. The table on the top left (B:C) calculates the profit for one trial production quantity. Cell C1 has a trial production quantity. Cell C2 has a random number. In cell C3, we simulate demand for this product with the function VLOOKUP.

◢	A	B	C	D	E	F	G
1		produced	20000			probability	demand
2		rand#	0.851499701		0<p>0.1	0%	10,000
3		demand	60,000		0.1<p>0.25	10%	20,000
4		unit prod cost	$ 2.50		0.25<p>0.6	25%	40,000
5		unit price	$ 6.00		0.6<p>	60%	60,000
6							
7		revenue	$120,000.00				
8		total var cost	$ 50,000.00				
9		profit	$ 70,000.00				
10							
11	mean	$ 35,000.00	$ 64,120.00	$105,740.00	$ 104,520.00		
12	st dev	$ -	$ 17,847.81	$ 63,670.29	$ 107,039.37		
13							
14	$ 70,000.00		10,000	20,000	40,000	60,000	
15	1		$35,000.00	$70,000.00	$140,000.00	$30,000.00	
16	2		$35,000.00	$70,000.00	$140,000.00	$210,000.00	
17	3		$35,000.00	$70,000.00	$140,000.00	$210,000.00	
18	4		$35,000.00	$70,000.00	$140,000.00	$210,000.00	
19	5		$35,000.00	$10,000.00	$140,000.00	$30,000.00	
20	6		$35,000.00	$70,000.00	$140,000.00	$210,000.00	

The table on the lower left is a what-if table which simulates each possible production quantity (10,000, 20,000, 40,000 or 60,000) some 1,000 times and calculates profit for each trial number (1 to 1,000) and each production quantity (10,000, etc.).

Finally, row 11 calculates the mean profit for the four different production quantities. In this example, the results show that production of 40,000 units results in maximum profits.

What you need to know

The VLOOKUP function in C3 matches up the value in C1 with the closest match in the first column of table F2:G5. The corresponding value from the second column in table F2:G5 is then entered in C3.

The what-if table is a Data Table that uses cell C1 (20,000) for the row input, and an empty cell (say, G14) for the column input. How does this work? Consider the values placed by the what-if table in its fourth column. For each of these cells, Excel will use a value of 20,000 (cell C1).

Consider cell D15: the column input cell value of 1 is placed in a blank cell (G14) and the random number in cell C2 recalculates. The corresponding profit is then recorded in cell D15. Next the column cell input value of 2 is placed in the blank cell G14, and the random number in C2 again recalculates. The corresponding profit is entered in cell D16. And so on.

What you need to do

1. Select A14:E1014. Use a Data Table with C1 as row input and G14 (or any other empty cell) as column input. (See Appendix 3 for more details). The formula is =TABLE(C1,G14).

2. In B11: =AVERAGE(B15:B1014). Copy to the right.

3. In B12: =STDEV(B15:B1014). Copy to the right.

4. Hit *Sh F9* several times and notice, as shown in the picture below, that a production of 40,000 usually gives the best profit (in row 11). Even if another cell is higher, its risk is probably much higher (as expressed in the SD shown in row 12).

5. Try changing input cells in the top section and check the outcome.

11	mean	$	35,000.00	$ 64,120.00	$107,480.00	$ 104,460.00
12	st dev	$	-	$ 17,847.81	$ 61,811.57	$ 103,260.70
13						
14	$ 70,000.00		10,000	20,000	40,000	60,000

34. Missing or Exceeding Targets

What the simulation does

Open file 4-Financial.xlsx on sheet "Sensitivity." Let's say we are trying to predict the number of periods until a currently unprofitable company becomes profitable.

We have a goal here for managing expense growth rates and a goal for increasing sales growth rates—but, of course, we do not know whether or not we will meet our objectives.

A what-if table can help us. It shows us at a glance the effects of missing and/or exceeding our target numbers. The red numbers are losses after 4 years (cell B4).

	A	B	C	D	E	F	G	H	I	J	K	L
1		Amount	Growth rate									
2	Revenues	1,000,000	25%									
3	Expenses	1,400,000	3%									
4	Year	4										
5												
6	$865,693.92	12.0%	12.5%	13.0%	13.5%	14.0%	14.5%	15.0%	15.5%	16.0%	16.5%	
7	1.0%	$116,673.75	$144,961.03	$173,628.00	$202,678.04	$232,114.55	$261,940.94	$292,160.64	$322,777.09	$353,793.75	$385,214.09	
8	1.5%	$87,610.39	$115,897.67	$144,564.64	$173,614.68	$203,051.19	$232,877.58	$263,097.28	$293,713.73	$324,730.39	$356,150.73	
9	2.0%	$58,114.34	$86,401.62	$115,068.59	$144,118.63	$173,555.14	$203,381.53	$233,601.23	$264,217.68	$295,234.34	$326,654.68	
10	2.5%	$28,181.31	$56,468.59	$85,135.56	$114,185.60	$143,622.11	$173,448.50	$203,668.20	$234,284.65	$265,301.31	$296,721.65	
11	3.0%	-$2,192.97	$26,094.31	$54,761.28	$83,811.32	$113,247.83	$143,074.22	$173,293.92	$203,910.37	$234,927.03	$266,347.37	
12	3.5%	-$33,012.84	-$4,725.56	$23,941.41	$52,991.45	$82,427.96	$112,254.35	$142,474.05	$173,090.50	$204,107.16	$235,527.50	
13	4.0%	-$64,282.62	-$35,995.34	-$7,328.37	$21,721.67	$51,158.18	$80,984.57	$111,204.27	$141,820.72	$172,837.38	$204,257.72	
14	4.5%	-$96,006.68	-$67,719.40	-$39,052.43	-$10,002.39	$19,434.12	$49,260.51	$79,480.21	$110,096.66	$141,113.32	$172,533.66	
15	5.0%	-$128,189.39	-$99,902.11	-$71,235.14	-$42,185.10	-$12,748.59	$17,077.80	$47,297.50	$77,913.95	$108,930.61	$140,350.95	
16	5.5%	-$160,835.15	-$132,547.87	-$103,880.90	-$74,830.86	-$45,394.35	-$15,567.96	$14,651.74	$45,268.19	$76,284.85	$107,705.19	
17	6.0%	-$193,948.38	-$165,661.10	-$136,994.13	-$107,944.09	-$78,507.58	-$48,681.19	-$18,461.49	$12,154.96	$43,171.62	$74,591.96	
18	6.5%	-$227,533.53	-$199,246.25	-$170,579.28	-$141,529.24	-$112,092.73	-$82,266.34	-$52,046.64	-$21,430.19	$9,586.47	$41,006.81	
19	7.0%	-$261,595.05	-$233,307.77	-$204,640.80	-$175,590.76	-$146,154.25	-$116,327.86	-$86,108.16	-$55,491.71	-$24,475.05	$6,945.29	
20	7.5%	-$296,137.44	-$267,850.16	-$239,183.19	-$210,133.15	-$180,696.64	-$150,870.25	-$120,650.55	-$90,034.10	-$59,017.44	-$27,597.10	
21												

What you need to know

A what-if table will show us profits or losses for two different growth rates—one for revenues (C2) and one for expenses (C3)—after a certain amount of years (B4).

Since what-if tables can only be two dimensional, the year variable has to be manually changed. (Simulation 29 and Simulation 37 show you how to deal with 3 variables in a different way.)

What you need to do

1. The formula for profit in cell A6 is simple: (Revenues * (1 + Growth Rate Revenues) ^ Years) – (Expenses * (1 + Growth Rate Expenses) ^ Years).

2. So place in cell A6: =(B2*(1+C2)^B4)-(B3*(1+C3)^B4).

3. Select A6:K20 and create a Data Table with C2 for row input and C3 for column input. (See Appendix 3 for more details.)

4. Apply Conditional Formatting to the Data Table: Highlight Cell Rules | Less Than | 0.

5. Use *Sh F9*, and change some inputs in the top section.

6. In 6 years, this company would be doing much better for both variables (see below).

	A	B	C	D	E	F	G	H	I	J	K	L
1		Amount	Growth rate									
2	Revenues	1,000,000	25%									
3	Expenses	1,400,000	3%									
4	Year	6										
5												
6	$2,143,024.05	12.0%	12.5%	13.0%	13.5%	14.0%	14.5%	15.0%	15.5%	16.0%	16.5%	
7	1.0%	$487,694.47	$541,158.32	$595,823.54	$651,711.64	$708,844.41	$767,243.93	$826,932.55	$887,932.96	$950,268.11	#########	
8	1.5%	$443,002.12	$496,465.96	$551,131.18	$607,019.29	$664,152.05	$722,551.57	$782,240.20	$843,240.60	$905,575.75	$969,268.91	
9	2.0%	$397,195.30	$450,659.14	$505,324.37	$561,212.47	$618,345.24	$676,744.75	$736,433.38	$797,433.79	$859,768.94	$923,462.09	
10	2.5%	$350,251.90	$403,715.74	$458,380.97	$514,269.07	$571,401.84	$629,801.35	$689,489.98	$750,490.39	$812,825.54	$876,518.69	
11	3.0%	$302,149.47	$355,613.31	$410,278.54	$466,166.64	$523,299.41	$581,698.92	$641,387.55	$702,387.96	$764,723.11	$828,416.26	
12	3.5%	$252,865.23	$306,329.07	$360,994.30	$416,882.40	$474,015.17	$532,414.68	$592,103.31	$653,103.72	$715,438.87	$779,132.02	
13	4.0%	$202,376.06	$255,839.90	$310,505.13	$366,393.23	$423,526.00	$481,925.51	$541,614.14	$602,614.55	$664,949.70	$728,642.85	
14	4.5%	$150,658.51	$204,122.35	$258,787.58	$314,675.68	$371,808.45	$430,207.96	$489,896.59	$550,897.00	$613,232.15	$676,925.30	
15	5.0%	$97,688.79	$151,152.63	$205,817.86	$261,705.96	$318,838.73	$377,238.24	$436,926.87	$497,927.28	$560,262.43	$623,955.58	
16	5.5%	$43,442.76	$96,906.60	$151,571.82	$207,459.93	$264,592.69	$322,992.21	$382,680.84	$443,681.24	$506,016.39	$569,709.55	
17	6.0%	-$12,104.07	$41,359.77	$96,025.00	$151,913.10	$209,045.87	$267,445.38	$327,134.01	$388,134.42	$450,469.57	$514,162.72	
18	6.5%	-$68,976.53	-$15,512.69	$39,152.54	$95,040.64	$152,173.41	$210,572.92	$270,261.55	$331,261.96	$393,597.11	$457,290.26	
19	7.0%	-$127,199.81	-$73,735.96	-$19,070.74	$36,817.36	$93,950.13	$152,349.64	$212,038.27	$273,038.68	$335,373.83	$399,066.98	
20	7.5%	-$186,799.45	-$133,335.61	-$78,670.38	-$22,782.28	$34,350.49	$92,750.00	$152,438.63	$213,439.04	$275,774.19	$339,467.34	
21												

35. Two-Dimensional Filters

What the simulation does

Open file 4-Financial.xlsx on sheet "FilterTable." Let's say we have a table of data and we are trying to break out—or filter—results. It's easy enough to do this using one variable, but we want to filter for two variables simultaneously. Since what-if tables can be two-dimensional, we can also use them for two-dimensional filters.

We use three tables to set up this calculation. The database table is to the left. The filter table is located bottom-left, while the filtering what-if table can be found to the right.

	A	B	C	D	E	F	G	H	I	J	K
1	Product	Month	Cost	Sold	Total						
2	Lime	January	$ 0.35	946	$ 331.10						
3	Diet Lime	January	$ 0.35	762	$ 266.70						
4	Orange	January	$ 0.35	224	$ 78.40						
5	Diet Orange	January	$ 0.35	1	$ 0.35						
6	Kiwi	January	$ 0.35	715	$ 250.25		$ 4,127.20	January	February	March	
7	Diet Kiwi	January	$ 0.35	506	$ 177.10		Lime	$ 331.10	$ 318.50	$ 294.00	
8	Apple	January	$ 0.35	354	$ 123.90		Diet Lime	$ 266.70	$ 312.90	$ 154.70	
9	Diet Apple	January	$ 0.35	542	$ 189.70		Orange	$ 78.40	$ 324.10	$ 143.15	
10	Lime	February	$ 0.35	910	$ 318.50		Diet Orange	$ 0.35	$ 164.85	$ 71.75	
11	Diet Lime	February	$ 0.35	894	$ 312.90		Kiwi	$ 250.25	$ 172.55	$ 38.15	
12	Orange	February	$ 0.35	926	$ 324.10		Diet Kiwi	$ 177.10	$ 96.60	$ 92.05	
13	Diet Orange	February	$ 0.35	471	$ 164.85		Apple	$ 123.90	$ 15.75	$ 211.05	
14	Kiwi	February	$ 0.35	493	$ 172.55		Diet Apple	$ 189.70	$ 105.35	$ 194.25	
15	Diet Kiwi	February	$ 0.35	276	$ 96.60						
16	Apple	February	$ 0.35	45	$ 15.75						
17	Diet Apple	February	$ 0.35	301	$ 105.35						
18	Lime	March	$ 0.35	840	$ 294.00						
19	Diet Lime	March	$ 0.35	442	$ 154.70						
20	Orange	March	$ 0.35	409	$ 143.15						
21	Diet Orange	March	$ 0.35	205	$ 71.75						
22	Kiwi	March	$ 0.35	109	$ 38.15						
23	Diet Kiwi	March	$ 0.35	263	$ 92.05						
24	Apple	March	$ 0.35	603	$ 211.05						
25	Diet Apple	March	$ 0.35	555	$ 194.25						
26							no spaces in header names!				
27	Product	Month	Cost	Sold	Total						
28											
29											

What you need to know

Filtering in Excel can be done with a filter section—which is usually called an advanced filter (A27:E28). The filter has a copy of the database headers or labels (without spaces!) and a row below it to enter specific filters. In this example, we leave the second row (Row 28) empty because we let the what-if table to the right do the filtering work. The what-if table uses the cells A28 as column input and B28 as row input.

Depending on whether we want a sum or some other summary calculation, we use the DSUM function (or DAVERAGE, DMAX, etc.). All such D-functions do their math based on a filter specified in their third argument, whereas the second argument designates the field name of the database field that we want to summarize (in our case cell E1, the Total column label).

What you need to do

1. Place in G6: =DSUM(A1:E25,E1,A27:E28). You can replace DSUM with DAVERAGE, DMAX, DMIN, DCOUNT, etc.

2. Select D6:G14 and start a Data Table with B28 for row input and A28 for column input. (See Appendix 3 for more details.)

3. The array formula that was automatically placed in range H7:J14 is now: =TABLE(B28,A28).

4. It is also possible to place certain criteria in the filter. See the example below for sales over 400.

	A	B	C	D	E	F	G	H	I	J
1	Product	Month	Cost	Sold	Total					
2	Lime	January	$ 0.35	946	$ 331.10					
3	Diet Lime	January	$ 0.35	762	$ 266.70					
4	Orange	January	$ 0.35	224	$ 78.40					
5	Diet Orange	January	$ 0.35	1	$ 0.35					
6	Kiwi	January	$ 0.35	715	$ 250.25		$ 3,504.90	January	February	March
7	Diet Kiwi	January	$ 0.35	506	$ 177.10		Lime	$ 331.10	$ 318.50	$ 294.00
8	Apple	January	$ 0.35	354	$ 123.90		Diet Lime	$ 266.70	$ 312.90	$ 154.70
9	Diet Apple	January	$ 0.35	542	$ 189.70		Orange	$ -	$ 324.10	$ 143.15
10	Lime	February	$ 0.35	910	$ 318.50		Diet Orange	$ -	$ 164.85	$ -
11	Diet Lime	February	$ 0.35	894	$ 312.90		Kiwi	$ 250.25	$ 172.55	$ -
12	Orange	February	$ 0.35	926	$ 324.10		Diet Kiwi	$ 177.10	$ -	$ -
13	Diet Orange	February	$ 0.35	471	$ 164.85		Apple	$ -	$ -	$ 211.05
14	Kiwi	February	$ 0.35	493	$ 172.55		Diet Apple	$ 189.70	$ -	$ 194.25
15	Diet Kiwi	February	$ 0.35	276	$ 96.60					
16	Apple	February	$ 0.35	45	$ 15.75					
17	Diet Apple	February	$ 0.35	301	$ 105.35					
18	Lime	March	$ 0.35	840	$ 294.00					
19	Diet Lime	March	$ 0.35	442	$ 154.70					
20	Orange	March	$ 0.35	409	$ 143.15					
21	Diet Orange	March	$ 0.35	205	$ 71.75					
22	Kiwi	March	$ 0.35	109	$ 38.15					
23	Diet Kiwi	March	$ 0.35	263	$ 92.05					
24	Apple	March	$ 0.35	603	$ 211.05					
25	Diet Apple	March	$ 0.35	555	$ 194.25					
26										
27	Product	Month	Cost	Sold	Total		no spaces in header names!			
28				>400						
29										

36. Scenarios

What the simulation does

Open file 4-Financial.xlsx on sheet "Scenarios." Predictions of expenses and revenues are subject to lots of uncertainty. Nevertheless, let's say we want to predict these under a few defined scenarios, such as the most likely, best case and worst case scenarios, in order to project a range of possible profit levels.

	A	B	C	D	E	F	G	H	I	J	K	L
1	most likely scenario			worst case		best case		uncertainty			scenario combinations	
2		1		4		6					1-4-6	146
3	Volume	1,500		1,400		2,200		2,014.35				
4	Cost/unit	$ 2.50		$ 2.75		$ 3.25		$3.16			Min	$ 77,015.26
5	Profit/unit	$ 50.00		$ 55.00		$ 65.00		$56.45			25%	$ 90,687.95
6	Overhead	$ 800.00									Median	$ 104,664.60
7											75%	$ 111,175.96
8	Revenues	$75,000.00		$77,000.00		$143,000.00		$113,713.26			Max	$ 124,838.96
9	Expenses	$4,550.00		$4,650.00		$7,950.00		$7,161.74				
10									Volume	Revenues	Expenses	Profit
11	Profit	$70,450.00		$72,350.00		$135,050.00		$106,551.52	2,014	$ 113,713.26	$ 7,161.74	$ 106,551.52
12									1,415	$ 86,532.85	$ 5,282.17	$ 81,250.68
13		most likely		worst case		best case			2,087	$ 127,182.44	$ 6,817.41	$ 120,365.04
14	1	2	3	4	5	6			1,504	$ 84,222.94	$ 5,560.58	$ 78,662.36
15	1,500	2,000	1,200	1,400	2,100	2,200			2,028	$ 129,654.70	$ 6,456.60	$ 123,198.10
16	$ 2.50	$ 3.00	$ 2.30	$ 2.75	$ 2.70	$ 3.25			1,620	$ 101,131.01	$ 5,755.89	$ 95,375.12
17	$ 50.00	$ 60.00	$ 47.00	$ 55.00	$ 53.00	$ 65.00			2,043	$ 115,189.20	$ 6,564.53	$ 108,624.67
18									1,990	$ 110,593.28	$ 7,127.25	$ 103,466.04
19									2,114	$ 132,366.78	$ 7,527.82	$ 124,838.96
20									1,644	$ 102,715.48	$ 5,862.71	$ 96,852.77
21									1,633	$ 101,801.45	$ 5,723.44	$ 96,078.01
22									1,990	$ 115,555.75	$ 6,927.09	$ 108,628.66
23									1,424	$ 83,325.96	$ 4,951.97	$ 78,373.99
24									1,524	$ 97,969.32	$ 5,114.38	$ 92,854.94

We use several tables to set up this calculation. The top left table has 3 dropdown boxes (B2, D2, F2) where we choose 3 scenarios. The main calculations occur in the Data Table in the lower-right corner. It is two-dimensional, but has a "hidden" third dimension—in this example a set of six different scenarios—displayed in the left-lower section (A14:F17).

Through cell B2, a specific "likely" scenario can be chosen; through cell D2, a "worst case" scenario and, through cell F2, a "best case" scenario. There are actually six scenarios—two for each case—but this set can be expanded, of course, and its values can be changed.

All values in column H depend on the 3 scenarios chosen in the cells B2, D2, and F2. But "results may vary." So we run these probability predictions at least some 100 times in a Data Table.

Finally, in the top right table, we summarize the results of our runs *(by averaging?)* based on each scenario and have derived our possible profit scenarios.

What you need to know

This calculation uses HLOOKUP, which stands for Horizontal lookup. It is similar to VLOOKUP, only it searches horizontal data rather than columnar data. HLOOKUP is used in the top left table to locate the correct input in the scenario table A14:F17. Because the scenario numbers are in a row (row 14), we need a *horizontal* lookup—HLOOKUP, not VLOOKUP.

What you need to do

1. There is Data Validation in B2 (1,2), D2 (3,4), and F2 (5,6).

2. Place in cell B3 a lookup formula that we can copy down to cell B5:
    =HLOOKUP(B$2,$A$14:$F$17,ROW(A2),0).

3. In D3: =HLOOKUP(D$2,$A$14:$F$17,ROW(C2),0). Copy.

4. In F3: =HLOOKUP(F$2,$A$14:$F$17,ROW(E2),0). Copy.

5. In H3 we simulate random values between the worst and best case scenario: =D3+RAND()*(F3-D3).
    Copy down to H5.

6. In cell H8: =H3*H5. In cell H9: =B6+H3*H4.

7. In cell H11: =H8-H9. This calculates the prediction for the given scenarios based on a single random
    run.

8. Create links in I11 (=H3), J11 (=H8), K11 (=H9), and L11 (=H11). These will regulate the outcome of
    100 runs.

9. Select range H11:L111 at once and implement a Data Table with no row input and an empty cell (e.g.
    F11) for column input: =TABLE(,F11).

10. In the cells L4 through L8 we create an overview of the 100 profits generated in the Data Table:
    =MIN($L$11:$L$111) and =PERCENTILE($L$11:$L$111, 0.25), and so on.

11. K2 shows the chosen scenarios: =B2 & "-" & D2 & "-" & F2.

12. Cell L2 changes this into a 3-digit number: =B2&D2&F2. In Simulation 68, we will use this number to
    "remember" the outcome of each combination of three scenarios.

13. Hitting *Sh F9* will show you how each scenario combination has still some uncertainty in its outcome.
    Running the Data Table some 1,000,000 times, would dampen the variation.

14. Try also to change scenario combinations.

37. Moving Averages

What the simulation does

Open file 4-Financial.xlsx on sheet "MovingAvg." Let's say we want to calculate a moving average on a set of data, but we wish to change the period of the moving average without having to re-calculate the average each time we make a change.

This example calculates a moving average based on a specific period (specified in cell E1), and plots both the data and the moving average on the chart to the right of the data. This period (E1) can be changed by clicking on the buttons to the right of cell E1.

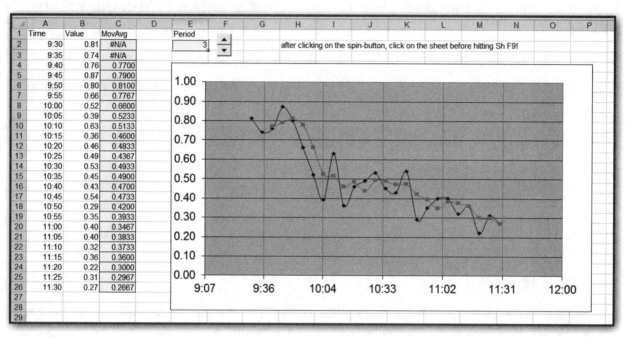

What you need to know

The data we are averaging is in column B, while the average is in column C. To start the moving average calculation in the correct row, we use the function ROW in the moving average column to start calculating the average in the correct row number. If this row number is greater than or equal to E2 + 1 (1 is for the column headers), then the average will be calculated, otherwise place #N/A in the cell. #N/A is from the function NA, which makes that data point not show up in the chart.

The difficult part is how to determine the range that has to be averaged. This is done with the function OFFSET, which returns an offset range of cells and has 5 arguments. The 1st argument determines where to start the range (B2 in our case). The 2nd argument controls the number of rows up or down (in our case, minus E2 + 1). The 3rd argument is the number of columns to the left or right (0 in our case). The 4th and 5th arguments are optional and specify the numbers of rows (height) and the number of columns (width); left empty, the height and width are assumed to be the same as for the starting cell (B2).

The moving average curve in the chart obviously starts after the indicated period as specified in cell E1.

What you need to do

1. Place the following formula in cell C2:
   =IF(ROW()>=($E$2+1),AVERAGE(OFFSET(B2,-$E$2+1,0,$E$2)),NA()). It might be helpful to know that the *Analysis Toolpak* also includes a *Moving Average* feature to compute moving averages without using formulas.

2. Copy this formula down to C26. In our example, with a delay period of 3, the average should kick in when the cell can offset -3+1 rows up—which is in cell C4 (for a period of 4, it would be in cell C5, etc.)

3. Position a spin-button next to E2. (See Appendix 5 for more details.) Set Min to 0, Max to 10, and Linked Cell to E2.

4. After clicking on the spin-button, you must click on the sheet before hitting *Sh F9*, if the file is set to manual calculation.

5. Based on a delay period of 7, the curve would obviously be much less fluctuating (see below).

6. You could also apply *Exponential Smoothing* by using the *Analysis Toolpak*. It is a weighted-average technique that uses a weighting, or damping, factor (by default 0.3). Be aware, though, this tool puts formulas, not values, in your cells.

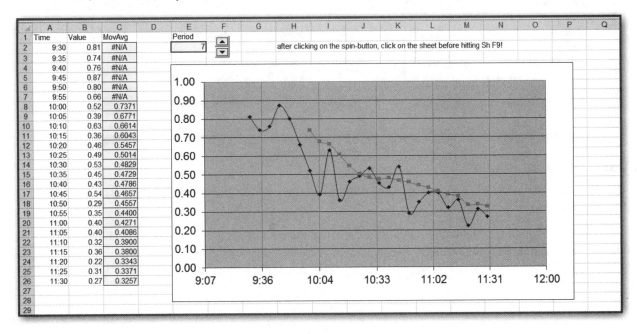

38. Return on Investment

What the simulation does

Open file 4-Financial.xlsx on sheet "ReturnOI." Let's say we want to calculate our return on an investment but also take into consideration the cost of inflation and taxes to our investment.

This sheet simulates the return on investment (ROI) when buying bank CDs for a certain amount of money (B1), with the assumption that these have a fixed interest rate (B2), a certain fixed inflation rate (B4), and that we are taxed at 25% for CD profits (B3).

We also assume that we want to keep our CD value at its original power by, at least theoretically, putting in more money each year (B8).

We do all of this for a certain number of years (B6). In the what-if table to the right, we can see at what return rates and inflation rates our investment becomes profitable.

	A	B	C	D	E	F	G	H	I	J	K
1	CD value	$ 100,000.00									
2	CD interest	8%									
3	Taxes	25%									
4	Inflation rate	10%									
5											
6	Number of years	10		-3.11%	5%	6%	7%	8%	9%	10%	CD return
7	After inflation	$ 34,867.84		4%	3%	9%	14%	20%	25%	31%	
8	To keep power	$ 65,132.16		5%	-2%	3%	9%	14%	20%	25%	
9	CD interest	$ 80,000.00		6%	-6%	-1%	4%	9%	15%	20%	
10	Taxes on profit	$ 20,000.00		7%	-9%	-4%	1%	6%	10%	15%	
11	ROI (return on investment)	-3.11%		8%	-12%	-7%	-3%	2%	7%	12%	
12				9%	-15%	-10%	-5%	-1%	4%	9%	
13				inflation							
14											

What you need to know

The core part of this simulation is calculating the return on investment (ROI) in cell B11, based on all the cells above it.

We also use that same calculation to create a two-dimensional what-if table based on a variable for CD interest and a variable for the inflation rate.

What you need to do

1. In cell B7: =B1*(1-B4)^B6.

2. In cell B8: =B1-B7.

3. In cell B9: =B1*B2*B6.

4. In cell B10: =B9*B3.

5. In cell B11: =(B9-B8-B10)/(B1+B8).

6. In cell D6: =B11.

7. Select D6:J12 and start a Data Table with B2 for row input and B4 for column input.

8. Place Conditional Formatting in the Data Table: Highlight Cell Rules | Less than 0.

9. In 20 years, the overall results would be a bit better—that is, fewer negative numbers (see below).

	A	B	C	D	E	F	G	H	I	J	K
1	CD value	$ 100,000.00									
2	CD interest	8%									
3	Taxes	25%									
4	Inflation rate	10%									
5											
6	Number of years	20		17.12%	5%	6%	7%	8%	9%	10%	CD return
7	After inflation	$ 12,157.67		4%	12%	22%	32%	41%	51%	60%	
8	To keep power	$ 87,842.33		5%	7%	16%	25%	34%	43%	52%	
9	CD interest	$ 160,000.00		6%	2%	11%	20%	29%	37%	46%	
10	Taxes on profit	$ 40,000.00		7%	-1%	8%	16%	25%	33%	42%	
11	ROI (return on investment)	17.12%		8%	-3%	5%	13%	21%	30%	38%	
12				9%	-5%	3%	11%	19%	27%	35%	
13				inflation							
14											

39. Employee Stock Options

What the simulation does

Open file 4-Financial.xlsx on the sheet called "StockOptions." Companies must determine and report the fair value of stock options they use to compensate employees. But because employee stock options cannot be traded publicly, their fair value is not readily available and must be estimated using option-pricing models. One could do this by building a lattice model that makes the necessary calculations in Excel.

To calculate the fair value of issued stock options, we develop a stock-price tree. At each node, there is either an upward movement in price or a downward movement in price. After 4 years, there are 16 nodes. In year 1, the probability of reaching 1 of the 2 nodes is 0.5 (E2), in year 2, the probability of reaching 1 of the 4 nodes is 0.25 (F2), etc. The end nodes depend on the nodes in the previous years.

How much the price goes up or down depends on the variables in the left top corner. The stock price increases by the risk-free rate, 3% (B7); is unaffected by the assumed 0% expected dividend yield (B8); and then either increases or decreases by 30% due to the expected volatility (B6).

	A	B	C	D	E	F	G	H	I	J	K	L	M	N	O	P	Q	R	S
1	Current stock price	$30.00		Year 0	Year 1	Year 2	Year 3	Year 4		intrinsic	present		$ 8.56	10%	20%	30%	40%	volatility	
2	Price of option	$30.00		1.0000	0.5000	0.2500	0.1250	0.0625		value	value		2%	$ 3.70	$ 5.59	$ 8.23	$ 10.89		
3													3%	$ 4.43	$ 6.30	$ 8.56	$ 11.22		
4								$96.44		$ 66.44	$3.69		4%	$ 5.13	$ 6.99	$ 8.88	$ 11.54		
5	Expected option life	4					$72.02						5%	$ 5.79	$ 7.66	$ 9.24	$ 11.84		
6	Volatility	30%						$51.93		$ 21.93	$1.22		risk-free rate						
7	Risk-free rate	3%				$53.79													
8	Dividend yield	0%						$51.93		$ 21.93	$1.22								
9							$38.78												
10	Fair option value	$ 8.56						$27.96		$ -	$0.00								
11					$40.17														
12								$51.93		$ 21.93	$1.22								
13						$38.78													
14								$27.96		$ -	$0.00								
15					$28.96														
16								$27.96		$ -	$0.00								
17						$20.88													
18								$15.06		$ -	$0.00								
19				$30.00															
20								$51.93		$ 21.93	$1.22								
21						$38.78													
22								$27.96		$ -	$0.00								
23					$28.96														
24								$27.96		$ -	$0.00								
25						$20.88													
26								$15.06		$ -	$0.00								
27				$21.63															
28								$27.96		$ -	$0.00								
29						$20.88													
30								$15.06		$ -	$0.00								
31					$15.60														
32								$15.06		$ -	$0.00								
33						$11.24													
34								$8.11		$ -	$0.00								

What you need to know

Assume, at the grant date, year 0, the stock price is $30 (cell B1 and D19). The model assumes also that stock prices will increase at the risk-free interest rate minus the expected dividend yield, then either *plus* or *minus* the price volatility for the stock.

In column J, we calculate the intrinsic value of each end node. In column K, we calculate the present value with the function PV as follows: –PV(risk-free rate in B7, option life in B4, , intrinsic value in column J * probability in H2).

Remember, in annuity functions, cash you pay out is represented by a negative number, but cash you receive is a positive number; therefore, we use the negative version of PV(…).

The "fair option value" is the sum total of all possible present values in column K—either positive or 0. Based on this value, we use a Data Table to see the effect of different volatilities and risk-free rates.

What you need to do

1. Place in cell E11: =D19*(1+$B$7-$B$8)*(1+$B$6). Copy this formula to all *positive* nodes (the ones upward).

2. In cell E27: =D19*(1+$B$7-$B$8)*(1-$B$6). Copy to all *negative* nodes (the ones downward). Notice the negative sign in the last argument.

3. In cell J4: =IF(H4>$B$2,H4-$B$2,0). Copy formula down.

4. In cell K4: =–PV($B$7,4,,J4*$H$2). Copy down.

5. In cell B10: =SUM(K4:K34). This is the "fair option value."

6. Place in cell M1 a link to cell B10: =B10. This is going to be the origin of a Data Table.

7. Select Range M1:Q5 and start a Data Table with the volatility (B6) as row input and the risk-free rate (B7) as column input: =TABLE(B6,B7).

8. Conditional Formatting highlights the current situation in the Data Table with the following formula: =N2=$M$1.

9. Changing any variables in column B should update the situation (*Sh F9*).

40. Value at Risk

What the simulation does

Open file 4-Financial.xlsx on sheet "ValueAtRisk." *Value-at-Risk*, or *VaR*, is a risk measure that answers the question "What is my potential loss."

Specifically, it is the potential maximum loss in a portfolio (and a certain standard deviation) at a given confidence interval over a given period of time (which could be a day, a month, or a year).

	A	B	C	D	E
1	Portfolio	$ 100.00			
2	Avg return	0.152			
3	SD	0.135			
4	Confidence	99%			
5					
6	Confidence	Min. return	New value	Value at Risk (VaR)	
7	99%	-0.16206	$ 83.79	$ 16.21	
8	95%	-0.07006	$ 92.99	$ 7.01	
9	90%	-0.02101	$ 97.90	$ 2.10	
10	85%	0.01208	$ 101.21	$ (1.21)	
11	80%	0.03838	$ 103.84	$ (3.84)	
12	75%	0.06094	$ 106.09	$ (6.09)	
13	70%	0.08121	$ 108.12	$ (8.12)	
14	65%	0.09998	$ 110.00	$ (10.00)	
15	60%	0.11780	$ 111.78	$ (11.78)	
16	55%	0.13504	$ 113.50	$ (13.50)	
17	50%	0.15200	$ 115.20	$ (15.20)	
18					

What you need to know

We calculate the minimum expected return with respect to the confidence level chosen (i.e. if your confidence level is 99%, then you are 99% sure that your return will be above this). This is done with the function NORMINV (although investments do not always follow a normal distribution!).

What we have for a result is the *VaR* for a single time period (say, one trading day). To convert that value to a longer range, simply multiply the *VaR* by the square root of the number of single periods within the longer period. Say, you calculated the *VaR* for one day and want it for a month, use the number of trading days in a month, say 22, and multiply your *VaR* with √22.

Be aware, though, that *VaR* is not your worst case loss. At a confidence level of 95%, the *VaR* is your minimum expected loss 5% of the time—not your maximum expected loss. So be prepared for surprises.

What you need to do

1. Place in cell B7: =NORMINV(1-B4,B2,B3). This is your minimum return at a 99% confidence level (cell B4).

2. Place in cell C7: =B1*(B7+1). This would be the new value.

3. Place in cell D7: =B1-C7. This is the *Value-at-Risk* at a 99% confidence level.

4. To see the result for lower confidence level, we use a Data Table again.

5. Select range A7:D17 and start a Data Table with no row input, but B4 as column input: =TABLE(,B4).

6. If these are the results for one day, you could add a column (e.g. F) for the results in a month with 22 trading days: =D7*SQRT(22).

7. It is clear that you can change the variables in B1:B3 at any time and watch their impact.

41. Asian Options

What the simulation does

Open file 4-Financial.xlsx on sheet "AsianOption." Let's say we want to value an Asian option, which is valued by determining the average underlying price over a period of time. To price an Asian option by its mean, we need to know, at least to some degree, the path that the stock takes as time progresses. To simplify things, we will track the stock over 5 years in yearly increments.

To derive the average value, we multiply the initial stock price (column B) by the first randomly generated log-normal number (with the functions EXP and NORMINV) to obtain a value for year 1 (I won't go into further explanations). The result must be multiplied by the second randomly generated number (column C), and so on.

To make the predictions a bit more reliable, we give it 10 trials in this simulation (rows 7:16). For each trial, we calculate the average (column I) and the payoff (column J). In real life, we would need many more trials.

Then we calculate the average payoff (J18) and its standard deviation (J19). The graph only shows 5 of the 10 trials for 6 yrs.

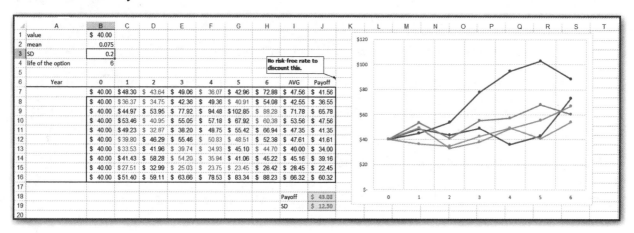

What you need to know

Simply put, an option contract is an agreement between two people that gives one the right to buy or sell a stock at some future date for some preset price.

An Asian option (or "average value option") is a special type of option contract. The payoff is determined by the average underlying price over some pre-set period of time. This is different from the usual European options and American options which are valued at the expiration of the contract.

One advantage of Asian options is that these reduce the risk of market manipulation. Another advantage is the relatively low cost of Asian options. Because of the averaging feature, Asian options reduce the volatility inherent in the option; therefore, Asian options are typically cheaper than European or American options.

What you need to do

1. Place in cell B7: =$B$1.

2. Place in cell C7: =B7*EXP(NORMINV(RAND(), $B$2-0.5*$B$3^2, $B$3)). Copy this formula to the right, to H7.

3. Place in cell I7: =AVERAGE(B7:H7).

4. Place in cell J7: =MAX(0,I7-$B$4).

5. Select range A7:J16 and start a Data table with no row input and any empty cell (e.g. cell A5) as a column input: =TABLE(,A5).

6. Place in cell J18: =AVERAGE(J7:J16).

7. Place in cell J19: =STDEV(J7:J16).

8. At each new series of runs (*Sh F9*), the results can vary widely (see below). That is why we would need many more runs to get more reliable results.

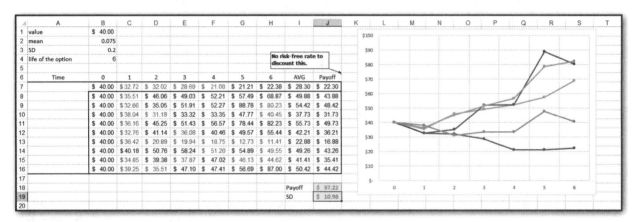

42. Black-Scholes Model

What the simulation does

Open file 4-Financial.xlsx on sheet "BlackScholes." The Black-Scholes formula is designed to give the value of an option on a security, such as a stock. It is calculated based on the price of the stock today (cell C2), the exercise price of the option (D2), the duration of the option in years (E2), the volatility of the stock (F2), and the annual risk-free rate (G2). The Black-Scholes model works with some fancy formulas which you can use in Excel to return the Black-Scholes Option value.

	A	B	C	D	E	F	G	H	I
1			price today	exercise price	duration (yrs)	volatility	risk-free rate (yr)	d1	d2
2			50.00	50.00	0.25	20.0%	5.0%	0.1750	0.0750
3	Call	$ 2.31						N(d1)	N(d2)
4	Put	$ 1.69						0.5695	0.5299
5									
6		$ 2.31	Call		$ 1.69	Put			
7		10%	$ 1.33		10%	$ 0.71			
8		15%	$ 1.82		15%	$ 1.20			
9		20%	$ 2.31		20%	$ 1.69			
10		25%	$ 2.80		25%	$ 2.18			
11		30%	$ 3.29		30%	$ 2.67			
12		35%	$ 3.78		35%	$ 3.16			
13		40%	$ 4.28		40%	$ 3.66			
14		45%	$ 4.77		45%	$ 4.15			
15		50%	$ 5.26		50%	$ 4.64			
16		volatility			volatility				
17									

What you need to know

Options are divided into two categories: calls and puts. *Calls* increase in value when the underlying security is going up, and they decrease in value when the underlying security declines in price. *Puts* increase in value when the underlying security is going down and decrease in value when it is going up.

A *call* (cell B3) gives you the right to buy a stock from the investor who sold you the call option at a specific price on or before a specified date. For instance, if you bought a 50 October call option, the option would come with terms telling you that you could buy the stock for $50 (the strike price) any time before the third Friday in October (the expiration date). If the stock rises anywhere above $50 before the third Friday in October, you can buy the stock for less than its market value. Or if you do not want to buy the stock yourself or exercise the option, you can sell your option to someone else for a profit. But if the stock never rises above $50, your option won't be worth anything.

A *put* option (cell B4) gives you the right to sell a stock to the investor who sold you the put option at a specific price, on or before a specified date. For instance, if you bought, the option would come with terms telling you that you could sell the stock for $50 (the strike price) any time before the third Friday in October (the expiration date). What this means is, if the stock falls anywhere below $50 before the third Friday in October, you can sell the stock for more than its market value.

To simulate how this works out for different volatility values, we create two what-if tables—one for *calls* given different volatility conditions, and one for *puts* given different volatility values.

What you need to do

1. Place in H2 the calculation for the *d*-factor: =(LN(C2/D2)+(G2+(F2^2)/2)*E2)/(F2*SQRT(E2)). The values for *d1* and *d2* are used to calculate the probabilities that the stock price at expiration will be a certain number of standard deviations above or below the standardized mean (i.e., 0).

2. Place in cell I2: =H2-(F2*SQRT(E2)).

3. Place in H4: =NORMSDIST(H2). The variables N(d1) and N(d2) are probabilities of the stock price being used at a certain price relative to where it is now

4. Place in I4: =NORMSDIST(I2).

5. Place in B3: =C2*H4-D2*EXP(-G2*E2)*I4.

6. Place in B4: =B3+D2*EXP(-G2*E2)-C2.

7. Place in B6 a link to B3, and in E6 a link to B4.

8. Start a Data Table from cell B6: =TABLE(A6,F2).

9. Start a Data Table from cell E6: =TABLE(D6,F2).

Expansion

43. Offspring of Two Rabbits

What the simulation does

Open file 5-Expansion.xlsx on sheet "FeedRabbits." The question you may have to face is this: How much food do we need to keep the offspring of 2 laboratory rabbits alive after X generations? The answer is: in the beginning not much, but rather soon an unexpectedly huge amount of food.

Let us assume the population starts with a male and a female (B1) and grows at a net rate of 2.4 per generation (B2). After 25 generations (B28), the population has reached the astonishing number of 6,401,931,729 individuals (C28).

This is called exponential growth, which creates a curve with a shape as shown in the top graph. The growth starts slowly but gradually grows enormously fast. If you would put an exponential trend line through the data, its formula would be $y = 2e^{0.8755x}$

We limited the growth rate to a maximum of 2.8, since the computer could easily run into overflow situations.

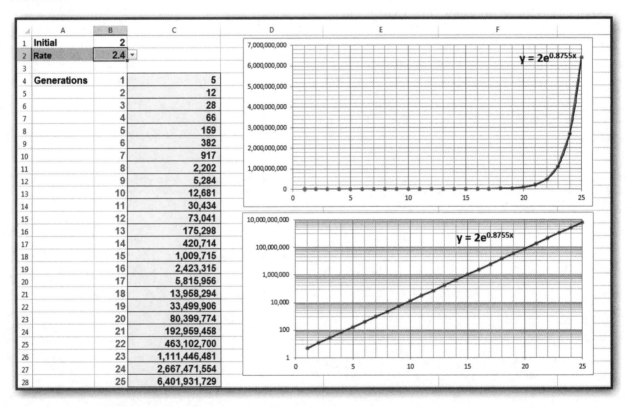

What you need to know

For exponential growth, we could change the (vertical) Y-axis into a logarithmic scale, which changes the exponential curve into a seemingly linear curve as shown in the second graph.

If you would add a trend-line to the second curve, make sure it is exponential, not linear: $y = 2e^{0.8755x}$ (that is, based on a growth rate of 2.4).

What you need to do

1. Place in cell C4: =$B$1*$B$2^B4.

2. Copy the formula down to cell C28.

3. Validate cell B2 with a list if you want: 2,2.2,2.4,2.6,2.8.

4. Any change in growth rate should change the entire picture (perhaps after hitting *Sh F9*).

5. With a growth rate of 2.8, the food needs do rise dramatically: from 6,401,931,729 in the previous graph to 301,981,806,790 in the graph below.

6. Be aware: The graph may look the same, but the Y-axis has been expanded enormously.

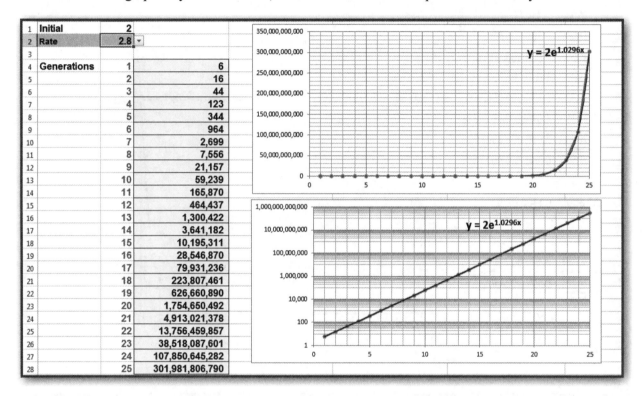

44. Extrapolation

What the simulation does

Open file 5-Expansion.xlsx on sheet "Extrapolation." The rows 2:9 show historical figures for the size of the world population.

Based on this information, row 10 predicts what the size of the world population will be in 2050. This is called extrapolation.

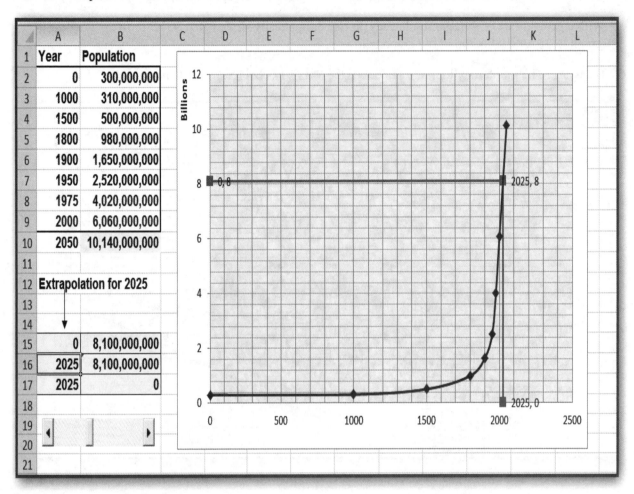

What you need to know

Extrapolation can be done in two ways. If you can figure out the equation behind the observed, or known, figures, you can apply that equation to the new figure (in this case, the year 2050).

If you do *not* know the equation, you can use the two most recent observations (in this case, 1975 and 2000), assume a linear relationship between the two, and calculate the new, approximate value in cell B10.

The function to do the latter is TREND. We used it before, in Simulation 22, for a case of interpolation, but it also works for extrapolation; however, extrapolation is always more risky than interpolation. It is a multi-cell array function. Based on observed X-values and observed Y-values, it can be used for a new, unobserved X-value to predict what the extrapolated Y-value would be.

The lower tabel to the left (A15:B17) holds three sets of coordinates for additional extrapolations. This section can be manipulated with a scroll-bar control.

What you need to do

1. Place in cell D10: =TREND(B8:B9,A8:A9,A10). Do not forget to accept the array function with *Ctr Sh Enter*.

2. Place in cell B16: =TREND(B8:B9,A8:A9,A16).

3. Link cell B15 to B16, and cell A17 to A16.

4. Add a scroll-bar control. (For more details see Appendix 5). Set Min to 1975, Max to 2100, and Linked-Cell to cell A16.

5. The farther away the extrapolation goes, the more unreliable it becomes, of course (see below).

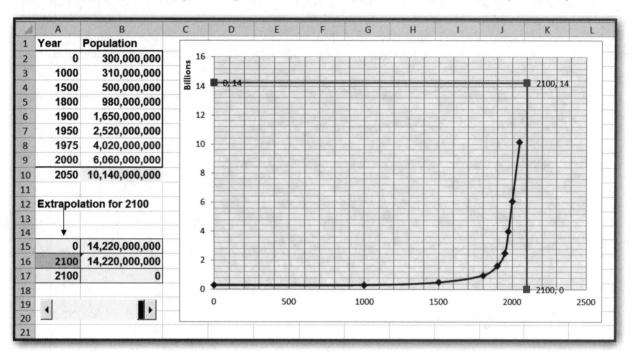

45. Predator-Prey Cycle

What the simulation does

Open file 5-Expansion.xlsx on sheet "PredatorPrey." In "real" life, populations do not grow in an exponential and unlimited way as they may under artificial circumstances (like in Simulation 44). There are always limiting factors such as food supply and the presence of predators.

This idea has led to the so-called Lotka-Volterra model, dealing specifically about the relationship between predator and prey. It makes a number of assumptions: 1.The prey population finds ample food at all times. 2. The food supply of the predator population depends entirely on the prey populations. 3. The rate of change is proportional to the population size.

After some manipulation, we could deduce two simplified equations for the size of the prey population (done in column B) and the size of the predator population (in column C) in a certain generation (column A). Notice how this may lead to a stable relationship: Each species goes to a minimum before rising to a maximum, but the two curves are shifted relative to each other. Notice also how the minima and maxima are constant.

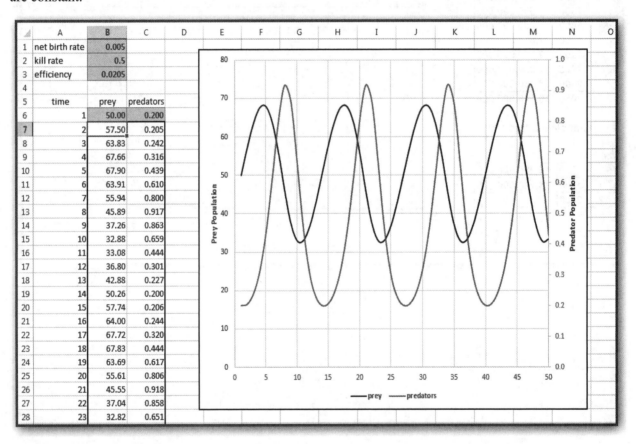

What you need to know

The prey are assumed to have an unlimited food supply, and to reproduce exponentially unless subject to predation. The rate of predation upon the prey is assumed to be proportional to the rate at which the predators and the prey meet. Consequently, the change in the prey's numbers is given by its own growth minus the rate at which it is preyed upon. On the other hand, the change in growth of the predator population is fueled by the food supply, minus natural death.

What you need to do

1. Place in B7: =(1-$B$1*(B6-100))*B6-$B$2*B6*C6. Copy down. The left Y-axis is for the size of the prey population.

2. Place in cell C7: =$B$3*B6*C6. Copy the formula down.

3. The actual outcome depends on the variables and parameters that were entered in the dark-colored cells.

4. When you change any of these variables slightly, you may sometimes just see minor effects, but you may also lose stability in the system. Reset each value after changing it.

5. When you change certain parameters more drastically, the population may either explode or become extinct.

6. When you change the net birth rate from 0.005 to 0.01, for instance, you will see the pattern shown below.

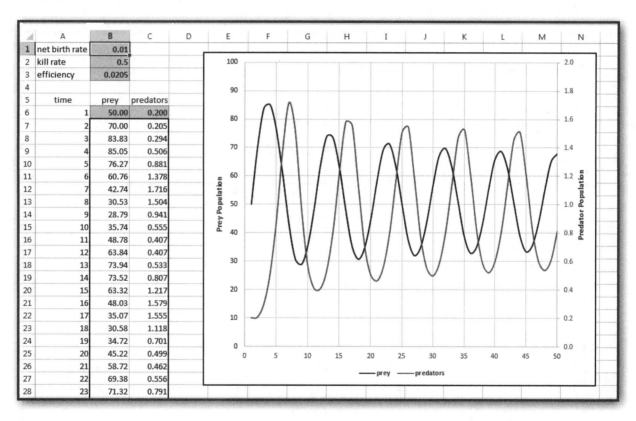

46. Homeostasis

What the simulation does

Open file 5-Expansion.xlsx on sheet "Homeostasis." In human biology, homeostasis is the process used by the body to maintain a stable internal environment. Examples are plenty—the regulation of body temperature, control of blood glucose levels, and regulation of salt and water balance. Usually these variables stay within narrow margins. When they deviate, control mechanisms correct the deviation by either enhancing aberrations with positive feedback or depressing them with negative feedback. This process is simulated in column B and the top graph.

This process can sometimes adjust to new challenges by reducing spikes in a particular value. This is simulated in column C and the second graph. It resembles a decreasing tremor

Sometimes the opposite happens. The process runs out of control by extreme changes of a variable or by defects in the control mechanism. This phenomenon is simulated in column D and the bottom graph. Diabetes is probably the best example. Enormous spikes in glucose intake may cause the system to go haywire. It looks like an increasing tremor.

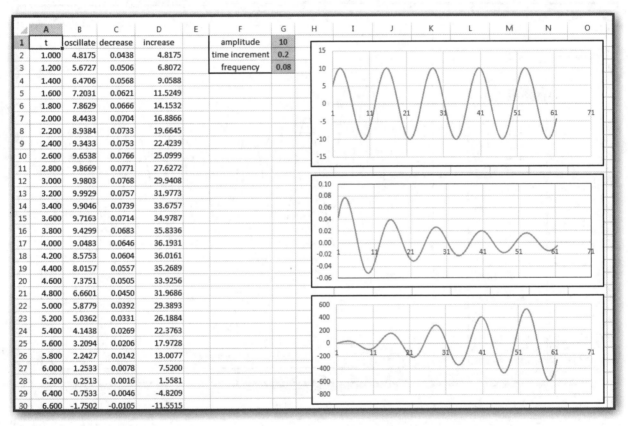

	A	B	C	D	E	F	G
1	t	oscillate	decrease	increase		amplitude	10
2	1.000	4.8175	0.0438	4.8175		time increment	0.2
3	1.200	5.6727	0.0506	6.8072		frequency	0.08
4	1.400	6.4706	0.0568	9.0588			
5	1.600	7.2031	0.0621	11.5249			
6	1.800	7.8629	0.0666	14.1532			
7	2.000	8.4433	0.0704	16.8866			
8	2.200	8.9384	0.0733	19.6645			
9	2.400	9.3433	0.0753	22.4239			
10	2.600	9.6538	0.0766	25.0999			
11	2.800	9.8669	0.0771	27.6272			
12	3.000	9.9803	0.0768	29.9408			
13	3.200	9.9929	0.0757	31.9773			
14	3.400	9.9046	0.0739	33.6757			
15	3.600	9.7163	0.0714	34.9787			
16	3.800	9.4299	0.0683	35.8336			
17	4.000	9.0483	0.0646	36.1931			
18	4.200	8.5753	0.0604	36.0161			
19	4.400	8.0157	0.0557	35.2689			
20	4.600	7.3751	0.0505	33.9256			
21	4.800	6.6601	0.0450	31.9686			
22	5.000	5.8779	0.0392	29.3893			
23	5.200	5.0362	0.0331	26.1884			
24	5.400	4.1438	0.0269	22.3763			
25	5.600	3.2094	0.0206	17.9728			
26	5.800	2.2427	0.0142	13.0077			
27	6.000	1.2533	0.0078	7.5200			
28	6.200	0.2513	0.0016	1.5581			
29	6.400	-0.7533	-0.0046	-4.8209			
30	6.600	-1.7502	-0.0105	-11.5515			

What you need to know

The simulation was done by using the SIN function in rather simple formulas. To create a sine curve, we could use its most basic equation as a function of time (t): $A * sin(2\pi f t)$, where A, the amplitude, is the peak deviation of the function from zero; f, the frequency, is the number of oscillations (cycles) that occur each second of time; and $2\pi f$, the angular frequency, is the rate of change of the function argument in units of radians per second.

What you need to do

1. Place in cell A3: =A2+$G$2. Copy down to cell A305. This adds a certain time increment to each previous time cell.

2. Place in cell B2: =$G$1*SIN(2*PI()*A2*$G$3). Double-click the formula down. This creates a regular sine wave based on the parameters for amplitude (G1) and frequency (G3). This pattern is typical for homeostasis.

3. Place in cell C2: =(1/(A2+$G$1))*SIN(2*PI()*A2*$G$3). Double-click the formula down. The main difference with the previous formula is that the amplitude gradually decreases.

4. Place in cell D2: =($G$1*A2)*SIN(2*PI()*A2*$G$3). Copy down. In this case, the amplitude increases gradually. This is a situation where the control mechanism runs out of control.

5. Try various values for the input range G1:G3. Below, the frequency parameter was changed from 0.08 into 0.2.

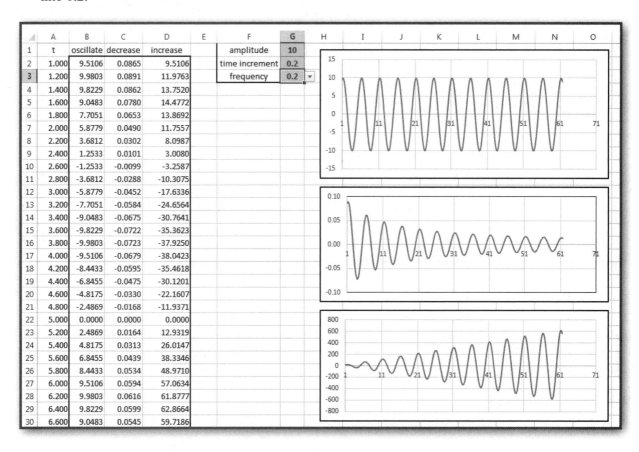

47. Taking Medication

What the simulation does

Open file 5-Expansion.xlsx on sheet "Medication." When taking medication, we want to reach a rather steady concentration of the medicine inside the body. The concentration rises each time we take a pill, but then it also declines because the body metabolizes and/or excretes it.

We simulate this process based on at least 5 parameters. The three important ones are the number of pills a day (B1), the strength of each pill (B2), and the elimination factor (B3). You could change these variables to find out what the best regimen is.

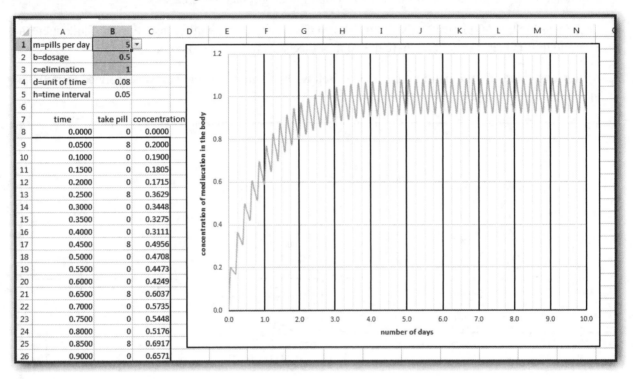

What you need to know

The simplest model would be as follows: If $u(t)$ is the concentration of the medication in the body, then $du = b\,f(t)\,dt - cu\,dt$. In words: the change in concentration equals (the amount of medication entering the body at time t during the period dt) minus (the amount of medication leaving the body during a small time interval dt). Instead of differentiating the equation, we use an Excel simulation.

What you need to do

1. Place in cell A9: =A8+$B$5. Copy down to cell A208.

2. Place in B9 a formula that determines when to take a pill:
    =IF(AND(A9>INT($B$1*A9)/$B$1,A9<INT($B$1*A9)/$B$1+$B$4),8,0). Copy down.

3. Determine in C9 the concentration at a specific point in time: =C8+$B$5*($B$2*B9-$B$3*C8). Copy down.

4. The graph shows that the concentration gradually increases—especially during the first three days—until it reaches a rather stable range. Each day should have 5 peaks for 5 pills (B1).

5. Notice how a regimen of "2 pills a day" reaches a stability range sooner but at a lower average concentration (see the first graph below).

6. Notice also how "3 pills a day" creates a "strange" daily pattern, until you change the unit of time (B4) to 0.06.

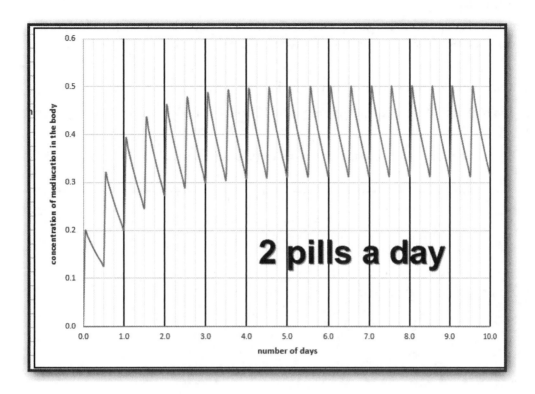

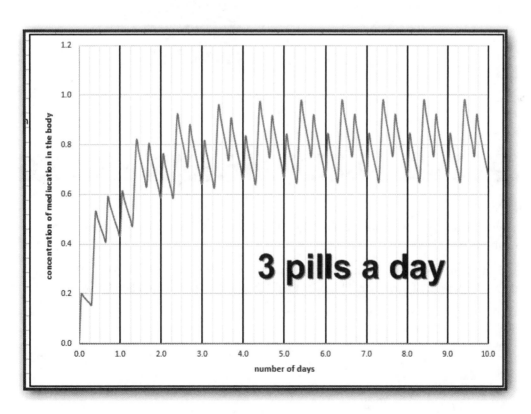

48. Population Pyramid

What the simulation does

Open file 5-Expansion.xlsx on sheet "Pyramid." On this sheet, we simulate how a population pyramid may change over the course of 100 years. The simulation is based on several grossly oversimplified assumptions.

Assumption #1: The population starts at 100,000 (cell D11).

Assumption #2: The birth rate is partially randomized (row 12) and is based on participation by everyone over 20 years old.

Assumption #3: Every age group has a certain survival value (column B) which is subject to small fluctuations.

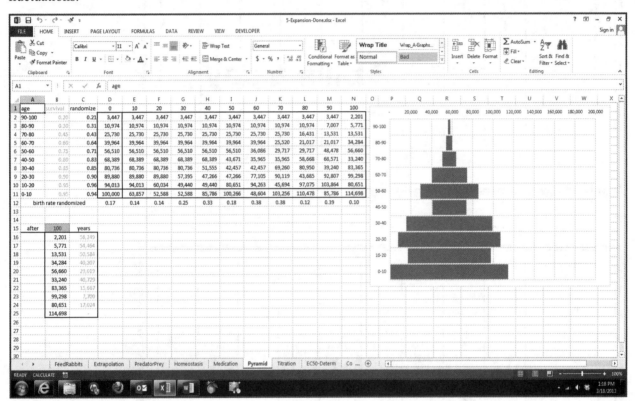

What you need to know

In cell B15, you determine after how many years (0 to 100) you would like to plot a population pyramid in the chart shown to the right.

The cells B16:B25 show the results in column N if you choose 100 years, or column M for 90 years, etc. They determine the width/length of each bar. The cells C16:C25 calculate how far each bar should be offset to the right.

What you need to do

1. Place in cell C2: =NORMINV(RAND(),B2,0.02). Copy down to C11. This randomizes the survival rate of each cohort.

2. Place in cell D12: =RANDBETWEEN(10,40)/100. This assumes birth rates vary between 0.1 and 0.4 per adult per 10 years.

3. In D10: =D11*$C11. Copy *upwards* to D2. This calculates the volume of each ten-year cohort, based on a gross oversimplification (but good enough for now).

4. In E11: =SUM(D$2:D$9)*D$12. Copy to N11. This assumes that all adults are included in the birth rate multiplier.

5. In E2: =D3*$C3. Copy this formula all the way to N10.

6. In B16: =HLOOKUP($B$15,$D$1:$N$11,ROW(A2),0). Copy down to B25. This looks up all age group sizes after the number of years chosen in cell B15.

7. In C16: =(MAX($B$16:$B$25)-B16)/2. This calculates the offset for each bar in the bar chart.

8. By using (*Sh*) *F9*, you can create an enormous variety of population pyramids. Some pyramids have a solid basis, others a rather weak one. Famine and other disasters can leave their marks on certain age groups.

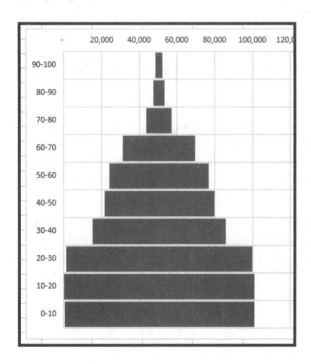

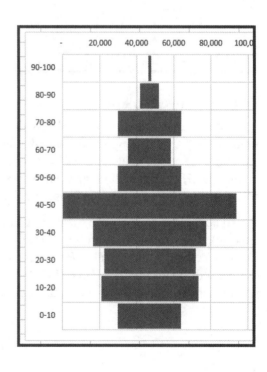

49. Titration

What the simulation does

Open file 5-Expansion.xlsx on sheet "Titration." On this sheet, we pretend that we do not know the chemical equation as to how to calculate the fraction of non-dissociated acid (column B) at a certain pH (column A). Instead we use an equation that creates a logistic (or s-shaped or sigmoidal) curve—which is a curve very common in science, but unknown to Excel. We try to simulate how any changes in variables that we use in the equation affect the shape of the curve.

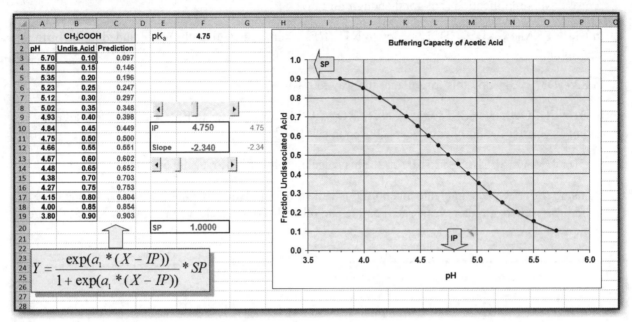

What you need to know

Strong acids are almost completely dissociated in aqueous solutions, but weak acids are not. The constant called pK_a is the logarithmic acid dissociation constant. Acids with a pK_a value of less than about -2 are said to be strong acids. A weak acid has a pK_a value in the approximate range -2 to 12 in water. Depending on the pH of the solution, they can accept or release hydrogen ions—in other words, they can buffer the solution. Acetic acid, for instance, is a weak acid with a pK_a of 4.75 (cell F1).

The logistic equation we use here is shown in the left lower section of the sheet (we will use it again later on). The variable $a1$ represents the slope of the curve—that is, its steepness up or down (in this case -2.34, in cell F12). The variable IP stands for the inflection point, when upwards turns into downwards, or reversed (in this case 4.75, in cell F10). And the variable SP represents the saturation point, the highest point where the curve levels off (in this case 1, in cell F20).

What you need to do

1. Place in cell A3: =$F$1+LOG((1-B3)/B3). Copy this formula down to A19. The formula creates exponential growth.

2. Place in C3 a simplified formula for s-shaped curves:
   =EXP($F$12*(A3-$F$10))/(1+EXP($F$12*(A3-$F$10))) *$F$20. (Shown in the left lower corner of the sheet.)

3. The prediction curve should more or less coincide with the observation curve, if the logistic equation is correct.

4. To change variables in the equation, we use scroll-bar controls—in this case only for the variables slope and IP, but you can add another one for SP if you want. (See Appendix 5.)

5. Set the IP control as follows: Min to 1, Max to 100,000, and Linked Cell to F8.

6. Place in cell F10: =F8/10000.

7. Set the Slope control as follows: Min to 1, Max to 10,000, and Linked Cell to F14.

8. Place in cell F12: =-F14/1000.

9. Notice the effect of changing IP or Slope (or SP).

10. Small changes in the slope can be quite dramatic, as you can see in the graph below.

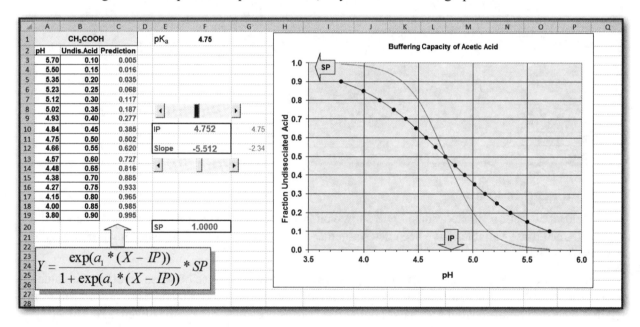

50. EC50 Determination

What the simulation does

Open file 5-Expansion.xlsx on sheet "EC50-Determ." The term "half maximal effective concentration" (EC50) refers to the concentration of a drug, antibody, or toxicant which induces a response halfway between the baseline and maximum after a specified exposure time. It is commonly used as a measure of a drug's *effective* potency. (IC50, on the other hand, is the "half maximal *inhibitory* response.")

The curves for EC50 are of the logistic, s-shaped, or sigmoidal type, so we can use the same equation again as we discussed in Simulation 49. But this time, we also need to locate the half-way point for EC50 in cell B15.

Based on that information, we calculate the three sets of coordinates for EC50, which turns out to be -9.59.

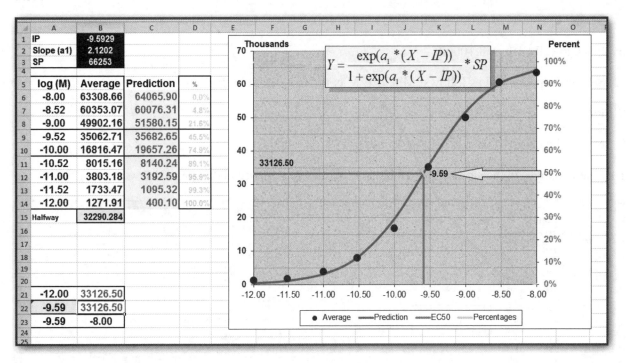

What you need to know

Later on, in section VII Iterations, I will show you how I came up with the input of the three variables in B1:B3. Once those variables have been determined correctly, we can use the logistic equation to predict the values in column C.

The logistic equation gives us as set of predicted values. The difference between an observed value and a predicted value is called a residual. Residuals can even each other out, for some are positive and some negative. The sum of all squared residuals should be as low as possible—if possible, even zero.

What you need to do

1. Place in cell C6 the following logistic equation:
    =EXP($B$2*(A6-$B$1))/(1+EXP($B$2*(A6-$B$1)))*$B$3.

2. Copy this formula down to C14.

3. In cell D6:
    =1-(B6-MIN($B$6:$B$14))/(MAX($B$6:$B$14)-MIN($B$6:$B$14)). Copy down.

4. Place in cell B15: =B14+(B6-B14)/2.

5. In cell A21: =MIN(A6:A14).

6. In cell B23: =MAX(A6:A14).

7. In cell A22: =TREND(A9:A10,B9:B10,B15).

8. Link cell A23 to A22.

9. In cell B22: =EXP($B$2*(A22-$B$1))/(1+EXP($B$2*(A22-$B$1)))*$B$3.

10. Link cell B21 to B22.

11. Apparently -9.59 is the outcome for EC50 determination in this case—at the halfway point of 33126.50 (50%).

12. Without the right equation, we would not have a curve that "fits" the observed data (see below).

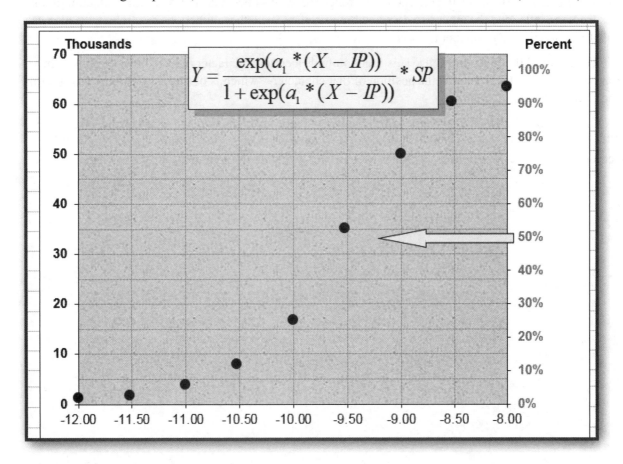

$$Y = \frac{\exp(a_1 * (X - IP))}{1 + \exp(a_1 * (X - IP))} * SP$$

51. Converter

What the simulation does

Open file 5-Expansion.xlsx on sheet "Converter." This is a simple sheet that converts measurements done in feet and inches into meters of the metric system.

It does so by using simple formulas and functions in the cells B2:B6. Based on the end calculation in B6, it creates a two-dimensional what-if table for conversions from feet and inches.

	A	B	C	D	E	F	G	H	I	J	K	L	M	N
1	ft-in	1'10"												
2	feet	1												
3	ft->m	0.3048												
4	inches	10												
5	in->m	0.254												
6	total in m.	0.5588	0 in	1 in	2 in	3 in	4 in	5 in	6 in	7 in	8 in	9 in	10 in	11 in
7		0 ft	0.0000 m	0.0254 m	0.0508 m	0.0762 m	0.1016 m	0.1270 m	0.1524 m	0.1778 m	0.2032 m	0.2286 m	0.2540 m	0.2794 m
8		1 ft	0.3048 m	0.3302 m	0.3556 m	0.3810 m	0.4064 m	0.4318 m	0.4572 m	0.4826 m	0.5080 m	0.5334 m	0.5588 m	0.5842 m
9		2 ft	0.6096 m	0.6350 m	0.6604 m	0.6858 m	0.7112 m	0.7366 m	0.7620 m	0.7874 m	0.8128 m	0.8382 m	0.8636 m	0.8890 m
10		3 ft	0.9144 m	0.9398 m	0.9652 m	0.9906 m	1.0160 m	1.0414 m	1.0668 m	1.0922 m	1.1176 m	1.1430 m	1.1684 m	1.1938 m
11		4 ft	1.2192 m	1.2446 m	1.2700 m	1.2954 m	1.3208 m	1.3462 m	1.3716 m	1.3970 m	1.4224 m	1.4478 m	1.4732 m	1.4986 m
12		5 ft	1.5240 m	1.5494 m	1.5748 m	1.6002 m	1.6256 m	1.6510 m	1.6764 m	1.7018 m	1.7272 m	1.7526 m	1.7780 m	1.8034 m
13		6 ft	1.8288 m	1.8542 m	1.8796 m	1.9050 m	1.9304 m	1.9558 m	1.9812 m	2.0066 m	2.0320 m	2.0574 m	2.0828 m	2.1082 m
14		7 ft	2.1336 m	2.1590 m	2.1844 m	2.2098 m	2.2352 m	2.2606 m	2.2860 m	2.3114 m	2.3368 m	2.3622 m	2.3876 m	2.4130 m
15														

What you need to know

The entry in cell B1 is basically text that we need to split in the feet part and the inches part. Functions to do so are LEFT, MID, and RIGHT. The LEFT function, for instance, takes only a certain amount of characters from the left—and the other two do something similar. Since these functions return text, we also need the VALUE function to make them numeric.

We also need the function FIND. This function finds a certain character (say, the feet symbol '), in a certain text (say, 1'10"). It returns the position of that character—which is position 1 or higher. If it returns 0, the character was not found.

The function CONVERT converts values between numerous kinds of units—for instance, from feet ("ft") or inches ("in") to meters ("m"). To find out how to refer to other kinds of units, see Help on this function. (P.S. In older Excel version, CONVERT is only available through the Analysis Toolpak.)

What you need to do

1. Place in cell B2: =LEFT(B1,FIND("'",B1)-1). Make sure the first argument of FIND has a single quote within two double quotes. This returns the number of feet.

2. Place in cell B3: =CONVERT(VALUE(B2),"ft","m").

3. Cell B4 has the most heavily nested formula on this sheet:
   =IF(ISNUMBER(VALUE(LEFT(RIGHT(B1,3),1))),LEFT(RIGHT(B1,3),2),MID(RIGHT(B1,3),2,1)).
   This returns the number of inches. (For more information on nested functions see Appendix 2.)

4. If you want to find out how this heavily nested function operates, select a nested function in the formula bar and hit *F9*. This shows the result for that function. You can do so for other nested functions as well. Make sure you hit *Esc* when done (otherwise the formula is replaced with the value it found). More on this in Simulation 65.

5. The formula in Cell B5 does a conversion again, this time from inches to meters:
   =CONVERT(VALUE(B4),"in","m").

6. Cell B6 does a simple summation: =B3+B5.

7. Select B6:N14 and implement a Data Table with B4 as row input and B2 as column input.

8. Inside the table, the "m" at the end of each cell value was done with a custom format: Format Cells | Number | Custom: 0.0000" m".

9. Apply condition formatting to C7:N14: Cell Value | Equal to | =$B$6.

10. To make sure that new entries in cell B1 always have a feet symbol between feet and inches, create the following data validation: =FIND("'",B1)<>0. This excludes that the feet symbol is not (<>) found.

11. As a consequence, when testing for 10 inches only, you must enter something like 0'10". It does not matter whether there is space between 0' and 10".

52. Conditional Training

What the simulation does

Open file 5-Expansion.xlsx on sheet "Training." In this simple simulation, we train animals by giving them stimulus 0 or 1 (column A) in a random fashion. Only stimulus 1 comes with a reward if the animal responds correctly ("Y" in column D). In column B we count the correct negative responses (0 and "N"), and in column C the correct positive responses (1 and "Y"). Future responses are based on what the animal learned from previous experiences. Some kinds of animals learn faster than others, which can be simulated in cell F4.

Once animals had 10 correct responses (in E) in a row (either 0-N or 1-Y) and no more lapses, we consider them "trained" (F).

	A	B	C	D	E	F	G	H	I	J
1	stimulus	count 0-N	count 1-Y	response	correct					
2	0	1	0	N						
3	1	1	0	Y		learning speed				
4						10				
5	0	1	0	N	+					
6	0	2	1	Y	-					
7	1	2	1	Y	+					
8	1	2	2	Y	+					
9	1	2	3	Y	+					
10	1	2	4	Y	+					
11	0	2	5	N	+					
12	0	3	5	N	+					
13	0	4	5	Y	-					
14	0	4	5	N	+			stimulus	incentive	response
15	0	5	5	N	+					
16	0	6	5	N	+					
17	1	7	5	Y	+					
18	0	7	6	N	+					
19	1	8	6	Y	+					
20	1	8	7	Y	+					
21	1	8	8	Y	+					
22	0	8	9	N	+					
23	1	9	9	Y	+					
24	1	9	10	Y	+	trained		1	-1	N
25	1	9	11	Y	+	trained		1	-1	N
26	0	9	12	N	+	trained		0		Y
27	0	10	12	N	+	trained		0		Y
28	1	11	12	Y	+	trained		1	0	N
29	1	11	13	Y	+	trained		1	0	N

What you need to know

It has been found that animals, once trained, often do no longer respond when the award ceases to appear, unless it comes in an unpredictable way. So the best strategy is to *randomly* reinforce the behavior. Columns H:J simulate this. This phenomenon may remind you of gamblers who keep going for the unpredictable.

What you need to do

1. Place in cell A5: =IF(RAND()>0.5,1,0). This creates a stimulus of 0 or 1 in a random fashion. Copy down to cell A104.

2. Place in cell B5: =COUNTIFS($A$2:A2,0,$D$2:D2,"N"). This keeps track of 0-N combinations. Copy formula down.

3. Place in cell C5: =COUNTIFS($A$2:A2,1,$D$2:D2,"Y"). This keeps track of 1-Y combinations. Copy formula down.

4. We generate a response in cell D5 based on experiences:
   =IF(A5=0,IF((RAND()+B3/$F$4)>0.5,"N","Y"),IF((RAND()+C3/$F$4),"Y","N")). We still use a random number but "dampen" it with past experiences (in B3 and C3) divided by the learning factor (in cell F4). Gradually randomness plays no longer a role in the animal's response.

5. Place a plus or minus in cell E5 to evaluate the response:
   =IF(OR(AND(A5=1,D5="Y"),AND(A5=0,D5="N")),"+","-")

6. Place in cell F15:
   =IF(AND(COUNTIF(E5:E14,"-")=0,COUNTIF(E15:$E$104,"-")=0),"trained",""). This checks in the previous 10 responses and all the following responses for correct answers (so no 0s). Once that is the case, we consider the animal "trained" enough.

7. After reaching that stage some animals easily quit when the reward ceases to appear, unless they get randomly assigned. The following is for those situations.

8. Place in cell H15: =IF(F15="trained",A15,""). Copy down.

9. Place in cell I15: =IF(H15=1,INT(1-2*RAND()), ""). This determines randomly if there is a reward (0) or not (-1).

10. In cell J15: =IF(F15="trained",D15,""). I decided to keep the original, trained responses in effect. Change this if you want.

11. *Sh F9* will simulate various training processes, even for different learning speeds (cell F4). Some animals learn faster.

53. Epidemics

What the simulation does

Open file 5-Expansion.xlsx on sheet "Epidemic." In this simple simulation, we follow the course of an epidemic (e.g. the flu) based on certain variables in column H.

In general, epidemics follow a more or less fixed pattern. Initially only a few people get sick, but soon the number of sick cases rises exponentially until stabilization sets in, and more and more people recover.

We need some essential parameters, although they may not always be exactly known. We will only focus on transmission rate, recovery rate, and death rate—without going into issues such as mutation rate for the virus or bacterium.

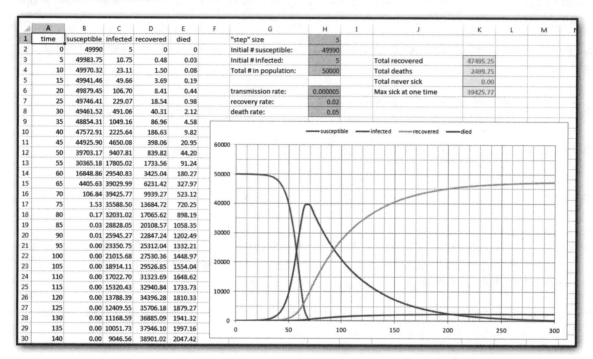

What you need to know

The model that we apply is the standard *SIR* model, commonly used for many infectious diseases. The name of the model reflects the three groups of individuals that it models: *S*usceptible people, *I*nfected people, and *R*ecovered people.

There are a number of important thresholds in this model. Reaching, or failing to reach, these thresholds is a crucial feature of managing the spread of infectious diseases. The system is sensitive to some changes and not to others, so this may give some insight into when and where the problem should be attacked.

In order to make the appropriate calculations, we use the Euler's method, without explaining it any further. You can find it explained elsewhere.

What you need to do

1. Place in cell A3: =A2+$H$1. This adds a "step" period of any value (in our case 5, for hours or days or whatever). Copy down to cell A302.

2. Place in cell B3: =B2-($H$6*B2*C2)*$H$1. This formula is derived with Euler's method. Copy the formula down to see what happens to the number of susceptible people.

3. Place in cell C3: =C2+($H$6*B2*C2-$H$7*C2)*$H$1. Copy the formula down to see how the number of infected people changes.

4. Place in cell D3: =D2+((1-$H$8)*$H$7*C2)*$H$1. Copy the formula down to estimate the number of recovered people.

5. Place in cell E3: =E2+($H$8*$H$7*C2)*$H$1. The number of deaths depends heavily on the death rate (cell H8), in addition to the number of recovered people and their recovery rate (cell H7).

6. Place in cell K3: =D302. This is the latest number of recovered people. We have set the limit to row 302—that is, 300 time periods—but for certain situations you may need more.

7. Place in cell K4: =E302. This is the latest number of deaths.

8. Place in cell K5: =B302. This is the last value in the column of susceptible people.

9. Place in cell K6: =MAX(C2:C302). This is the highest number of sick people per period of time in column C.

10. Change some variables in the cells H1:H8 and watch their effect on the epidemic. (You may have to hit *Sh F9*).

11. Obviously, this simulation is still rather deterministic. We could have included probabilities, but I leave that up to you.

Monte Carlo Simulations

54. How Random Is Random?

What the simulation does

Open file 6-MonteCarlo.xlsx on the sheet called "Random." The Monte Carlo method calculates approximate solutions of physical or mathematical problems by statistical sampling procedures based on the use of random numbers.

This poses the question: How random are Excel's random numbers? Most random numbers used in computer programs are *pseudo-random*, which means they are generated in a predictable fashion using a mathematical formula.

This is fine for many purposes, but it may not be random in the way you might expect. So let us find out in a simulation how useful and reliable the RAND function is for statistical purposes.

In the screen shot below, we created 1,000 random numbers and repeated this 20 times—which gives us 20,000 random numbers with a frequency distribution shown at the bottom. For a good simulation, though, we would need at least 1,000,000 runs.

	A	B	C	D	E	F	G	H	I	J	K	L	M	N	O	P
1	0.73591		frequency table				105	105	112	86	82	104	86	97	109	114
2	0.095837		0.1	105			99	118	98	102	95	92	113	90	100	93
3	0.543817		0.2	105			92	94	86	99	123	113	103	103	92	95
4	0.954797		0.3	112			96	95	86	90	115	111	90	104	94	119
5	0.032865		0.4	86			122	95	85	101	97	110	93	96	101	100
6	0.367615		0.5	82			89	115	92	120	86	89	101	87	116	105
7	0.999927		0.6	104			86	80	121	88	99	92	110	109	105	110
8	0.327502		0.7	86			114	110	101	94	104	99	89	96	108	85
9	0.967063		0.8	97			102	102	104	89	99	86	108	91	110	109
10	0.408956		0.9	109			103	97	104	87	94	100	97	112	96	110
11	0.882584		1	114			90	93	95	109	98	115	101	102	100	97
12	0.067123			0			92	100	99	123	97	110	98	91	98	92
13	0.48253						94	102	95	112	99	99	104	97	95	103
14	0.23505						105	105	100	105	97	85	100	102	105	96
15	0.943113						98	91	106	103	78	103	108	101	112	100
16	0.165281						101	106	90	110	108	83	97	96	103	106
17	0.422745						98	120	98	95	95	99	96	105	95	99
18	0.522054						106	109	108	89	119	86	89	97	96	101
19	0.292004						112	89	101	111	90	108	115	90	91	93
20	0.198021						100	111	105	106	100	73	102	112	98	93
21	0.874201															
22	0.316444						0.1	0.2	0.3	0.4	0.5	0.6	0.7	0.8	0.9	1
23	0.87766						99.56	102.06	98.89	100.11	99.17	98.67	99.06	98.67	101.94	101.89
24	0.514307															

What you need to know

Pseudo-random number generators (PRNGs) are algorithms that can automatically create long runs of numbers with good random properties but eventually the sequence repeats (or the memory usage grows without bound).

The string of values generated by such algorithms is generally determined by a fixed number called a seed. One of the most common pseudo-random-number-generators (PSNG) is the linear congruential generator, which uses the recurrence $X_{n+1} = (aX_n + b) \bmod m$ to generate numbers. The maximum number of numbers the formula can produce is the modulus, m.

Let us not forget that the first 10,000 digits of π look random from the point of view of any tests concerning the existence of patterns, yet we know they are completely determined—whereas "real" random numbers come from atmospheric noise or so.

What you need to do

1. Select cell A1, type A1000 in the Name Box (just above it), and hit *Sh Enter*. This selects the cells A1:A1000. Type in the formula bar =RAND(), and hit *Ctr Enter*.

2. Select D2:D12 (not D11) at once and implement this formula: =FREQUENCY(A1:A1000,C2:C11). Use *Ctr Sh Enter*.

3. Select G1:P1 at once: =TRANSPOSE(D2:D11). *Ctr Sh Enter*.

4. Select F1:P20 (yes, starting in the empty cell F1) and implement a Data Table with no row input and an empty cell (e.g. E1) for column input: =TABLE(,E1).

5. Place in G22:P22 the same formula as you did in step 3.

6. Place in G23: =AVERAGE(G1:G18). Copy to cell P23.

7. Give range G23:P23 a conditional format for when the average frequency of 1/10 * 1,000 runs is between 98 and 102: Cell Value | Between | 98 | and | 102.

8. Using *Sh F9*, you will see that all bins have very similar frequencies—which means RAND produces a fairly nice equal, uniform distribution. So use it in most of your simulations.

9. Had we executed 1,000,000 runs, we would have gotten more reliable results. Try it out if you want.

55. Brownian Motion

What the simulation does

Open file 6-MonteCarlo.xlsx on the sheet called "BrownianMotion." It is a simulation of how a grain of pollen—or a molecule, for that matter—takes a "random walk" on the surface of the water.

Dealing with the uncertain and the unknown is the realm of probability, which helps us to put a meaningful numerical value on things we do not know. Although a single random event is not predictable, the aggregate behavior of random events is (see also Simulation 6).

Column B displays random X-changes and column C displays random Y-changes. In D and E, we start at coordinates 0,0 and keep adding the random changes from the previous columns. In Q:S we repeat each run 14 times and display in column T whether we ended up close to 0,0 again (within a range of 1).

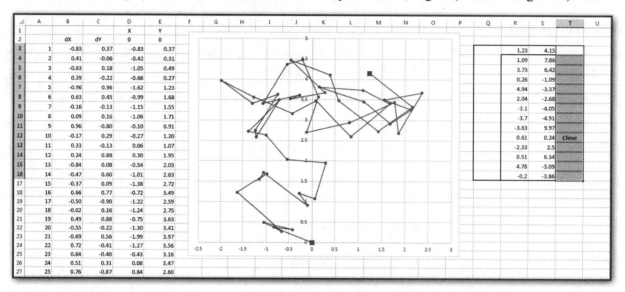

What you need to know

Brownian motion was discovered in the early 1800s by botanist Robert Brown, who noticed under his microscope how grains of pollen appeared to constantly and randomly move in a jittery way on the surface of the water. In his 1905 paper, Albert Einstein hypothesized that Brownian motion was caused by actual atoms and molecules hitting the grains of pollen, impelling them to take a "random walk" on the surface of the liquid. Einstein's work eventually led to the inherently probabilistic nature of quantum mechanics.

What you need to do

1. Place in B3: =ROUND(1-2*RAND(),2). Copy down to B52.

2. Do the same for column C.

3. Place in D3: =D2+B3. Copy down to D52 and E52.

4. Link R2 to D52 and T2 to E52.

5. Select range Q3:S16 and start a Data Table with no row input and an empty cell (e.g. Q1) as column input: =TABLE(,Q1).

6. In cells T3: =IF(AND(R3>-1,R3<1,S3>-1,S3<1),"Close",""). Copy down to T18.

7. Apply Conditional Formatting to $D$3:$E$52 with the formula =$T$3="Close".

8. Notice how Brownian motions can be very jittery—sometimes they center around the coordinates 0,0 but more often they veer to the sides or to the corners. The chance that they end up close to the spot where they started is very improbable.

9. In the case shown below, begin and end of the random walk are close together, but most of the walk is done in the left upper quadrant. Random walks are just fascinating.

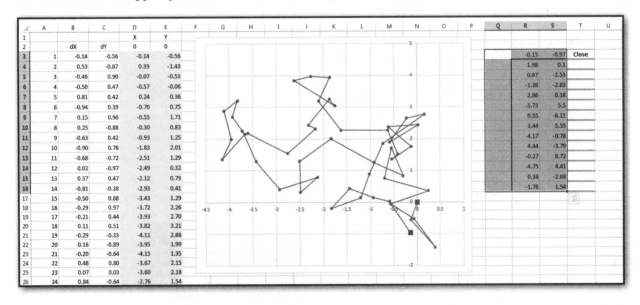

56. A Traffic Situation

What the simulation does

Open file 6-MonteCarlo.xlsx on sheet "Commute." A Monte Carlo simulation really illustrates how we can tame the uncertainty of the future with ranges and probabilities, but it also shows how impossible it is to be extremely precise.

We simulate driving 2 miles on a highway, with 90% probability we will average 65 MPH, but with a 10% probability that a traffic jam will result in an average speed of 20 MPH (column A).

Then there is a traffic light that goes through a 120 second cycle with 90 seconds for "red" and 30 seconds for "green." If we hit it on green then there is no delay, but if we hit it on red we must wait for green (column B).

Finally, we have 2 more miles to go: 70% of the time at 30 MPH, 10% at 20 MPH, 10% at 40 MPH, and 10% of the time it takes us 30 minutes (column C).

	A	B	C	D	E	F	G	H	I	J	K	L
1	1st stretch	Traffic light	2nd stretch	seconds	minutes		cumul.	secs				
2	111	55.08	240	406.08	6.77		0	240		median	6.46	
3	111	0.00	240	351.00	5.85		70	360		average	6.86	
4	111	60.41	240	411.41	6.86		80	180		75%	7.03	
5	111	80.86	240	431.86	7.20		90	1800		100%	11.35	
6	111	0.00	240	351.00	5.85							
7	111	6.94	240	357.94	5.97							
8	111		40	361.90	6.03							
9	111		40	381.28	6.35							
10	111		40	431.83	7.20							
11	111		40	402.03	6.70							
12	111		40	433.94	7.23							
13	111	0.00	240	351.00	5.85							
14	360	0.00	240	600.00	10.00							
15	111	35.19			44							
16	111	50.68			69							
17	111	22.95			23							
18	360	37.64			63							
19	111	0.00			85							
20	111	76.59	240	427.59	7.13							
21	360	0.00	240	600.00	10.00							
22	111	69.97	240	420.97	7.02							
23	360	81.93	240	681.93	11.37							
24	111	0.88	240	351.88	5.86							
25	111	14.60	240	365.60	6.09							

Drive 2 miles on a highway, with 90% probability you will be able to average 65 MPH the whole way, but with a 10% probability that a traffic jam will result in average speed of 20 MPH.

a traffic light through a 120 second cycle where RED lasts 90 seconds and GREEN lasts 30 seconds. If we hit it on green then there's no delay, but if we hit it on red we wait until it turns green.

2 more miles on a surface street. 70% of the time you travel at 30 MPH. 10% of the time you average 20 MPH, 10% of the time you average 40 MPH, and 10% of the time there's a traffic jam that takes you 30 minutes to travel these two miles."

What you need to know

Instead of using a fixed value for input variables, we can model an input variable with a probability distribution and then run the model a number of times and see what impact the random variation has on the output (see Appendix 4 for more information on Monte Carlo simulations).

It is wise to run at least 1,000 iterations of Monte Carlo models. This is to ensure that we have a statistical chance of getting sufficient outliers (extreme values) to make the variance analysis meaningful. This is important because as the number of iterations increases, the variance of the average output decreases.

What you need to do

1. Place in cell A2: =IF(RAND() < 0.9, 111, 360). Copy down.

2. Place in cell B2: =MAX(0, (RAND() * 120) - 30). And copy.

3. In C2: =VLOOKUP(RAND(),$G$2:$H$5, 2). Copy down. (For more info on VLOOKUP see Simulation 32.)

4. In D2: =SUM(A2:C2). Copy down. This is the total time in seconds.

5. In E2: =D2/60. Copy down. This is the total time in minutes.

6. In K2: =MEDIAN(E:E).

7. In K3: =AVERAGE(E:E). The average travel time.

8. In K4: =PERCENTILE(E:E,J4). This is the 75% margin.

9. In K5: =PERCENTILE(E:E,J5). This is the 100% margin.

10. Each time you hit *Sh F9*, the sheet simulates a new travel commute situation, based on the data and probabilities you have specified.

11. P.S. It might be wise to set Table calculation to manual for this file because of the thousands of calculations: File | Options | Formulas | Automatic except for Data Tables. This file will still save and open slowly because of its numerous calculations. So be patient! Or set calculation to manual.

57. Uncertainties in Sales

What the simulation does

Open file 6-MonteCarlo.xlsx on sheet "SalesRisks." Monte Carlo simulations are computerized mathematical techniques that allow people to account for risks in quantitative analysis and decision making.

In this case, the decision-maker supplies sales data and probabilities (the yellow cells in columns A and B).

Based on this information, we simulate distributions with a range of possible outcomes (center section) and the probabilities they will occur for any choice of action (right section).

Volume

Probability	Volume	Engine Bins	Volume
70%	300,000	0.00	300,000
15%	275,000	0.70	275,000
15%	325,000	0.85	325,000
100%			

Conversion

Probability	Rate	Engine Bins	Rate
70%	2.5%	0.00	2.5%
10%	2.1%	0.70	2.1%
10%	2.3%	0.80	2.3%
10%	2.7%	0.90	2.7%
100%			

Average Order

Probability	Amount	Engine Bins	Amount
70%	$ 75.00	0.00	$ 75.00
15%	$ 73.00	0.70	$ 73.00
15%	$ 77.00	0.85	$ 77.00
100%			

Yellow cells can be changed.

Simulations

Volume	Conversion	Avg Order	Total
300,000	2.1%	$ 75.00	$ 472,500
300,000	2.5%	$ 75.00	$ 562,500
300,000	2.5%	$ 75.00	$ 562,500
325,000	2.5%	$ 75.00	$ 609,375
300,000	2.5%	$ 75.00	$ 562,500
300,000	2.3%	$ 75.00	$ 517,500
300,000	2.5%	$ 75.00	$ 562,500
300,000	2.3%	$ 75.00	$ 517,500
300,000	2.5%	$ 75.00	$ 562,500
300,000	2.5%	$ 75.00	$ 562,500
300,000	2.5%	$ 75.00	$ 562,500
325,000	2.5%	$ 75.00	$ 609,375
325,000	2.5%	$ 75.00	$ 609,375
300,000	2.5%	$ 75.00	$ 562,500
300,000	2.5%	$ 77.00	$ 577,500
275,000	2.3%	$ 77.00	$ 487,025
300,000	2.3%	$ 75.00	$ 517,500
300,000	2.5%	$ 77.00	$ 577,500
300,000	2.1%	$ 77.00	$ 485,100
300,000	2.3%	$ 75.00	$ 517,500
300,000	2.5%	$ 75.00	$ 562,500
325,000	2.5%	$ 77.00	$ 625,625
300,000	2.3%	$ 75.00	$ 517,500
300,000	2.5%	$ 73.00	$ 547,500
300,000	2.5%	$ 75.00	$ 562,500
300,000	2.1%	$ 75.00	$ 472,500
300,000	2.1%	$ 75.00	$ 472,500

Last year base	$569,993		Average Sales Day	$ 553,627
			Minimum Sales Day	$ 421,575
			Maximum Sales Day	$ 675,675

Probabilities

Comp		Sales		Probability	Positive	22.3%
-25%	-30%	$427,495	$ 398,995	0.1%	Negative	77.7%
-20%	-25%	$455,994	$ 427,495	1.1%		
-15%	-20%	$484,494	$ 455,994	7.2%		
-10%	-15%	$512,994	$ 484,494	3.6%	Sales will exceed:	
-7%	-10%	$530,093	$ 512,994	11.1%	$400,000	100.0%
-5%	-7%	$541,493	$ 530,093	0.7%	$450,000	98.8%
-2%	-5%	$558,593	$ 541,493	8.7%	$500,000	90.4%
0%	-2%	$569,993	$ 558,593	45.3%	$569,993	22.3%
0	0	$569,993	$ 569,993	0.0%	$600,000	11.9%
0%	2%	$569,993	$ 581,393	8.5%	$650,000	0.6%
2%	5%	$581,393	$ 598,493	1.9%	Sales will be under:	
5%	7%	$598,493	$ 609,893	9.5%	$600,000	88.1%
7%	10%	$609,893	$ 626,992	1.7%	$575,000	77.8%
10%	15%	$626,992	$ 655,492	0.1%	$569,993	77.7%
15%	20%	$655,492	$ 683,992	0.6%	$500,000	9.6%
20%	25%	$683,992	$ 712,491	0.0%	$450,000	1.2%
25%	30%	$712,491	$ 740,991	0.0%	$425,000	0.1%

What you need to know

The situation is basically simple. The major functions we need to achieve such kinds of predictions in this case are RAND, VLOOKUP, COUNT, and COUNTIF. Again we use 1,000 simulations in the center section to reach more reliable predictions.

What you need to do

1. In cell F3: =VLOOKUP(RAND(),$C$3:$D$5,2). Copy down to cell F1002. (For more info on VLOOKUP see Simulation 32.)

2. In cell G3: =VLOOKUP(RAND(),$C$10:$D$13,2). Copy down to cell G1002.

3. In cell H3: =VLOOKUP(RAND(),$C$18:$D$20,2). Copy down to cell H1002.

4. In cell I3: =F3*G3*H3. Copy down to cell I1002.

5. In cell M8: =$M$2+($M$2*K8). Copy down to cell M24.

6. In cell N8: =$M$2+($M$2*L8). Copy down to cell N24.

7. Place in cell O8: =(COUNTIF($I$3:$I$10002,"<="&M8)-(COUNTIF($I$3:$I$10002,"<"&N8))) / (COUNT($I$3:$I$10002)). Copy down to cell O24.

8. Place in cells Q2, Q3, and Q4: =AVERAGE(I3:I10002), followed by =MIN(…) and =MAX(…).

9. Place in cell Q7: =(COUNTIF($I$3:$I$10002,">"&M2) /(COUNT($I$3:$I$10002))).

10. Place in cell Q8: =(COUNTIF($I$3:$I$10002,"<"&M2) /(COUNT($I$3:$I$10002))).

11. In cell P15 and P21: =M2. This was last year's base.

12. In cell Q12: =(COUNTIF($I$3:$I$10002,">"&P12) /(COUNT($I$3:$I$10002))). Copy down to cell Q17.

13. In cell Q19: =(COUNTIF($I$3:$I$10002,"<"&P19) /(COUNT($I$3:$I$10002))). Copy down to cell Q24.

14. This file will save and open slowly because of its numerous calculations, unless you change calculation settings.

58. Exchange Rate Fluctuations

What the simulation does

Open file 6-MonteCarlo.xlsx on sheet "ExchangeRate." The profit of a certain company depends on a fluctuating exchange rate between the American and Australian dollar—or whatever. So we need to simulate such variations.

The average profit we predict in cell I2 is based on normally distributed fluctuations in exchange rate.

	A	B	C	D	E	F	G	H	I	J
1		**Input**				**Profit**				
2	Units Sold	100,000				$ 126,434,782.61		**Average G3:G1008**	$ 126,454,304.01	
3					0.90	$ 129,196,145.90		**25% percentile**	$ 124,570,295.32	
4	Unit price U$	$ 1,200.00			0.94	$ 129,137,818.36		**75% percentile**	$ 128,288,712.60	
5	Exchange Rate A$/U$	0.92			0.93	$ 125,081,800.83				
6	SD exchange rate	0.02			0.93	$ 131,120,135.74		95% confidence		
7					0.96	$ 125,919,621.17		rate higher than	0.88	
8	Unit Cost	$ 40.00			0.93	$ 124,028,406.78		rate lower than	0.96	
9					0.90	$ 127,754,314.46				
10	Total Cost U$	4,000,000			0.92	$ 125,759,023.18		exchange rate	frequency	
11					0.91	$ 129,771,414.98		0.86	0	
12	Revenue U$	130,434,783			0.91	$ 124,599,941.73		0.88	18	
13					0.91	$ 133,242,250.56		0.90	127	
14	**Profit**	$ 126,434,782.61			0.93	$ 122,829,564.40		0.92	356	
15					0.93	$ 126,740,481.73		0.94	340	
16					0.93	$ 123,709,893.66		0.96	147	
17					0.93	$ 128,423,602.68		0.98	18	
18					0.93	$ 125,918,244.07		not covered	0	
19					0.90	$ 126,469,089.82				
20					0.89	$ 126,487,197.21				
21					0.92	$ 125,098,300.74				
22					0.93	$ 127,271,836.30				
23					0.93	$ 129,295,683.32				
24					0.90	$ 127,279,535.09				

What you need to know

We need to simulate in column E at least some 1,000 random exchange rates according to a normal distribution with a mean of 0.92 (cell B5) and a standard deviation that we set to something like 0.2 (cell B6).

This is done with the statistical function NORMINV as follows: =NORMINV(RAND(),0.92,0.02). It creates random numbers with a normal distribution around a certain mean (0.92 in this case) and with a certain standard deviation (0.02 in this case). We did something similar in Simulation 13.

What you need to do

1. The calculations in column C are rather basic.

2. Cell F2 has a link to the profit in cell B14.

3. Place in cell E3: =NORMINV(RAND(),0.92,0.02), and copy down to cell E1008. We could have placed the hard coded values in separate cells, of course.

4. Select E2:G1008 and implement a Data Table with *no* (!) row input and cell B5 for column input.

5. Calculate in cell I2 the average profit of all 1,000 simulations: =AVERAGE($F$3:$F$1008).

6. In cells I3 and I4, we calculate the 25th and 75th percentile.

7. In cells I7 and I8, we calculate the lower and higher margins for the exchange rate, based on a 95% confidence: between =B5-1.96*B6 and =B5+1.96*B6. (See Simulation 13 why we chose 1.96.)

8. To prove that NORMINV did create a normally distributed set of exchange rates, we calculate frequencies. Select I11:I18: =FREQUENCY(E3:E1008,H11:H17).

9. Hitting *Sh F9* shows us how profits vary depending on randomly fluctuating exchange rates.

10. It is very unusual that 4 random exchange rates exceed 0.98. To the left, we happen to have a case of four. They are "outliers" that we do not really want to miss (see Simulation 73 for more on this).

11. This file will save and open slowly because of its numerous calculations, unless you change calculation settings.

H	I
Average G3:G1008	$ 126,485,268.97
25% percentile	$ 124,465,733.30
75% percentile	$ 128,401,714.72
95% confidence	
rate higher than	0.88
rate lower than	0.96
exchange rate	frequency
0.86	0
0.88	24
0.90	139
0.92	337
0.94	334
0.96	149
0.98	19
not covered	4

59. Cost Estimates

What the simulation does

Open file 6-MonteCarlo.xlsx on sheet "CostEstimate." The cells A2:C3 are based on manual input, with the low estimates in row 2 and the high estimates in row 3.

For each of the columns A, B, and C, we simulate normally distributed values with a mean between low (row 2) and high (row 3) as well as a standard deviation of 2 units on either side. This time, we use only 100 simulations—which is rather risky.

Column D calculates the monthly costs for each simulation.

Cells G2 and G3 show the 5th and 95th percentile of all simulated monthly costs.

We also added a frequency distribution for every 5th percentile level. Based on 100 simulations, each level should have 5 cases (column H).

	A	B	C	D	E	F	G	H
1	Time (Secs)	Annual Cost	Monthly Volume	Monthly cost			Percentile 5%-95%	
2	120	200000	10000				$ 2,795,598,546	
3	240	300000	12000				$ 4,897,225,255	
4	211.41	$ 262,376	11,236.00	$ 4,794,221,905				
5	151.43	$ 265,377	11,193.33	$ 3,460,058,972				
6	193.99	$ 274,824	11,094.04	$ 4,549,643,371				
7	159.75	$ 238,545	10,660.79	$ 3,125,015,256		5%	$ 2,795,598,546	5
8	186.80	$ 290,509	10,980.61	$ 4,583,667,660		10%	$ 2,987,967,310	5
9	182.05	$ 299,953	11,532.82	$ 4,844,256,393		15%	$ 3,110,558,409	5
10	209.45	$ 211,993	10,205.50	$ 3,485,751,883		20%	$ 3,166,738,998	5
11	204.69	$ 234,327	10,489.12	$ 3,870,123,707		25%	$ 3,289,089,725	5
12	193.67	$ 227,349	11,734.03	$ 3,974,237,919		30%	$ 3,400,609,335	5
13	167.94	$ 264,006	11,044.71	$ 3,766,893,276		35%	$ 3,476,759,365	5
14	198.38	$ 244,442	11,120.57	$ 4,148,178,073		40%	$ 3,675,706,394	5
15	227.99	$ 226,945	10,911.94	$ 4,343,080,505		45%	$ 3,736,772,744	5
16	196.16	$ 269,689	10,794.11	$ 4,392,548,873		50%	$ 3,875,519,578	5
17	215.51	$ 254,863	10,908.12	$ 4,608,637,490		55%	$ 3,933,178,276	5
18	179.30	$ 273,501	11,420.94	$ 4,308,185,526		60%	$ 3,993,311,904	5
19	197.10	$ 248,188	10,882.28	$ 4,094,800,516		65%	$ 4,096,795,587	5
20	217.97	$ 284,596	11,568.19	$ 5,520,051,800		70%	$ 4,144,167,028	5
21	189.16	$ 277,545	11,337.12	$ 4,578,600,100		75%	$ 4,335,396,918	5
22	169.92	$ 266,699	11,345.86	$ 3,955,159,875		80%	$ 4,423,127,413	5
23	207.42	$ 267,476	11,437.25	$ 4,881,003,723		85%	$ 4,553,986,880	5
24	206.49	$ 260,037	10,876.95	$ 4,492,641,736		90%	$ 4,704,959,300	5
25	162.23	$ 258,497	11,294.00	$ 3,643,272,033		95%	$ 4,897,225,255	5
26	158.61	$ 274,974	10,301.01	$ 3,455,807,719				5
27	164.97	$ 276,223	11,446.59	$ 4,012,417,911				

What you need to know

In the columns A, B, and C we use NORMINV again (see Simulation13). It creates random numbers with a certain SD around a certain mean.

The mean would be the sum of high and low divided by 2. The SD would be high minus low divided by 4; thus we cover two times the SD on either side of the mean, which equates to nearly 97.5% surface of a normal distribution (see Simulation 13 on this).

What you need to do

1. Place the following formula in cell A4: =NORMINV(RAND(), SUM(A$2:A$3)/2,(MAX(A$2:A$3)-MIN(A$2:A$3))/4). Make sure you "lock" row references but not column references (see Appendix 1 for more information on "locking").

2. Copy this formula down to A103 and then C103.

3. In cell D4: =A4/130*B4*C4. Copy this down to cell D103.

4. In G2 5th percentile: =PERCENTILE($D$4:$D$103,0.05).

5. In G3 95th percentile: =PERCENTILE($D$4:$D$103,0.95).

6. In G7: =PERCENTILE($D$4:$D$103,F7). Copy this formula down to G25.

7. Select the cells H7:H26 and create the following formula: =FREQUENCY(D4:D103,G7:G25). Use *Ctr Sh Enter*.

8. Upon hitting *Sh F9*, almost every cell changes, except for the manual input cells A2:C3, as well as for column H, which shows 20 x 5 = 100.

9. Again, this file will save and open slowly because of its numerous calculations, unless you change calculation settings.

60. Market Growth

What the simulation does

Open file 6-MonteCarlo.xlsx on sheet "MarketGrowth." When talking about GDP growth (*Gross Domestic Product*), the relationship between GDP growth and market growth, and the increase in market share, we are dealing with three uncertain inputs. The obvious approach is to use the best estimate of each of these inputs.

A better approach might be using a probability distribution, rather than using the single best estimate. Monte-Carlo modelling would use the probability distributions of the inputs. Rather than using the distributions themselves as inputs, the distributions are used to generate random inputs.

Based on a certain market volume (cell D1) and a certain market share (cell F1), we calculate possible sales volumes (column G). We use random distributions in 100 runs to estimate GDP growth (column A), the relationship between GDP and market size (column B), and the market share growth (column E).

We repeat this set of runs another 100 times, in column J. After 10,000 runs, we get an estimate of the minimum and maximum sales volumes in column M. Needless to say that these figures can still vary quite a bit, because Monte Carlo simulations become more reliable when based on at least 1,000,000 runs.

	A	B	C	D	E	F	G	H	I	J	K	L	M
1			Market	4,000,000	Share	40%							
2	GDP Growth	Multiple	Market	New Market Size	Market Share Growth	New Market Share	Sales Volume			100 x 100 = 10,000 runs only			
3	2.5245	2.9414	7.4257	33,702,601	-0.001	0.399	13,445,547		8,730,145.77	8,730,146		MIN	2,227,725
4	1.9801	3.3614	6.6558	30,623,115	-0.013	0.387	11,836,313		2	7,190,286		MED	6,658,351
5	1.8177	4.5485	8.2680	37,071,821	0.033	0.433	16,056,360		3	5,941,166		MAX	11,184,144
6	2.7907	-1.7363	-4.8456	-15,382,504	-0.018	0.382	-5,871,948		4	8,640,388			
7	2.0695	-0.2010	-0.4160	2,336,051	-0.007	0.393	918,022		5	6,580,790			
8	2.7069	-2.8226	-7.6405	-26,561,969	0.018	0.418	-11,100,330		6	11,184,144			
9	0.5539	-0.7650	-0.4237	2,305,151	0.012	0.412	948,740		7	9,741,678			
10	2.5794	5.4634	14.0924	60,369,617	-0.007	0.393	23,742,204		8	7,946,415			
11	1.8746	2.9217	5.4769	25,907,753	0.001	0.401	10,401,292		9	4,977,133			
12	1.1822	-5.2886	-6.2523	-21,009,286	0.010	0.410	-8,610,250		10	7,129,781			
13	1.3981	2.9935	4.1853	20,741,357	0.027	0.427	8,853,290		11	7,167,134			
14	1.4571	-8.7849	-12.8002	-47,200,783	0.050	0.450	-21,248,434		12	5,892,245			
15	1.8097	9.1128	16.4912	69,964,634	0.050	0.450	31,457,233		13	2,901,411			
16	2.0004	8.3462	16.6958	70,783,372	0.050	0.450	31,819,119		14	8,269,278			
17	1.4115	-3.7255	-5.2583	-17,033,397	0.032	0.432	-7,353,341		15	7,004,652			
18	0.3902	-5.0085	-1.9542	-3,816,726	0.022	0.422	-1,612,094		16	5,347,690			
19	1.6581	6.7380	11.1720	48,688,045	0.006	0.406	19,762,119		17	6,098,079			
20	0.6944	3.0586	2.1238	12,495,207	0.004	0.404	5,047,244		18	5,636,848			

What you need to know

The model we use is basically very simple:

- C3: market growth = GDP growth × multiple
- D3: market size = current size × (market growth + 1)
- F3: market share = current market share + gain
- G3: sales volumes = market size × market share

What you need to do

1. Place in cell A3: =NORMINV(RAND(),2,1).

2. Place in cell B3: =NORMINV(RAND(),1.5,5).

3. Place in cell C3: =A3*B3.

4. Place in cell D3: =$D$1*(C3+1).

5. Place in cell E3: =NORMINV(RAND(),2%,2%).

6. Place in cell F3: =$F$1+E3.

7. Place in cell G3: =D3*F3.

8. Place in the cells I3 and J3: =G104.

9. Start in cell I3 a Data Table with no row input and an empty cell for column input: =TABLE(,H2).

10. Place in cell M3: =MIN($J$3:$J$102).

11. Place in cell M4: =MEDIAN($J$3:$J$102).

12. Place in cell M5: =MAX($J$3:$J$102).

13. Each time you hit Sh F9, you will see new estimates. But again, "results may vary." Sometimes you may even get into a minimum that is negative.

14. Try many more runs if you want to reduce the uncertainty.

100 x 100 = 10,000 runs only					
4,562,167.38	4,562,167		MIN	525,617
	2	7,321,424		MED	6,356,797
	3	5,184,209		MAX	11,144,304

61. Integration with Monte Carlo

What the simulation does

Open file 6-MonteCarlo.xlsx on sheet "Integration." Consider a circle inscribed within a square with sides of *s* units. The radius of the circle equates to *s*/2.

One-thousand darts (F2) are randomly thrown at the diagram and then we count the number that fall within the circle (F3).

This is basically an integration problem (with an analytical solution), but we can simulate it with a Monte Carlo technique that gives us an approximation of the analytical integral.

The advantage of using this example is that we can compare the simulation result (F4) with the analytical result (F5), telling us how close we came to the "real" solution.

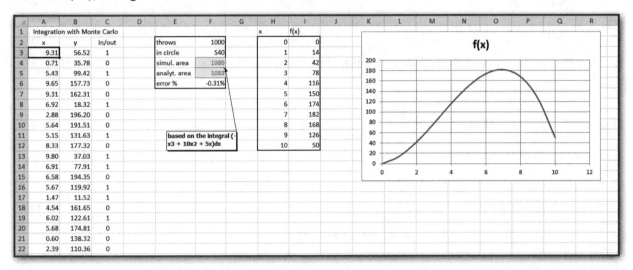

What you need to know

I won't explain this part, but the integral would be $(-x^3 + 10x^2 + 5x)dx$. This formula is used in the cells of columns C and I. The graph plots the analytic solution based on columns H and I. The curve is within a 10 by 200 rectangle (columns A and B).

We will use the RAND function again to determine the position of all darts.

Cell F6 shows us how far the simulated solution deviates from the analytical solution.

What you need to do

1. Place in cell A3: =RAND()*10. Copy down to A1002. This is for the X-position of the dart.

2. Place in cell B3: =RAND()*200. Copy down to B1002. This is for the Y-position of the dart.

3. Place in cell C3: =IF(B3>-A3^3+10*A3^2+5*A3,0,1). Copy down to C1002. This calculation determines whether the dart is inside or outside the circle by using the integral formula: 1 is "in," 0 is "out."

4. Cell F2 counts the number of darts thrown: =COUNT(A:A).

5. Cell F3 sums all the 1s for "in": =SUM(C:C).

6. Cell F4 calculates the area under the curve: =2000*F3/F2.

7. Cell F5 tells us what the analytical result would be (for comparison reasons): =-(1/4)*10^4+(10/3)*10^3+(5/2)*10^2.

8. Cell F6 calculates the error percentage: =(F4-F5)/F5.

9. Each time you hit *Sh F9*, the columns A:F recalculate. Notice how the error keeps changing too, since we "only" used 1,000 simulations. Sometimes you may hit the "perfect" solution.

10. An error percentage of ± 4 is very unusual but never impossible when dealing with probabilities (see to the left).

11. This file will save and open slowly because of its numerous calculations. You may have to be patient!

throws	1000
in circle	565
simul. area	1130
analyt. area	1083
error %	4.31%

Iterations

62. Circular References

What the simulation does

Open file 7-Iterations.xlsm on sheet "Circular." This file has macros (VBA) in it; if you enable them, you will not get warnings about circular references—otherwise you will.

Excel does not accept circular references (for instance, never put =SUM(C2:C4) in cell C4).

In this case, however, we do want to calculate 5% of the net-income for charity. This would create a circular reference because cell C9 would take 5% of C12, but C12 includes C9 in its calculation. So we do want a circular reference here.

A similar story for cell F2: If E2 and F2 are empty, then cell F2 puts a time stamp into itself if there isn't one yet. So cell F2 is referring to itself!

Cell H1 has a similar problem: If column E has a higher value than cell H1, then cell H1 replaces its own value with the higher value.

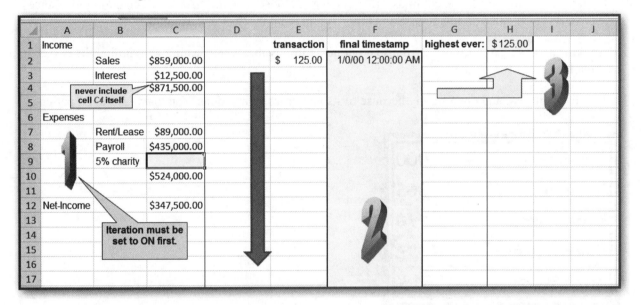

What you need to know

So far we have already been working with some kind of "iterations" by using more and more rows or columns. But this time we need another kind of iterations.

In all of the cases used on this sheet, Excel needs to perform iterations on its own. You can enable iterations by setting them to ON in the following way: File | Options | Formulas | Enable Iteration | Max 1 (for now).

Had you enabled macros for this file, VBA would have done so already for this sheet. But VBA is beyond the scope of this book. When you leave the sheet, VBA turns iteration back OFF. Otherwise you should do that step manually.

124

What you need to do

1. Place in cell C9: =5%*C12. This formula is only possible when iteration is set to ON.

2. Place in cell F2: =IF(E2="","",IF(F2="",NOW(),F2)).

3. Place in cell H1: =MAX(E:E,H1).

4. Type new transaction amounts in column E and watch how time stamps kick in automatically and how H1 goes up each time there is a higher value in column E.

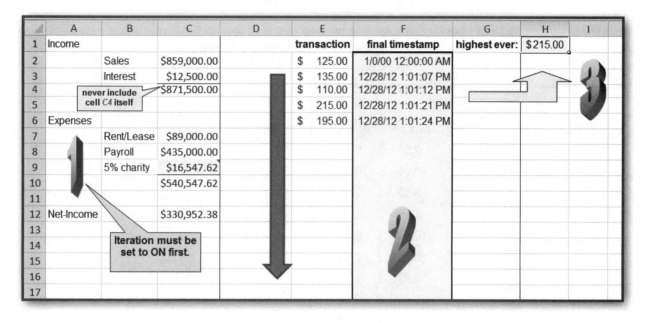

63. Win or Lose?

What the simulation does

Open file 7-Iterations.xlsm on sheet "Gambling." On this sheet we can start a gambling game that determines randomly at each time interval (say, 2 seconds) whether we win or lose (column C) and how much we have gained or lost so far (column D).

In cell B1, you can determine when to start the game ("yes"), so cell C1 gets filled with the current date and time. From that moment on, each hit of (*Sh*) *F9*, at the right time interval, creates a new row with a random value between -$1.00 and +$1.00.

The total column shows how much money they have gained or lost so far. Unfortunately for gamblers, they do not know when a positive total changes into a negative one, otherwise they could stop the game in time.

	A	B	C	D
1	START?	yes	/2/2013 5:54	total
2			$ 0.54	$ 0.54
3			$ (0.06)	$ 0.47
4			$ 0.52	$ 0.99
5			$ 0.26	$ 1.26
6			$ (0.60)	$ 0.65
7			$ (0.58)	$ 0.07
8			$ 0.93	$ 1.00
9			$ (0.92)	$ 0.08
10			$ 0.17	$ 0.24
11			$ (0.05)	$ 0.20
12			$ (0.29)	$ (0.10)
13			$ (0.05)	$ (0.15)
14			$ 0.29	$ 0.14
15			$ (0.55)	$ (0.41)
16			$ (0.12)	$ (0.54)
17			$ 0.67	$ 0.13
18			$ (0.30)	$ (0.17)
19			$ 0.11	$ (0.06)
20			$ (0.98)	$ (1.04)

What you need to know

Excel treats date and time as a sequential, serial number with decimals for the time. January 1, 2013, for instance, is the number 41275—which stands for the number of days since January 1, 1900. The next day would be 41275+1, and so on. So 41275.5 would be 1/1/2013 at noon.

The function TODAY() only creates today's date number, whereas the function NOW() also includes the time part.

Since most cells are going to have references to themselves, we need *Iterations* turned ON and set to a maximum of 1.

What you need to do

1. Apply Data Validation to cell B1: Data | Data Validation | List | yes,no.

2. Place in cell C1: =IF(B1="no","",IF(C1="",NOW(),C1)). Notice the (circular) self-reference.

3. Place in cell C2: =IF(NOW()>$C$1+ROW()/50000, IF(C2="",1-2*RAND(),C2),""). I decided on 50,000, but changing this makes the time interval shorter or longer.

4. Copy the formula in C2 down as far as you want (I copied down to C101).

5. Place in cell D2 a cumulative total: =SUM($C$2:C2). Copy down.

6. If you want this total to show up only if the cell to its left is not empty, adjust the formula: =IF(C2<>"",SUM($C$2:C2)).

7. Make sure *Iterations* is set to ON with a maximum of 1, before you change B1 from "no" into "yes."

8. Each time you hit (*Sh*) *F9*, a new random dollar amount kicks in (you may want to adjust the timing, though).

	A	B	C	D
1	START?	yes	▼ /2/2013 8:10	total
2			$ (0.55)	$ (0.55)
3			$ 0.41	$ (0.14)
4			$ (0.27)	$ (0.41)
5			$ 0.76	$ 0.35
6			$ 0.15	$ 0.51
7			$ 0.22	$ 0.73
8				$ 0.73
9				$ 0.73
10				$ 0.73

64. Circular Gradients

What the simulation does

Open file 7-Iterations.xlsm on sheet "Gradient." This graph is based on the four corner values in square A8:E12. We want to simulate a gradient pattern between these four points.

Gradients are very common in life: a gradient of temperatures, a gradient of altitudes, a gradient of pressure, a gradient of concentrations, a gradient of colors, a gradient of allele frequencies in a population, and so on.

The variation in space of any quantity can be represented (e.g. graphically) by a slope. The gradient represents the steepness and direction of that slope.

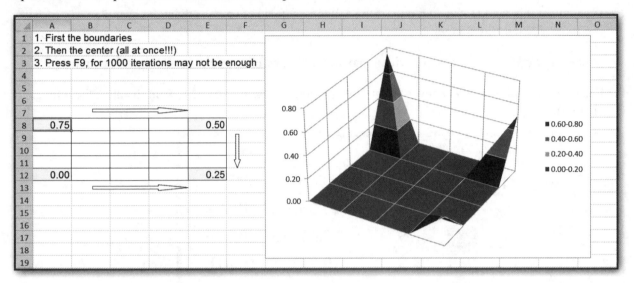

What you need to know

The problem in our simulation is how to determine the values in between those four corner points. The solution is using Excel's iteration capacity.

First we work on the empty cells in the top row, then in the bottom row, in the left column, and finally in the right column.

All we need in order to do so is the AVERAGE function, but since the cells that have to be determined are included in that function as well—a circular reference—we need iterations.

Once this is done for the outer sections, we can tackle the middle section. It could very well be that 1,000 iterations are not enough, especially not when the grid has a finer structure.

What you need to do

1. Make sure iteration is ON and set for at least 1,000 iterations.

2. Place in cell B8: =AVERAGE(A8:C8). Copy to C8 and D8.

3. Place in cell E9: =AVERAGE(E8:E10). Copy to E10 + E11.

4. Place in cell B12: =AVERAGE(A12:C12). Copy to the cells C12 and D12.

5. Place in cell A9: =AVERAGE(A8:A10). Copy to A10 + A11.

6. Now the center part. Place in cell B9: =AVERAGE(A8:C10).

7. Copy this formula down to cell B11, and then to the right to cell D11.

8. The end result will look like the graph below.

9. At any time can you change any of the four corner values, and a new gradient pattern will kick in.

10. You may want to make sure there were enough iterations by hitting *Sh F9* until the pattern does not change anymore.

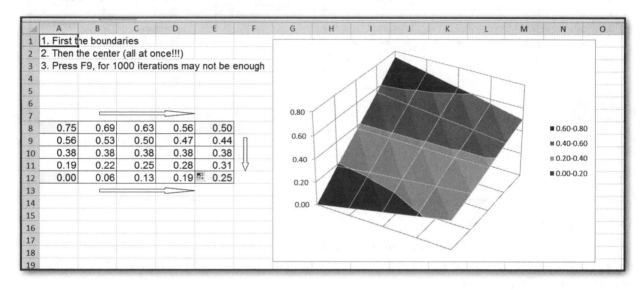

65. Single-Cell Arrays

What the simulation does

Open file 7-Iterations.xlsm on sheet "SingleCellArrays." There are formulas in Excel that use internal *arrays* to create their own "iterations" in order to get a result in one single cell. They often combine multiple operations into one operation.

In the left panel, we average mean values that are based on different numbers of replicates, which requires that we take into consideration the number of cases each average value is based on. This is called *weighting*. A value based on 2 cases (cell B2) should not "weigh" as much as an average value based on 6 cases (B9 or B10). That is why the average in cell B13 in *not* correct. Weighting can be done with *array* formulas.

In the two right panels, we need also single-cell *array* formulas to compare a new list with an old list: Which patients are new (column G), which systolic blood pressure values (SBP) have changes (column H), and which patients have left (column L)?

	A	B	C	D	E	F	G	H	I	J	K	L
1	sample	mean	# replicates			current list					previous list	
1					Patient	SBP	new patient?	new SBP		Patient	SBP	still patient?
2	Sample1	24.97	2									
3	Sample2	20.54	4		Bush	120				Lincoln	123	gone
4	Sample3	21.17	3		Carter	139		145		Bush	120	
5	Sample4	27.99	2		Clinton	160				Kennedy	137	
6	Sample5	27.27	4		Eisenhower	148				Reagan	137	
7	Sample6	19.59	3		Ford	167		159		Nixon	140	
8	Sample7	28.00	4		Johnson	145				Carter	145	
9	Sample8	22.86	6		Kennedy	137				Johnson	145	
10	Sample9	24.77	6		Nixon	155		140		Truman	145	gone
11	Sample10	21.15	5		Reagan	137				Eisenhower	148	
12					Roosevelt	131	new	new		Ford	159	
13	Mean	23.83	incorrect		Washington	139	new	new		Clinton	160	
14	Mean	23.67	array formula									
15	Mean	23.67	XL function									
16												

What you need to know

There are some built-in Excel functions that do also array work. One of them is the function SUM-PRODUCT. It uses two or more arrays, multiplies corresponding components in the given arrays, and then returns the sum of those products.

Be aware, the formula =SUMPRODUCT(range1,range2) is a regular function), but it would be equivalent to the following *single*-cell-array formula: =SUM(range1*range2). The asterisk multiplies corresponding values from two different arrays. Keep in mind that, if you use the latter formula, you should not forget to use *Ctr Sh Enter*, otherwise you would get a #VALUE! error.

Sometimes, or actually very often, there are no regular Excel equivalents, so you have to come up with your own custom array formula. That is the bad news. The good news is that you can always check parts of an array formula by using the *F9* key after highlighting those parts in the formula bar.

What you need to do

1. Place in cell B14 a customized array function for a weighted average: =SUM(E10:E15*F10:F15)/SUM(F10:F15). Make sure you use *Ctr Sh Enter*. (You may need *Sh F9* next if calculation is set to manual.)

2. Place in cell B15 a regular Excel function that does array work: =SUMPRODUCT(E10:E15,F10:F15)/SUM(F10:F15). Make sure you do *not* use *Ctr Sh Enter*.

3. In cell G3 we look up the 1ˢᵗ patient of the new list in all the patients of the old list: =IF(OR(E3=$J$3:$J$13),"","new"). This is a single-cell *array* function that you can copy down.

4. Let's test the function: In the formula bar, you highlight everything inside the OR parentheses and then hit *F9*: {FALSE;TRUE;FALSE;FALSE;FALSE; FALSE;FALSE;FALSE;FALSE;FALSE;FALSE}. Do not forget to hit *Esc* when you are done, otherwise you replace the formula with hard-coded values. You can use this "trick" for other parts of the array formula as well—which is a nice way of checking how the array formula works, or why it does not work.

5. Place in H3 an array formula that finds the old SBP: =IFERROR(IF(OR(E3&F3=$J$3:$J$13&$K$3:$K$13),"" ,VLOOKUP(E3,$J$3:$K$13,2,0)),"new"). Copy down. The ampersand strings things together. So E3&F3 is: "Bush120".

6. Test parts of the formula again with *F9*. Make sure you include or exclude the proper parentheses. Don't forget *Esc*.

7. Place in cell L3: =IF(OR(J3=$E$3:$E$13),"","gone"). Copy down.

8. The array formulas take care now of any changes in the lists.

66. Data Management

What the simulation does

Open file 7-Iterations.xlsm on sheet "Sorting." Here are some powerful single-cell array formulas that may help us in data management. The ones under the left table find various SBP readings for a specific patient. The three tables to the right sort a listing of patients in three different ways. The first one sorts them without duplicates. The second one sorts them without blanks. The third one does the same as the first one, but the list is dynamic, made for future growth.

	A	B	C	D	E	F	G	H	I	J	K	L	M
1	Patient	DOB	Systolic BP			List1	sorted/unique		List2	sorted/no-blanks		List3/dyn.	sorted/unique
2	Bush	05/05/76	120			Reagan	Bush		Reagan	Bush		Bush	Bush
3	Carter	12/10/45	139			Nixon	Carter		Nixon	Carter		Carter	Carter
4	Clinton	09/06/82	160			Kennedy	Clinton		Kennedy	Clinton		Clinton	Clinton
5	Eisenhower	07/05/77	148			Johnson	Eisenhower		Johnson	Eisenhower		Eisenhower	Eisenhower
6	Ford	06/06/55	167			Johnson	Ford			Ford		Ford	Ford
7	Johnson	05/05/65	145			Ford	Johnson		Ford	Johnson		Johnson	Johnson
8	Clinton	09/06/82	155			Ford	Kennedy			Kennedy		Clinton	Kennedy
9	Kennedy	01/11/47	137			Eisenhower	Nixon		Eisenhower	Nixon		Kennedy	Nixon
10	Eisenhower	07/05/77	170			Eisenhower	Reagan			Reagan		Eisenhower	Reagan
11	Ford	06/06/55	164			Clinton			Clinton			Ford	Roosevelt
12	Johnson	05/05/65	152			Clinton						Johnson	Truman
13	Nixon	11/08/54	155			Carter			Carter			Nixon	
14	Reagan	08/06/61	137			Bush			Bush			Reagan	
15												Truman	
16	SBP Avg. Top 5		163.2									Roosevelt	
17													
18		SBP	SBP	SBP	SBP	SBP							
19	Ford	167	164	-	-	-							
20													
21													
22													
23													
24													
25													
26													

What you need to know

All the formulas used here are *single*-cell-array formulas. They are fully customized and allow you to do almost anything you want—but the syntax can get pretty complicated. Be aware that you can always test your trials by using the *F9* key in the formula bar (followed by the *Esc* key).

There are also some new functions. The function LARGE returns the kth largest value in a data set. Take, for instance, =AVERAGE(LARGE(C2:C14,{1,2,3,4,5})). Testing the LARGE part of the array formula with *F9*, would give us the following result: {170,167,164,160,155}.

Another new feature is the use of *range names*. The range F2:F14, for example, can be given the name *List1*—which actually stands for $F$2:$F$14. You can do this as follows: Formulas | Name Manager | New | Name: ... | Refers to: ...

What you need to do

1. Calculate in C16 the average of the "top five" SBPs: =AVERAGE(LARGE(C2:C14,{1,2,3,4,5})). Instead of {1,2,3,4,5} you could also use ROW(1:5) in this case. In all these cases, use the *F9* key to test the formula piece by piece.

2. In row 19 we display all the readings found for the patient chosen in A19. In B19: =IFERROR(INDEX($A$1:$C$14,SMALL(IF($A$19=$A$1:$A$14,ROW($A$1:$A$14),""), COLUMN(A1)),3),"-"). Copy to F19. Test each part with the *F9* key.

3. Let us assign some names: *List1* for F2:F14; *List2* for I2:I14.

4. The third list is a dynamic list that grows automatically when new names get added at the bottom. We do this as follows: Formulas | Name Manager | New | Name: *List3* | Refers to: =OFFSET($L$2,0,0,COUNTA($L:$L)-1).

5. Instead of using OFFSET, you could have used INDEX: =$L$2:INDEX($L:$L,COUNTA($L:$L),0).

6. Now we are ready to implement the three array formulas.

7. The single-cell array formula in G2 can be copied down: =IFERROR(INDEX(List1,MATCH(0,COUNTIF(List1,"<"&List1)- SUM(COUNTIF(List1,$G$1:G1)),0)),""). Test each part with *F9*. The first COUNTIF function, for instance, yields this: {12;11;10;8;8;6;6;4;4;2;2;1;0}. (You may also need *Sh F9* next if calculation is manual.)

8. The single-cell array formula in J2 can be copied down: =IFERROR(INDEX(List2,MATCH(0,IF (ISBLANK(List2),"",COUNTIF(List2,"<"&List2))-SUM(COUNTIF(List2,$J$1:J1)),0)),""). Test each part.

9. Copy the M2 formula down as far as you want: =IFERROR(INDEX(List3,MATCH(0,COUNTIF(List3,"<"&List3)-SUM (COUNTIF(List3,$M$1:M1)),0)),""). Test it.

67. Solving Equations

What the simulation does

Open file 7-Iterations.xlsm on sheet "Equations." Excel has a powerful tool, called *Solver*, which can perform numerous iterations to reach a formula result that you were looking for. It is an ideal simulation tool. In this example, we use ☑ Solver to solve three equations in rows 4:6 with three unknown Xs. We need to find the values of those 3 unknown Xs, if we want the Ys set to the values shown in column G.

We will do this in three different ways. In the top section, we apply Solver directly to columns A, G, and H. In the middle section, we apply Solver to column I, which has the squared residuals between what the 3 Ys are now (column H) and what they are supposed to be (column G). In the bottom section, we use "regular" Excel functions of the array type to solve the equations.

	A	B	C	D	E	F	G	H	I
1	3 equations with 3 unknown X's:				$Y = a_1X_1 + a_2X_2 + a_3X_3$				
2									
3	$X_{1\text{-}3}$		a_1	a_2	a_3		set Y to	formula for Y	
4	0.500		9.375	3.042	-2.437		9.231	6.511	
5	1.000		3.042	6.183	1.216		8.202	8.312	
6	0.500		-2.437	1.216	8.443		3.931	4.219	
7									
8									
9	we could also use the least squares method								
10									
11	$X_{1\text{-}3}$		a_1	a_2	a_3		set Y to	formula for Y	sq.resid.
12	0.500		9.375	3.042	-2.437		9.231	6.511	7.397377
13	1.000		3.042	6.183	1.216		8.202	8.312	0.012045
14	0.500		-2.437	1.216	8.443		3.931	4.219	0.083123
15							sum squared residuals		7.492545
16									
17	we could also use Excel functions to solve this								
18									
19	2 equations		9.375	3.042			9.231		
20	with 2		3.042	6.183			8.202		
21	unknowns		0.659	1.002					
22									
23	3 equations		9.375	3.042	-2.437		9.231		
24	with 3		3.042	6.183	1.216		8.202		
25	unknowns		-2.437	1.216	8.443		3.931		
26			0.896	0.765	0.614				

What you need to know

Solver is an add-in that you may have to activate. If so, you must do the following: File | Options | Add-Ins | Go | ☑ Solver. Now Solver can be found on the Data ribbon, way to the right.

Solver has quite some potential. First of all, you can determine which formula cell (only one) is your target, or your objective, and whether you want it to be set to its lowest or highest value, or rather to a specific value. Second, you determine which cell or cells should be allowed to change in order to reach your objective. Third, you can add certain constraints, such as "no decimals," "equal to," "greater than," or "less than."

Given those settings, Solver starts iterating based on the values put already in as an educated guess (column A).If there is a solution, Solver can probably find it, but perhaps after many more iterations than 1,000 or so. The button *Options* in Solver lets you change such settings (I will not go into further details).

What you need to do

1. Start Solver for the top section. Leave the objective setting empty in this case. The Changing Cells are $A$4:$A$6. And finally set one constraint: $H$4:$H$6 = $G$4:$G$6. Once you hit *Solve*, Solver will come up with a solution by setting $A$4:$A$6 to the values also shown in the range C26:E26.

2. Another approach to this problem would be using the least squared residuals method (see also Simulation 50). Place in cell I12: =(G12-H12)^2. Copy this formula down to I14. Then sum these three squared residuals in cell I15.

3. Instead of calculating all the individual cells I12:I14, we could have used just one formula in cell I15 in one step: =SUMXMY2(G12:G14,H12:H14). This function sums the squares of the differences in two corresponding ranges—in our case, what it is now and what it is supposed to be.

4. Apply Solver: Set the Objective $I$15 to either Min or the value of 0, by changing the cells $A$12:$A$14. Add one constraint again:$H$12:$H$14 = $G$12:$G$14.

5. In the cells C21:D21, we place a multi-cell array formula: =TRANSPOSE(MMULT(MINVERSE(C19:D20),G19:G20)). Make sure you select *both* cells and use *Ctr Sh Enter*. MMULTI returns a vertical array, so we add TRANSPOSE. This finds the settings for *a1* and *a2*, given only 2 equations.

6. In the cells C26:E26, we do this for 3 equations: =TRANSPOSE(MMULT(MINVERSE(C23:E25),G23:G25)).

68. Least Squares Method

What the simulation does

Open file 7-Iterations.xlsm on sheet "LeastSquares." We discussed this situation already in Simulation 50 when we were dealing with logistic (or sigmoidal or s-shaped) regression curves. We use the formula shown in the insert.

This time we want to find the best settings for the variables shown in C1:C3 as an educated guess. Solver may be able to help us find the best fit for this logistic curve.

The logistic equation is used in column D, and the residuals between observed values (column B) and predicted values (column C) are squared and summed in cell D15 (or alternatively in D16 with the function SUMXYM2).

Solver can help us set these bottom cells to a minimum by changing our educated guesses in C1:C3.

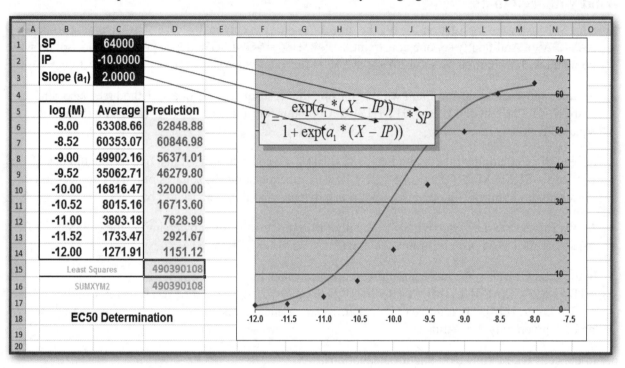

What you need to know

Our predictions are based on the logistic equation shown as an insert in the graph. The formula uses three variables in C1:C3 that need to be reset through a series of iterations, so that the sum of the squared residuals becomes as low as possible. That is where Solver comes to our aid.

Usually Solver does come up with a solution, providing our educated guesses were not too far off and we allow enough iterations. If Solver does come up with a solution, the logistic curve should more or less "hug" the observation points (assuming there are no outliers as discussed in Simulation 73).

What you need to do

1. Place in D6: =EXP($C$3*(B6-$C$2))/(1+EXP($C$3*(B6-$C$2)))*$C$1. This is the logistic equation shown in the insert and used earlier in Simulation 50.

2. Copy this formula down to cell D14.

3. Place in cell D15 a *single*-cell array formula to sum a set of squared residuals: =SUM((((C6:C14)-(D6:D14))^2). Use *Ctr Sh Enter*.

4. Or use instead in D16: =SUMXMY2(C6:C14,D6:D14). This function does not require *Ctr Sh Enter*.

5. Start Solver and set the Objective D15 (or D16) to a minimum, by changing cells C1:C3.

6. Solver came up with the solution shown below. The logistic curve looks fine, but the sum of the squared residuals did not get very low. It is the best Solver could do.

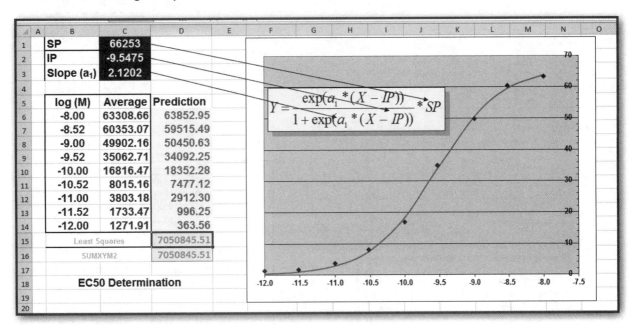

69. Combining Scenarios

What the simulation does

Open file 7-Iterations.xlsm on sheet "Scenarios." Most of this sheet was discussed and developed in Simulation 36. The only new part is the section in the left-lower corner, because it requires iteration.

The user has a choice of six different scenarios—1 and 2 for the most likely scenario, 3 and 4 for the worst-case scenario, and 5 and 6 for the best-case scenario. The current combination is shown in cell L2, but there are actually 8 possible combinations as is shown in B20:B27 (135, 136, etc.). By the way, each scenario setting can be changed, and the number of scenarios is also up to the user, but we limited ourselves to six in this simulation.

Each time the user tests a new combination of scenarios in row 2, the table in the left-lower corner "memorizes" the minimum predicted profit and the maximum predicted profit, so we can compare the different outcomes. However, these predictions are still very fluctuating, because we used only 100 runs.

	A	B	C	D	E	F	G	H	I	J	K	L
1	most likely scenario			worst case		best case		uncertainty			scenario combinations	
2		1		4		6					1-4-6	146
3	Volume	1,500		1,400		2,200		1,861.96				
4	Cost/unit	$ 2.50		$ 2.75		$ 3.25		$3.13			Min	$ 73,987.29
5	Profit/unit	$ 50.00		$ 55.00		$ 65.00		$58.39			25%	$ 89,484.32
6	Overhead	$ 800.00									Median	$102,096.24
7											75%	$114,840.53
8	Revenues	$75,000.00		$77,000.00		$143,000.00		$108,717.37			Max	$130,667.62
9	Expenses	$4,550.00		$4,650.00		$7,950.00		$6,621.13				
10									Volume	Revenues	Expenses	Profit
11	Profit	$70,450.00		$72,350.00		$135,050.00		$102,096.24	1,862	$108,717.37	$6,621.13	$102,096.24
12									2,122	$118,494.42	$7,392.18	$111,102.24
13	most likely		worst case		best case				1,826	$106,040.97	$6,121.20	$ 99,919.77
14	1	2	3	4	5	6			1,412	$ 82,707.92	$4,988.80	$ 77,719.13
15	1,500	2,000	1,200	1,400	2,100	2,200			1,658	$ 92,981.22	$5,527.87	$ 87,453.35
16	$ 2.50	$ 3.00	$ 2.30	$ 2.75	$ 2.70	$ 3.25			1,975	$126,311.95	$6,267.44	$120,044.51
17	$ 50.00	$ 60.00	$ 47.00	$ 55.00	$ 53.00	$ 65.00			2,000	$119,170.54	$6,947.93	$112,222.61
18									1,460	$ 81,674.69	$5,010.76	$ 76,663.93
19		scenarios	worst	best					2,125	$133,710.10	$7,513.52	$126,196.58
20		135	$ -	$ -					1,522	$ 83,705.85	$5,516.35	$ 78,189.51
21		136	$56,843.66	$132,417.02					1,733	$ 97,338.62	$5,833.12	$ 91,505.50
22		145	$ -	$ -	turn				1,436	$ 91,924.76	$5,216.25	$ 86,708.51
23		146	$73,987.29	$130,667.62	Iterations				1,526	$ 97,469.06	$5,683.38	$ 91,785.68
24		235	$ -	$ -	ON, set to				2,157	$128,165.07	$6,812.81	$121,352.26
25		236	$55,059.33	$130,774.96	a max of 1				1,435	$ 90,965.03	$4,769.21	$ 86,195.81
26		245	$ -	$ -					2,192	$132,093.08	$7,692.01	$124,401.06
27		246	$ -	$ -					1,805	$108,774.97	$6,358.61	$102,416.36
28									2,115	$131,051.83	$7,238.14	$123,813.69
29			$55,059.33	$132,417.02					1,485	$ 95,108.30	$5,335.37	$ 89,772.92

What you need to know

In order to record each new combination of scenarios, we need a formula that either updates its own value or leaves it as is—which creates a circular reference and requires *one* iteration.

If you have macros enabled, this sheet has already iteration turned on and set to a maximum of 1 (and it will be set back to default when leaving the sheet). If not, you must enable iterations by setting them to ON in the following way: File | Options | Formulas | Enable Iteration | Max 1 (for this sheet).

scenarios	worst	best	
135	$ -	$ -	
136	$56,843.66	$132,417.02	
145	$ -	$ -	**turn**
146	$73,987.29	$130,667.62	**Iterations**
235	$ -	$ -	**ON, set to**
236	$57,153.26	$132,965.51	**a max of 1**
245	$ -	$ -	
246	$72,648.66	$133,220.13	
	$56,843.66	$133,220.13	

What you need to do

1. Place in C20: =IF(B20=VALUE($L$2),$L$4,C20). Copy the formula down to C27. This records the *lowest* random profit for a specific combination of scenarios.

2. Place in D20: =IF(B20=VALUE($L$2),$L$8,D20). Copy down to cell D27. This records the *highest* random profit for a specific combination of scenarios.

3. Cell C29 finds the lowest value for all combinations of scenarios. We cannot use MIN here, because it might find 0. So we need the function SMALL here as an alternative:
   =SMALL(C20:C27,COUNTIF(C20:C27,0)+1).

4. Cell D29 is easier: =MAX(D20:D27).

5. Use a conditional format for C20:C27: Cell Value | Equal to | C29.

6. Do something similar for D20:D27: Cell Value | Equal to | D29.

7. Changing scenarios and hitting *Sh F9* will affect things (as shown to the left).

70. Logistics

What the simulation does

Open file 7-Iterations.xlsm on sheet "Logistics." The problem presented in this simulation involves the shipment of goods from three plants (A3:A5) to five regional warehouses (C:G), which is an issue of logistics.

Goods can be shipped from any plant to any warehouse, but it obviously costs more to ship goods over long distances than over short distances (C12:G14).

The problem is to determine the amounts to ship from each plant to each warehouse at minimum shipping costs in order to meet the regional demand, while not exceeding the plant supplies.

	A	B	C	D	E	F	G	H	I	J	K	L	M
1			Number to ship from plant A to warehouse B (at intersection):							Color Coding			
2	*Plants:*	Total	*San Fran*	*Denver*	*Chicago*	*Dallas*	*New York*						
3	S. Carolina	5	1	1	1	1	1					Target cell	
4	Tennessee	5	1	1	1	1	1						
5	Arizona	5	1	1	1	1	1					Changing cells	
6			—	—	—	—	—						
7	Totals per Whse		3	3	3	3	3					Constraints	
8													
9	Demands by Whse		180	80	200	160	220				123	Formulas	
10													
11	*Plants:*	Supply	Shipping costs from plant x to warehouse y (at intersection):										
12	S. Carolina	310	$10	$8	$6	$5	$4						
13	Tennessee	260	$6	$5	$4	$3	$6			Total shipments above demands			
14	Arizona	280	$3	$4	$5	$5	$9			Total cannot go beyond supplies			
15										Each shipment must be positive			
16	*Shipping:*	$83	$19	$17	$15	$13	$19						
17													
18		Solution: $ 3,200											
19													

What you need to know

The double underlined numbers are based on formulas, whereas the other numbers are manual input—and thus can be changed by Solver. The target cell holds the total shipping costs in B16, which should be as low as possible. The changing cells are the values found in white cells. The constraints are located in the yellow cells.

There are at least 3 constraints, but they may not always be obvious. #1. The total of shipments must be above demands. #2. The total of shipments cannot go beyond supplies. #3. Each shipment must be positive—something easy to overlook.

	A	B	C	D	E	F	G	H
1			Number to ship from pla					
2	*Plants:*	Total	*San Fran*	*Denver*	*Chicago*	*Dallas*	*New York*	
3	S. Carolina	=SUM(C3:G3)	1	1	1	1	1	
4	Tennessee	=SUM(C4:G4)	1	1	1	1	1	
5	Arizona	=SUM(C5:G5)	1	1	1	1	1	
6			—	—	—	—	—	
7	Totals per Whse		=SUM(C3:C5)	=SUM(D3:D5)	=SUM(E3:E5)	=SUM(F3:F5)	=SUM(G3:G5)	
8								
9	Demands by Whse		180	80	200	160	220	
10								
11	*Plants:*	Supply	Shipping costs from plan					
12	S. Carolina	310	10	8	6	5	4	
13	Tennessee	260	6	5	4	3	6	
14	Arizona	280	3	4	5	5	9	
15								
16	*Shipping:*	=SUM(C16:G16)	=C3*C12+C4*C13+C5*C	=D3*D12+D4*D13	=E3*E12+E4*E13	=F3*F12+F4*F13	=G3*G12+G4*G13+G	
17								

What you need to do

1. Hit *Ctr* ~ to see where the formulas are located (see above). Switch back from formula-view to value-view.

2. Start Solver. Cell B16 has to be set to a minimum, by changing cells $C$3:$G$5.

3. The 1st constraint is: $B$3:$B$5 <= $B$12:$B$14.

4. The 2nd constraint is: $C$3:$G$5 >= 0.

5. The 3rd constraint is: $C$7:$G$7 >= $C$9:$G$9.

6. Sometimes it is also necessary to make sure Solver comes up with integers instead of parts of a product. Try it if you want.

7. Solver found the best solution—which is the lowest shipping costs—with $3,200 for the total shipping costs.

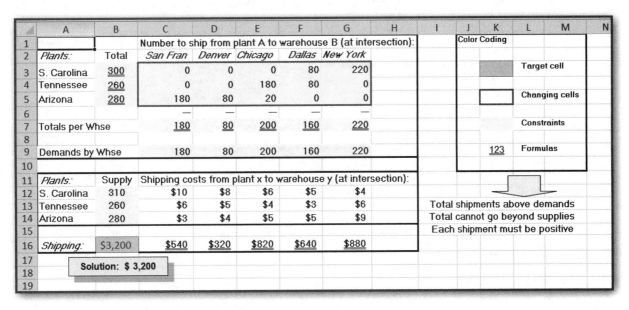

Extras

71. Area Code Finder

What the simulation does

Open file 8-Extras.xlsx on sheet "AreaCodeFinder." This sheet has much more on it than you might think at first sight. It has a listing of some 270 area codes with information about the state, city, and time zone. Those rows, starting in row 14, could be made hidden, but I decided to make their font white, so they are visible in the formula bar when you select one of their cells.

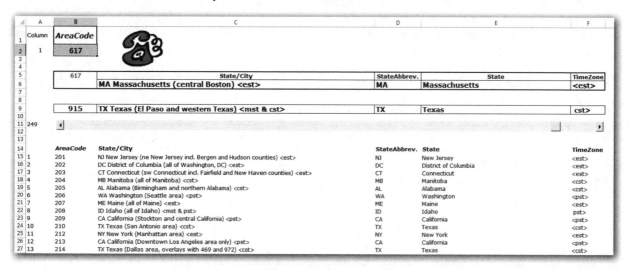

Typing a certain area code in B2 shows additional information about that particular area code in row 6. This could have been done with the function VLOOKUP, but I chose to use Excel's Data Table facility instead.

In addition, row 11 has a scroll bar that allows you to scroll through all the records and then displays one particular record in row 9.

What you need to know

All D-functions in Excel, such as DSUM, are ideal for data bases if you want to use a filter (see Simulation 35). One of those D-functions is DGET. It searches in a data base for a specific field under certain conditions as specified in a filter.

In our case, DGET is used in cell B5, at the origin of a Data Table. The filter used by DGET is located in B1:B2.

In row 9 we use VLOOKUP to find a record that starts with the number shown in cell A11. The number in A11 is controlled by a scroll bar just below it.

What you need to do

1. Place in cell B5: =DGET($B$11:$F$278,A2,$B$1:$B$2).

2. The 1st argument refers to the range that holds the listing of area code information.

3. The 2nd argument indicates which column is used in the function—either the column label enclosed between double quotation marks, or a number (without quotation marks) that represents the position of the column within the list: 1 for the first column, 2 for the second column, and so on. I used an invisible number 1 in cell A2.

4. The 3rd argument refers to a filter (in this case, located in B1:B2).

5. Select B5:F6 and implement a Data Table (see Appendix 3) with A2 for the row input and A5 for the column input.

6. Cell B2 has also a custom validation that prevents wrong area code entries: =ISERROR(B5)=FALSE. This validation will only work when calculation is set to *automatic*.

7. Changing the area code in cell B2 should bring up a new area code record.

8. Implement a scroll bar (see Appendix 5) with these settings: Min: 1, Max: 267, LinkedCell: A11, LargeChange: 5.

9. The formula in cell B9 finds the record with the number of A11: =VLOOK UP($A$11,$A$15:$F$281,COLUMN(B1),0). Copy this formula to the right, to cell F9.

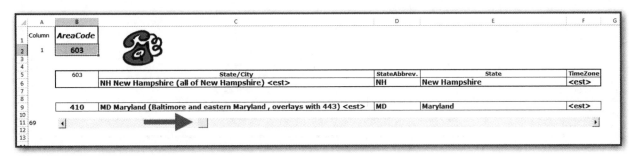

72. Graph Manipulation

What the simulation does

Open file 8-Extras.xlsx on sheet "GraphManipulation." On this sheet we filter the data we would like to be plotted in a graph. The graph plots historical data used by Ancel Keys, who "invented" the fat and heart disease connection around 1956. He selected from the table to the left a series of countries that were "in line" with his hypothesis: heart disease and mortality are strongly correlated with a high consumption of fat in a daily diet. The regression line is certainly exponential, combined with a high R-squared value (0.96), which makes the curve a nice fit.

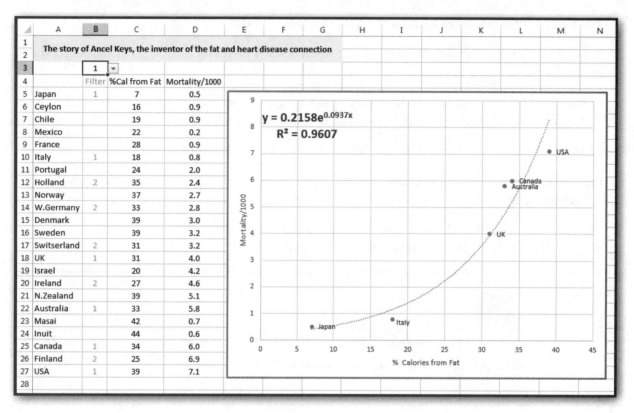

What you need to know

His story sounds great until we realize that his selection of countries was very biased. Had he used all the data available to him at the time (1956), he would have gotten a curve that does *not* show a strong correlation between his two variables (R-squared has plummeted from 0.96 to 0.14, as you can see below).

Sometimes it can be very legitimate to leave extreme values out—so-called outliers (more on those in Simulation 73). In this case, however, it is hard to call the ignored data outliers.

Nowadays, we know Ancel Keys did not only use biased data, but also forgot to factor in the existence of other variables—the consumption of sugar, for instance. These are called confounding factors or hidden variables. Always be on the lookout for those.

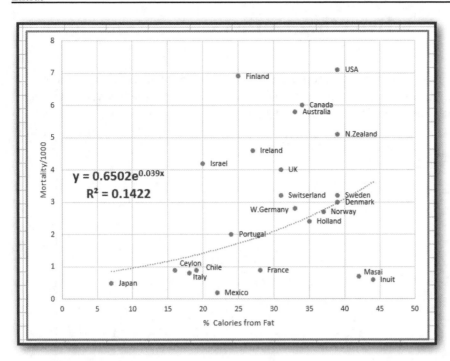

To switch from one graph to the other, we use a filter (regulated by cell B3 and the numbers below it). In this case there are 3 filter settings (0, 1, and 2). The "real secret" behind this filter, however, is hidden in the columns E and F behind the graph.

What you need to do

1. Start in E5 to E27: =IF($B$3=0,C5,IF($B$3=B5,C5,NA())).

2. Start in F5 to F27: =IF($B$3=0,D5,IF($B$3=B5,D5,NA())).

3. Filter 1 shows Ancel Keys' selection; filter 0 shows *all* the data available. Had you chosen filter 0, you would have actually found a very strong *negative* relationship (R-squared is high again, 0.96)—but again a spurious relationship.

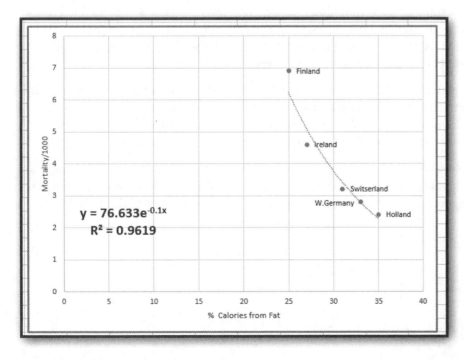

73. Detecting Outliers

What the simulation does

Open file 8-Extras.xlsx on sheet "Outliers." Outliers are defined as numeric values in any random data set that have an unusually high deviation from either the statistical mean or the median value. In other words, these numbers are relatively extreme. It requires sound statistics—not intuition—to locate them.

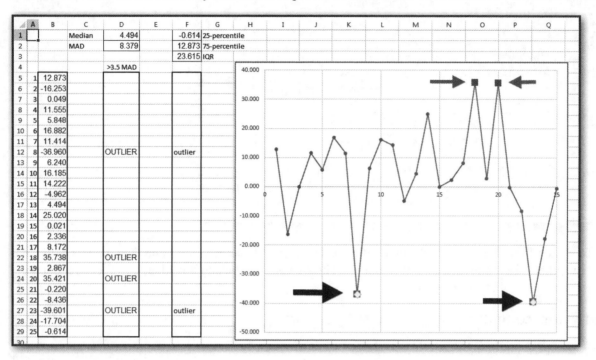

What you need to know

A rather simple rule is that all values outside a range of three times the standard deviation around the mean could be considered outliers—provided they follow a normal distribution.

In this simulation, however, we will use a more robust statistical detection of outliers by calculating the deviation for each number, expressed as a "modified Z-score," and testing it against a predefined threshold. Z-scores stand for the amount of standard deviation relative to the statistical median (in D1). MAD (in D2) stands for Median Absolute Deviation. Any number in a data set with the absolute value of modified Z-score exceeding 3.5 times MAD is considered an outlier. Column D shows the outcome.

In the 1970's the famous statistician John Tukey decided to give the term outlier a more formal definition. He called any observation value an outlier if it is smaller than the first quartile (F1) minus 1.5 times the *IQR* (F3), or larger than the third quartile (F2) plus 1.5 times the *IQR*. The Inter-Quartile Range, *IQR*, is the width of the interval that contains the middle half of the data. Column F shows the outcome.

The graph to the right shows the observed values marked with a *square* if it is an outlier according to the first method, or with a *diamond* if it is an outlier according to the second method. Most of the time, the first method detects more outliers than the second one (in this case, 4x for the first method and 2x for the second).

What you need to do

1. In cell B5 we create normally distributed values between around 30 with SD 15 and manipulate them randomly: =NORMINV(RAND(),30,15)*(1-2*RAND()). Copy down.

2. D1 shows the median of these numbers: =MEDIAN(B5:B29).

3. MAD in D2: =MEDIAN(ABS(MEDIAN(B5:B29)-B5:B29)). This is a single-cell array formula requiring *Ctr Sh Enter*.

4. In D5 we make a decision on each value: =IF(ABS(D$1-B5)>(3.5*D$2), "OUTLIER", ""). We consider any number with the absolute value of the modified Z-score exceeding 3.5 times MAD to be an outlier.

5. F1 has the 25-percentile: =PERCENTILE($B$5:$B$29,0.25). QUARTILE for quart #1 equals PERCENTILE for 25%.

6. F2 has the 75-percentile: =PERCENTILE($B$5:$B$29,0.75). QUARTILE for quart #3 equals PERCENTILE for 75%.

7. *IQR* in F3: =AVERAGE($B$5:$B$29)+(1.5*(F2-F1)). *IQR* is the width of the interval that contains the data's middle half.

8. F5 has the verdict: =IF(OR(B5>($F$2+1.5*$F$3),B5<($F$1-1.5*$F$3)),"outlier",""). Copy down.

9. The markers in the graph for the first method (in column D) are based on a hidden column I behind the graph (as shown in Simulation 72). In cell I15: =IF(D5="OUTLIER",B5,NA()).

10. The same for the second method (in column F). In cell J15: =IF(F5="outlier",B5,NA()).

74. False Positives

What the simulation does

Open file 8-Extras.xlsx on sheet "FalsePositives." Most tests for certain diseases produce sometimes positive results (T[+]) even though the person tested does *not* have the disease (D[-]). Those "positive" results are called "*false* positives."

In the left panel below, we calculate the *sensitivity* (C8) and the *specificity* (C9) of a certain test based on known test results—for instance based on a trial (B4:C5).

In the cells H4:H8 from the right panel, we use existing information about a certain test for a certain disease (in this case AIDS, but the same would hold for a drug test) and then we calculate what number of affected people we would find if we went for *universal* testing (in cells H9 and K9). You will be surprised to discover how low this percentage is! Then we use a Data Table to check the effect of changes in the test's sensitivity (row 12) and specificity (column F).

	A	B	C	D	E	F	G	H	I	J	K	L	M	N	O	P	Q
1		from data to diagnostics								from diagnostics to universal testing							
2																	
3		T+	T-	Total													
4	D+	283	51	334		new	population	300,000,000			T+	T-	Total				
5	D-	27	612	639		disease	w/ AIDS	500,000		D+	475,000	25,000	500,000				
6	Total	310	663	973			prevalence	0.001666667		D-	5,990,000	293,510,000	299,500,000				
7						new	sensitivity	0.95		Total	6,465,000	293,535,000	300,000,000				
8	sensitivity T+	SE =B2/D2	0.84731			test	specificity	0.98									
9	specificity T+	SP =C3/D3	0.95775				P(D+|T+)	7.35%			7.35%	P(D+|T+)					
10	prevalence D+	PR =D2/D4	0.34327														
11						P(D+|T+)											
12		T+	T-	Total		7.35%	80.0%		82.0%	84.0%	86.0%	88.0%	90.0%	92.0%	94.0%	96.0%	98.0%	SE
13	D+	SE*PR	(1-SE)*PR	PR		80.0%	0.66%		0.68%	0.70%	0.71%	0.73%	0.75%	0.76%	0.78%	0.79%	0.81%	
14	D-	(1-SP)*(1-PR)	SP*(1-PR)	(1-PR)		82.0%	0.74%		0.75%	0.77%	0.79%	0.81%	0.83%	0.85%	0.86%	0.88%	0.90%	
15	Total	P(T+)	P(T-)	1		84.0%	0.83%		0.85%	0.87%	0.89%	0.91%	0.93%	0.95%	0.97%	0.99%	1.01%	
16						86.0%	0.94%		0.97%	0.99%	1.02%	1.04%	1.06%	1.09%	1.11%	1.13%	1.16%	
17	P(D+|T+)	P(D+|T-)	P(D-|T+)	P(D-|T-)		88.0%	1.10%		1.13%	1.16%	1.18%	1.21%	1.24%	1.26%	1.29%	1.32%	1.35%	
18	=P(D+ and T+)/P(T+)	=P(D+ and T-)/P(T-)	=P(D- and T+)/P(T+)	=P(D- and T-)/P(T-)		90.0%	1.32%		1.35%	1.38%	1.42%	1.45%	1.48%	1.51%	1.55%	1.58%	1.61%	
19						92.0%	1.64%		1.68%	1.72%	1.76%	1.80%	1.84%	1.88%	1.92%	1.96%	2.00%	
20	P(D+|T+)	SE*PR / SE*PR + (1-SP)*(1-PR)				94.0%	2.18%		2.23%	2.28%	2.34%	2.39%	2.44%	2.50%	2.55%	2.60%	2.65%	
21	P(D+|T-)	(1-SE)*PR / (1-SE)*PR + SP*(1-PR)				96.0%	3.23%		3.31%	3.39%	3.46%	3.54%	3.62%	3.70%	3.78%	3.85%	3.93%	
22	P(D-|T+)	(1-SP)*(1-PR) / SE*PR + (1-SP)*(1-PR)				98.0%	6.26%		6.41%	6.55%	6.70%	6.84%	6.99%	7.13%	7.28%	7.42%	7.56%	
23	P(D-|T-)	SP*(1-PR) / (1-SE)*PR + SP*(1-PR)				SP												
24																	

What you need to know

This is basically an issue of "conditional probability." We want to find, for instance, the probability of having a disease (D[+]) "on condition of" having a positive test (T[+]). This is expressed as: $P(D^+|T^+)$, which you read as follows: the probability of event D[+] given event T[+]. Or we want to find the probability of *not* having a disease given a (*false*) positive test: $P(D^-|T^+)$. An analysis like this is done with the so-called Bayes Theorem.

This kind of analysis is explained in the left panel. Based on trial data (B4:C5), we can calculate how good the test is in *excluding* a disease (which is the *sensitivity* of the test, in cell C8) and how good the test in *finding* a disease (which is the *specificity* of the test, in cell C9). The *prevalence* of D[+] is the relative number of disease cases in a sample or population (in cell C10). The Hayes Theorem allows us to calculate the four different conditional probabilities based on sensitivity, specificity, and prevalence—as shown in the lower part of the left section. The basic "rule" is shown in A17:D18: $P(D^+|T^+) = P(D^+$ and $T^+) / P(T^+)$.

What you need to do

1. All calculations in the left panel are already done. They are of the simple type and explain the basics of the Bayes Theorem.

2. The right panel estimates that, in a population of 300 million people (H4), 500,000 individuals have AIDS (H5). A certain test for AIDS has a sensitivity of 0.95 (H7) and a specificity of 0.98 (H8). The rest is based on calculations explained next.

3. Place in H6: =H5/H4. This calculates the prevalence of the disease (the percentage of AIDS people in the population).

4. Place in cell H9: =(H7*H6)/(H7*H6+(1-H8)*(1-H6)). This is the calculation for $P(D^+|T^+)$, based on the formula in B18. In other words, if we would do general testing for AIDS in the entire population, we would find that the probability of having the disease, if one gets a positive test result, is only 7.35%. Doing general testing for a rather rare disease is not good policy because of the probability of *false*-positives.

5. We could have calculated this also with the grid of K5:M7. Place in M5: =H5. In M7: =H4. In M6: =M7-M5. In K5: =$H$7*M5. In L5: =M5-K5. In K6: =M6-L6. In L6: =H8*M6. In K7: =SUM(K5:K6). In L7: =SUM(L5:L6).

6. Based on this, we can calculate $P(D^+|T^+)$ in K9: =K5/K7.

7. In cell F12, we start an overview table for various test sensitivities and specificities: =H9 (or: =K9). To do so, select range F12:P22 and start a Data Table with H7 for row input and H8 for column input: =TABLE(H7,H8).

75. Probability of Beliefs

What the simulation does

Open file 8-Extras.xlsx on sheet "Beliefs." Probabilities have everything to do with uncertainty. So far we have been talking about probabilities in terms of *frequencies*. But there is another kind of probability and uncertainty: this one measures the degree to which we *believe* something. To say that there is a 98% probability that Shakespeare wrote Hamlet does not mean that if 100 Shakespeares were born, 98 of them would have written Hamlet. Apparently, this is not an uncertainty about frequencies but an uncertainty about beliefs. The initial probability of a hypothesis can and will be updated in the light of new relevant data.

Let us study what the fraction of a certain disease in the population is based on hypothetical possibilities of 5%, 15%, etc. (column A). We start assuming—a belief—that each possibility has the same probability, 0.1 (column B). Then we find out that, from the first 5 individuals that we studied, 4 (in cell C1) did have the disease, while 1 (in C2) did not. Based on these findings, we calculate how often doctors would find 4 out of 5 individuals with the disease in a population of 100 individuals (column C). Then we recalculate in column D the probabilities we had assumed in column B. It turns out that the highest probability is now concentrated around the 75% option. So we believe this is the hypothesis with the highest probability at this point.

	A	B	C	D	E	F	G	H	I	J	K	L	M	N	O	P	Q
1		YES	4														
2		NO	1														
3		out of	100														
4																	
5																	
6	hypo-	probability	number	corrected													
7	thesis	of belief	of cases	probability		23%	1	2	3	4	5	6	7	8	9	10	YES
8	5%	0.1	0.0006	0%		1	15%	18%	21%	23%	27%	31%	34%	36%	37%	38%	
9	15%	0.1	0.0430	0%		2	18%	18%	20%	23%	25%	28%	30%	31%	34%	38%	
10	25%	0.1	0.2930	1%		3	21%	20%	21%	23%	25%	27%	28%	31%	34%	35%	
11	35%	0.1	0.9754	3%		4	23%	23%	23%	24%	26%	26%	29%	31%	31%	33%	
12	45%	0.1	2.2553	7%		5	27%	25%	25%	26%	26%	28%	29%	30%	33%	34%	
13	55%	0.1	4.1178	12%		6	31%	28%	27%	26%	28%	28%	30%	31%	31%	34%	
14	65%	0.1	6.2477	19%		7	34%	30%	28%	29%	29%	30%	29%	32%	33%	33%	
15	75%	0.1	7.9102	23%		8	36%	31%	31%	31%	30%	31%	32%	31%	34%	35%	
16	85%	0.1	7.8301	23%		9	37%	34%	34%	31%	33%	31%	33%	34%	32%	35%	
17	95%	0.1	4.0725	12%		10	38%	38%	35%	33%	34%	34%	33%	35%	35%	33%	
18						NO											
19			33.7456	23%													
20																	

What you need to know

Apparently, there are two different views of probability. The so-called frequentist probability is the view in which probability is defined in terms of frequency in outcomes of repeated experiments (column C). The so-called Bayesian probability, on the other hand, is the view in which probability is interpreted as a measure of degree of belief—a belief one has about possible values of a certain feature (column D). In this Simulation, our ultimate goal is the latter view.

In the table to the right we will find out how various values in cell C1 (from 1 to 10 people *with* the disease)—shown in the top row of the table—and how various values in cell C2 (from 1 to 10 people *without* the disease)—shown in the left column of the table—lead us to different beliefs about the entire population.

What you need to do

1. Cells C1 and C2 have Data Validation for the values 1 to 10.

2. Cell C8 calculates how many out of 100 doctors would find 4 out of 5 people with the disease: =A8^$C$1*(1-A8)^$C$2*$C$3. Copy the formula down to cell C17.

3. Cell C19 sums all these cases: =SUM(C8:C17).

4. Cell D8 recalculates the new probabilities: =C8/$C$19. Copy.

5. Cell D19 locates the highest probability in the previous list: =MAX(D8:D17).

6. With conditional formatting in range D8:D17, we mark the cell with the highest probability: Top/Bottom Rules | Top: 1.

7. Based on this information, we can start a Data Table to simulate various values in cells C1 and C2, running from 1 to 10. To do so, select range F7:P17, implement a Data Table with C1 as row input and C2 as column input: =TABLE(C1,C2).

8. In range A8:A17, we apply conditional formatting to mark the option that corresponds with the highest value in column D: =ROW($A1)=MATCH($D$19,$D$8:$D$17,0).

9. In the Table range G8:P17, we mark the cell in column 4 (the value of cell C1) and row 2 (the value of cell C2) by using the formula: =AND(ROW(A1)=$C$2,COLUMN(A1)=$C$1).

10. Try changing values in C1 and C2 and watch the outcome.

76. Unbiased Sampling

What the simulation does

Open file 8-Extras.xlsx on sheet "SampleTechniques." When taking samples, the problem is that some are more likely to be chosen than others—so we call them biased samples. Unbiased sampling requires some bias-proof techniques. Therefore, we need the unbiased verdict of mathematical tools.

In this simulation, we use four different techniques to select telephone area codes at random. #1 assigns a random number, sorts by that number, and then takes the first or last *N* cases. #2 selects *X*% of the area codes randomly. #3 produces *N* cases randomly. #4 "weighs" each area code (say, depending on population density) and then performs a *weighted* sampling of *N* cases.

	A	B	C	D	E	F	G	H	I	J	K	L	M	N	O	P	Q	R	S
1	mere random			25% of random			only 10 codes						10 weighted area codes						
2	random	area code		area code	25%		area code	10x		cumul.	area code	weight	bar		sample of 10	weighted			
3	0.000	670		670	FALSE		670	417		0	203	1	+		225	++		1	+
4	0.002	611		611	FALSE		611	270		1	204	4	++++		210	+++		2	++
5	0.002	757		757	FALSE		757	811		5	205	2	++		217	+		3	+++
6	0.004	216		216	FALSE		216	504		7	206	1	+		219	+		4	++++
7	0.006	411		411	FALSE		411	709		8	207	1	+		210	+++			
8	0.010	307		307	FALSE		307	816		9	208	1	+		209	++++			
9	0.013	805		805	FALSE		805	450		10	209	4	++++		215	++++			
10	0.014	905		905	TRUE		905	513		14	210	3	+++		210	+++			
11	0.015	803		803	FALSE		803	937		17	212	1	+		204	++++			
12	0.018	606		606	FALSE		606	612		18	213	1	+		219	+			
13	0.022	843		843	FALSE		843			19	214	1	+						
14	0.023	308		308	TRUE		308			20	215	4	++++						
15	0.024	360		360	FALSE		360			24	216	2	++						
16	0.033	917		917	FALSE		917			26	217	1	+		order codes randomly				
17	0.035	314		314	FALSE		314			27	218	1	+		225	3			
18	0.035	784		784	TRUE		784			28	219	1	+		210	5			
19	0.037	920		920	TRUE		920			29	224	4	++++		217	4			
20	0.044	267		267	TRUE		267			33	225	2	++		219	6			
21	0.048	417		417	FALSE		417			35	228	1	+		210	1			
22	0.049	419		419	FALSE		419			36	240	1	+		209	10			
23	0.052	612		612	FALSE		612								215	9			
24	0.052	201		201	FALSE		201								210	7			
25	0.057	765		765	FALSE		765								204	8			
26	0.057	956		956	TRUE		956								219	2			
27	0.059	416		416	FALSE		416												

What you need to know

Case #4 may need some more explanation. In column J, we calculate the cumulative total of all previous weights. So area code 204 (in K4) is four times included in that total. In column O, we multiply the grand total (J22) with a random number between 0 and 1, and then we look up that value in range J3:K22 and determine its corresponding area code. In other words, the second area code, 204, can be found through the random numbers between >=1 and <5—which amounts to 4 chances of being picked (4x more than the first area code, 203).

What you need to do

1. Place in cell A3: =RAND(). Copy down to the last area code.

2. In order to sort by column A, without RAND recalculating again, we copy column A and paste it back as a value.

3. Consider the top or bottom *N* cases as your random samples.

4. For case #2, we want a certain percentage of area codes (say, 25% in cell E2). To do so, place in cell E3: =RAND()<$E$2. Copy down. Take the TRUE cases for your 25% sampling.

5. For case #3, we use an Excel tool: Data | Data Analysis | Sampling | Input Range: $G$3:$G$269 | ⊙ Random: 10 | Output Range: H3.

6. Case #4 is more complicated. Each area code has a certain weight in column L, depending on population density or so. With the help of a table in R3:S6, this weight was translated into a bar symbol (column M). So place in cell M3: =VLOOKUP(L3,$R$3:$S$6,2,0).

7. Column J is for a cumulative total. Place in J3 the value 0. Place in J4: =J3+L3. Copy this last formula down.

8. Column O creates a series of (10 or more) random area codes in accordance with their weight. To do so, place in O3: =VLOOKUP($J$22*RAND(), $J$3:$K$22, 2). Copy down.

9. If you also want to see their bar codes, place in cell P3: =VLOOKUP(VLOOKUP(O3,$K$3:$L$22,2,0),$R$3:$S$6,2,0). Copy this "double" VLOOKUP formula down.

10. *Sh F9* should give you each time a new set of weighted random area codes. Most of the time, you will see more four- and three-plusses than any other cases.

11. Starting in P17, we sort the selected codes *randomly*: =LARGE(ROW($1:$10)*NOT(COUNTIF($P$16:P16, ROW($1:$10))), RANDBETWEEN(1,11-ROW(P1))). Make sure to use *Ctr Sh Enter* before you copy the formula down.

12. How does this work? ROW($1:$10) creates the array {1, 2, 3, 4, 5, 6, 7, 8, 9, 10}. If the array formula had randomly selected the number 2 in cell P17, COUNTIF(..., ROW...)) in cell P18 would create this array: {0;1;0;0;0;0;0;0;0;0}, so number 2 cannot be selected anymore. Now ROW(...)*NOT(...) creates another array: {1;0;3;4;5;6;7;8;9;10}.

13. If you want N codes, use *$1:$N* 2x, and change 11 into N+1.

14. To start in Q15, replace P with Q (3x), and 16 with 14 (2x).

77. Numbering Records

What the simulation does

Open file 8-Extras.xlsx on sheet "AutoNumber." Assigning consecutive numbers to a series of records is a very common procedure. Here are some ways to do so in an easy way.

All white cells show the type of numbering. All yellow cells contain formulas—which can then be finalized by Copy | Paste Special | Values.

	A	B	C	D	E	F	G	H	I	J	K	L	M	N	O	P
1	1	1		001	001	001		1001	1001		1	1		1	1	
2	2	2		002	002	002		1002	1002		2	2		1	1	
3	3	3		003	003	003		1003	1003		3	3		1	1	
4	4	4		004	004	004		1004	1004		4	4		1	1	
5	5	5		005	005	005		1005	1005		5	5		1	1	
6	6	6		006	006	006		1006	1006		1	1		2	2	
7	7	7		007	007	007		1007	1007		2	2		2	2	
8	8	8		008	008	008		1008	1008		3	3		2	2	
9	9	9		009	009	009		1009	1009		4	4		2	2	
10	10	10		010	010	010		1010	1010		5	5		2	2	
11	11	11		011	011	011		1011	1011		1	1		3	3	
12	12	12		012	012	012		1012	1012		2	2		3	3	
13	13	13		013	013	013		1013	1013		3	3		3	3	
14	14	14		014	014	014		1014	1014		4	4		3	3	
15	15	15		015	015	015		1015	1015		5	5		3	3	
16																

What you need to know

The two functions we have not used yet are MOD and QUOTIENT. The MOD function returns the remainder after a number is divided by a divisor. For instance, =MOD(3, 2) returns the remainder of the division 3/2, which is 1.

The function QUOTIENT returns the integer portion of a division. Use this function when you want to discard the remainder of a division. In older versions of Excel, it used to be only available if the *Analysis Toolpak* had been activated.

In the table at the bottom (see the picture at the end), we create a *randomly* sorted list in the 4th column based on an unsorted list in the 3rd column. This is basically an issue of permutations. Permutations are different from combinations; in the latter case, the internal order is not significant.

The number of permutations can be calculated with the function PERMUT—in this case, =PERMUT(6,6), which equals 720.

What you need to do

1. Place in cell B1: =ROW(). Copy down. This produces a series of sequential numbers. We used the function ROW already in Simulations 14 and 31.

2. The assigned numbers will change when you sort the column, so you may want to replace the formula with values.

3. In column E, we like the sequential numbers to have leading zeros. To do so, place in cell E1: =RIGHT("000" & ROW(),3). Copy down (and replace with values if you want).

4. In column F, we use a simpler formula instead: =ROW(). The leading zeros were implemented through formatting: Format Cells | Custom | 000.

5. In column I, we want the sequential numbers to start with 1001. Place in cell I2: =ROW(A1001). Instead of using A1001, you could have used any column reference (for instance, B1001 or C1001).

6. In column L, we keep repeating a certain set of numbers (in this case 1 through 5). Place in cell L1: =MOD(ROW()-1,5)+1. If you replace 5 with 12, you would get the numbers 1 through 12 repeatedly, of course.

7. In column O, we wish to repeat each number a series of times. Place in cell O1: =QUOTIENT(ROW()-1,5)+1. Again, the number 5 stands for the number of repeats

8. Next we create a list that automatically sorts in a random order. Place in B19:B24 a series of random numbers.

9. The sorting work is done in the 4th column, starting in D19: =VLOOKUP(SMALL($B$19:$B$24,A19),$B$19:$D$24,2,0). Copy the formula down to cell D24.

10. Each time you hit *Sh F9*, the last column will display a new randomly sorted list—which is another permutation.

#	RAND	unsorted	sorted
1	0.1078	Top Mgmt	Administration
2	0.2763	Senior Mgmt	Top Mgmt
3	0.3157	Finance	Marketing
4	0.1419	Marketing	Senior Mgmt
5	0.3433	Sales	Finance
6	0.0947	Administration	Sales

78. Fiscal Year

What the simulation does

Open file 8-Extras.xlsx on sheet "FiscalYear." Excel has great functions to extract the year, month, and day part of a date—but amazingly enough, it has no function to find out to which *quarter* of the year such a date belongs.

For summary overviews, that is quite a limitation, though. This problem can be solved with a simple nested function such as *ROUNDUP(MONTH(any date)/3,0)*.

However, finding the correct quarter becomes much harder when your company does not have a regular fiscal year.

On this sheet, we determine in cell G2 when your fiscal year starts—let us assume it is in October (10). Column E has to do "the math."

	A	B	C	D	E	F	G	H	I	J	K	L
1	Account	Sale	Date	Year	Fiscal Quarter		Starts in		1	January	2	2013
2	Young	$ 146.91	February 3, 2001	2001	2001--Q2		9		2	February	2	2013
3	Jones	$ 155.05	April 15, 2001	2001	2001--Q3				3	March	3	2013
4	Burke	$ 41.55	June 25, 2001	2001	2001--Q4				4	April	3	2013
5	O'Brian	$ 172.39	September 4, 2001	2001	2002--Q1				5	May	3	2013
6	Brown	$ 189.73	November 14, 2001	2001	2002--Q1				6	June	4	2013
7	Brown	$ 219.95	December 1, 2001	2001	2002--Q2				7	July	4	2013
8	Roberts	$ 115.55	January 24, 2002	2002	2002--Q2				8	August	4	2013
9	Brown	$ 15.27	April 5, 2002	2002	2002--Q3				9	September	1	2014
10	Young	$ 56.45	June 15, 2002	2002	2002--Q4				10	October	1	2014
11	Jones	$ 103.95	August 25, 2002	2002	2002--Q4				11	November	1	2014
12	Minsky	$ 163.96	November 4, 2002	2002	2003--Q1				12	December	2	2014
13	Minsky	$ 63.96	November 4, 2002	2002	2003--Q1				1	January	2	2014
14	Jenkins	$ 48.29	January 14, 2003	2003	2003--Q2				2	February	2	2014
15	Jenkins	$ 88.19	March 14, 2003	2003	2003--Q3				3	March	3	2014
16	Russell	$ 19.43	March 26, 2003	2003	2003--Q3				4	April	3	2014
17	Caruso	$ 109.40	June 5, 2003	2003	2003--Q4				5	May	3	2014
18	Russell	$ 171.92	August 15, 2003	2003	2003--Q4				6	June	4	2014
19	Roberts	$ 45.77	October 25, 2003	2003	2004--Q1				7	July	4	2014
20	O'Brian	$ 146.32	January 4, 2004	2004	2004--Q2				8	August	4	2014
21	Jones	$ 65.92	March 15, 2004	2004	2004--Q3				9	September	1	2015
22	Young	$ 37.88	May 25, 2004	2004	2004--Q3				10	October	1	2015
23	Jones	$ 93.87	August 4, 2004	2004	2004--Q4				11	November	1	2015
24	Burke	$ 77.51	October 14, 2004	2004	2005--Q1				12	December	2	2015
25	O'Brian	$ 224.22	December 24, 2004	2004	2005--Q2							
26	Brown	$ 144.15	March 5, 2005	2005	2005--Q3							
27	Roberts	$ 24.67	May 15, 2005	2005	2005--Q3							
28	Brown	$ 257.14	July 25, 2005	2005	2005--Q4							
29	Jones	$ 18.13	October 4, 2005	2005	2006--Q1							
30												

What you need to know

This is going to be a heavily nested formula (see Appendix 2 for more details). It uses the functions YEAR, MONTH, IF, MOD, and INT. MOD was explained in Simulations 4 and 75. The last one, INT, rounds a number down to the nearest integer.

In addition, you may want to use the function TODAY, which returns the current day and therefore changes its outcome every day.

What you need to do

1. Cell G2 has Data Validation: =$I$1:$I$12.

2. The hard work is done in cell E2:
   =YEAR(C2) + IF(MONTH(C2)>=$G$2,1,0) & "--Q" & INT(1 + MOD(MONTH(C2) - $G$2,12)/3).
   This results in something like "2001--Q2". The ampersand (&) "hooks" all the pieces together. Adjust the formula to your needs.

3. Copy this formula down.

4. In case you are interested, cell K1 has the following formula: =INT(1+MOD(I1-$G$2,12)/3). Copy down.

5. Cell L1 has: =YEAR(TODAY())+COUNTIF($I$1:I1,$G$2).

6. Range I1:L24 has a conditional formatting formula: =AND(ROW()>=$G$2,ROW()<$G$2+12). Assign a fill color.

7. Range I1:L24 has another conditional formatting formula: =$L2<>$L1. Assign a bottom border line.

8. A different fiscal year (say 5, for May) would result in different quarters, of course, and a different color range, as you can see below.

	A	B	C	D	E	F	G	H	I	J	K	L
1	Account	Sale	Date	Year	Fiscal Quarter		Starts in		1	January	3	2013
2	Young	$ 146.91	February 3, 2001	2001	2001--Q4		5		2	February	4	2013
3	Jones	$ 155.05	April 15, 2001	2001	2001--Q4				3	March	4	2013
4	Burke	$ 41.55	June 25, 2001	2001	2002--Q1				4	April	4	2013
5	O'Brian	$ 172.39	September 4, 2001	2001	2002--Q2				5	May	1	2014
6	Brown	$ 189.73	November 14, 2001	2001	2002--Q3				6	June	1	2014
7	Brown	$ 219.95	December 1, 2001	2001	2002--Q3				7	July	1	2014
8	Roberts	$ 115.55	January 24, 2002	2002	2002--Q3				8	August	2	2014
9	Brown	$ 15.27	April 5, 2002	2002	2002--Q4				9	September	2	2014
10	Young	$ 56.45	June 15, 2002	2002	2003--Q1				10	October	2	2014
11	Jones	$ 103.95	August 25, 2002	2002	2003--Q2				11	November	3	2014
12	Minsky	$ 163.96	November 4, 2002	2002	2003--Q3				12	December	3	2014
13	Minsky	$ 63.96	November 4, 2002	2002	2003--Q3				1	January	3	2014
14	Jenkins	$ 48.29	January 14, 2003	2003	2003--Q3				2	February	4	2014
15	Jenkins	$ 88.19	March 14, 2003	2003	2003--Q4				3	March	4	2014
16	Russell	$ 19.43	March 26, 2003	2003	2003--Q4				4	April	4	2014
17	Caruso	$ 109.40	June 5, 2003	2003	2004--Q1				5	May	1	2015
18	Russell	$ 171.92	August 15, 2003	2003	2004--Q2				6	June	1	2015
19	Roberts	$ 45.77	October 25, 2003	2003	2004--Q2				7	July	1	2015
20	O'Brian	$ 146.32	January 4, 2004	2004	2004--Q3				8	August	2	2015
21	Jones	$ 65.92	March 15, 2004	2004	2004--Q4				9	September	2	2015
22	Young	$ 37.88	May 25, 2004	2004	2005--Q1				10	October	2	2015
23	Jones	$ 93.87	August 4, 2004	2004	2005--Q2				11	November	3	2015
24	Burke	$ 77.51	October 14, 2004	2004	2005--Q2				12	December	3	2015
25	O'Brian	$ 224.22	December 24, 2004	2004	2005--Q3							
26	Brown	$ 144.15	March 5, 2005	2005	2005--Q4							
27	Roberts	$ 24.67	May 15, 2005	2005	2006--Q1							
28	Brown	$ 257.14	July 15, 2005	2005	2006--Q1							
29	Jones	$ 18.13	October 4, 2005	2005	2006--Q2							
30												

79. Stock Market

What the simulation does

Open file 8-Extras.xlsx on sheet "StockMarket." The left section of this sheet is hard-coded data, comparing S&P 500 values (C) with the values of a traditional portfolio (B).

The right section analyses this information from the most recent month (12/1/06) down to the previous month (11/1/06 or further back in time). It "grows" if you copy its first row down as far as you want to go back in history.

In addition, when new records are added at the bottom of the left section, the first row in the right section will automatically update the history from the most recent data down.

	A	B	C	D	E	F	G	H	I	J	K	L
1	Month	Traditional	S&P 500		Month	Traditional	Trad-3mo	BenchMark	S&P500	S&P-3mo	BenchMark	
2	1/1/04	51.50	65.90		12/1/06	68.38	64.10	0.07	87.16	81.68	0.07	
3	2/1/04	52.17	66.81		11/1/06	67.41	62.48	0.08	85.95	79.63	0.08	
4	3/1/04	51.37	65.80		10/1/06	66.18	61.04	0.08	84.35	77.78	0.08	
5	4/1/04	50.60	64.77		9/1/06	64.10	60.99	0.05	81.68	77.30	0.06	
6	5/1/04	51.29	65.66		8/1/06	62.48	60.52	0.03	79.63	77.20	0.03	
7	6/1/04	52.26	66.93		7/1/06	61.04	62.33	-0.02	77.78	79.49	-0.02	
8	7/1/04	50.55	64.72		6/1/06	60.99	61.50	-0.01	77.30	78.43	-0.01	
9	8/1/04	50.73	64.98		5/1/06	60.52	60.81	0.00	77.20	77.47	0.00	
10	9/1/04	51.29	65.68		4/1/06	62.33	60.65	0.03	79.49	77.26	0.03	
11	10/1/04	52.17	66.68		3/1/06	61.50	59.12	0.04	78.43	75.27	0.04	
12	11/1/04	54.30	69.38		2/1/06	60.81	59.14	0.03	77.47	75.24	0.03	
13	12/1/04	56.12	71.74		1/1/06	60.65	56.99	0.06	77.26	72.50	0.07	
14	1/1/05	54.81	69.99		12/1/05	59.12	57.86	0.02	75.27	73.73	0.02	
15	2/1/05	55.97	71.47		11/1/05	59.14	57.36	0.03	75.24	73.14	0.03	
16	3/1/05	55.08	70.20									
17	4/1/05	54.05	68.87									
18	5/1/05	55.73	71.06									
19	6/1/05	55.80	71.16									
20	7/1/05	57.89	73.81									
21	8/1/05	57.36	73.14									
22	9/1/05	57.86	73.73									
23	10/1/05	56.99	72.50									
24	11/1/05	59.14	75.24									
25	12/1/05	59.12	75.27									
26	1/1/06	60.65	77.26									
27	2/1/06	60.81	77.47									
28	3/1/06	61.50	78.43									
29	4/1/06	62.33	79.49									
30	5/1/06	60.52	77.20									
31	6/1/06	60.99	77.30									
32	7/1/06	61.04	77.78									
33	8/1/06	62.48	79.63									
34	9/1/06	64.10	81.68									
35	10/1/06	66.18	84.35									
36	11/1/06	67.41	85.95									
37	12/1/06	68.38	87.16									

What you need to know

The only two new functions are COUNTA and INDEX. The COUNTA function works like COUNT, but it also counts cells with text in them, such as the headers over each column.

The function INDEX is a more sophisticated version of VLOOKUP. It looks in a table at a certain row position and a certain column position. It uses this syntax: *INDEX(table, row#, col#)*. Whereas VLOOKUP works only with column numbers, INDEX also uses row numbers, which is very important when we want to look at a record that is located 3 or 12 rows above another record (like in columns G and J).

This time we use the function ROW again, but for a different reason—to make the month go down: *row# − ROW(A1)+1*. Each time we copy that formula one row down, the formula subtracts one more row: − ROW(A2), then − ROW(A3), and so forth.

What you need to do

1. Place in cell E2 a formula to find the bottom date: =INDEX($A:$C,COUNTA($A:$A)-ROW(A1)+1,1).

2. Place in F2 a formula to find the corresponding value in column B:
    =INDEX($A:$C,COUNTA($A:$A)-ROW(B1)+1,2).

3. Place in G2 a formula for a value 3 rows up from the previous one:
    =INDEX($A:$C,COUNTA($A:$A)-ROW(C1)+1-3,2).

4. Place in cell H2: =F2/G2-1.

5. Place in I2 a formula to find the matching value in column C:
    =INDEX($A:$C,COUNTA($A:$A)-ROW(A1)+1,3).

6. Place in J2 a formula for a value 3 rows up from the previous one:
    =INDEX($A:$C,COUNTA($A:$A)-ROW(A1)+1-3,3).

7. Place in cell K2: =I2/J2-1.

8. Copy the cell range E2:K2 as far down as you want to go back in history.

9. Add new records at the end of the table in columns A:C, and notice how the table to the right nicely updates the history and its analysis.

80. Forecasting Temperatures

What the simulation does

Open file 8-Extras.xlsx on sheet "WeatherForecast." This is a very busy sheet that requires quite some work. It shows the monthly temperatures in Florida between 1980 and 2011 (left panel). I kept year 2011 separate in row 34, so we can make a prediction of its temperatures (T) based on historical records.

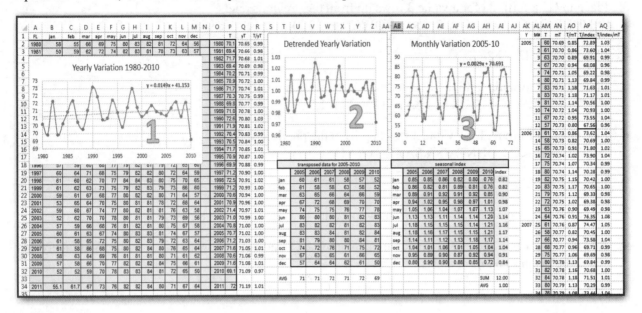

What you need to know

We use a very simple model based on three components: a yearly trend (yT), a monthly trend (mT), and a random component (rT). So $T = yT*mT*rT$. There are more sophisticated models but those are also much more complicated.

First we "de-trend" the original yearly temperatures by removing the yearly trend component (yT). Then we do something similar for the monthly temperatures by removing the monthly trend component (mT). Finally, we should be able to forecast 2011.

What you need to do

1. Place in cell P2: =AVERAGE(B2:M2). Copy down to P32.

2. Place in Q2:Q32 at once: =TREND(P2:P32,O2:O32). Don't forget *Ctr Sh Enter*. This calculates temperatures based on a linear yearly upward trend. This trend is plotted in graph #1.

3. Place in R2: =P2/Q2. This de-trends the yearly variations (T/yT). The result is plotted in graph #2.

4. Now we need to tackle the monthly variations—say, for 2005-2010. Select B27:M32 and transpose it into cell U19.

5. Calculate the averages of each year in cell U33: =AVERAGE(U20:U31). Copy the formula to cell Z33.

6. Next we calculate the monthly indexes—T in a specific month and year divided by the average of that year. So place in cell AC20: =U20/U$33. Copy this into the entire table.

7. AI20 creates a monthly index: =AVERAGE(AC20:AH20).

8. Copy AI20 down; their total should be 12, their average 1.

9. In the right panel (AK:AQ), we split each year (2005-2010) into 12 months. Each month needs a consecutive number (in AL), so we can use that number for the TREND function.

10. Copy U20:U31 and paste it into AM2:AM13. These are the monthly T's for 2005. Do something similar for the 4 other years (2006-2010). The result is plotted in graph #3.

11. Select range AN2:AN73: =TREND(AM2:AM73,AL2:AL73).

12. Place in AO2: =AM2/AN2 (which is T/mT). Copy down.

13. In column AP, we divide T for each year by the index for that particular year. Make sure you do this per year. In AP2: =AM2/$AI20 (and down to AP13). In AP14: =AM14/$AI20 (and down to AP25), and so on. The result is in graph #4.

14. In AQ2: =AP2/AN2 (which is *(T/index)/mT*). Copy down.

15. Now the 2011 forecast. In A38: =$AM$73 + ROW(A1). Copy down to A49. The month numbers must be consecutive.

16. In B38, we predict T for each month based on columns AL and AN:
    =TREND($AN$2:$AN$73,$AL$2:$AL$73,A38). Do this for *one* cell (*Ctr Sh Enter*) and then copy down.

17. Correct mT by multiplying with the month's index. Place in cell C38: =B38*AI20. Copy down to C49. This is *mT*index*.

18. Transpose the actual T's for 2011 (B34:M34) into D38:D49.

19. Although we used a rather crude model, our forecast is pretty close to the actual monthly temperatures in 2011. Was it worth all the work? You decide.

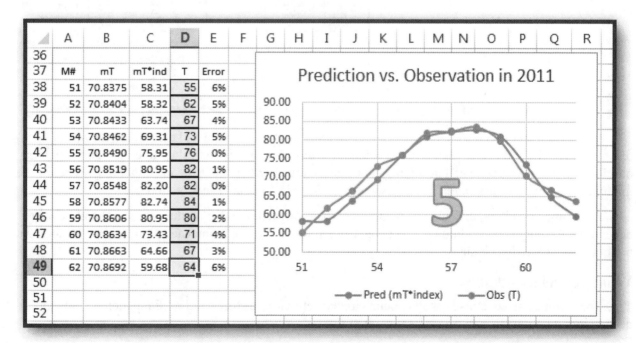

Miscellanea

81. Data Table with Memory

What the simulation does

Open file 81-DataTableMemory.xlsx in the folder Miscellanea. In column A, we randomly choose 0's or 1's, with a chance for 1's based on cell C1. The number of 1's is calculated in cell F1. Based on this calculation, a data table in columns E and F runs all of this again for the next 9 percentages. When you change the percentage in C1 to 2%, column E shows the next 9 percentages from 3% to 11%.

	A	B	C	D	E	F	G	H	I	J

A1 ✕ ✓ *fx* =IF(RAND()<=$C$1,1,0)

	A	B	C	D	E	F	G	H	I	J
1	0		1%			9		Min	Max	
2	0				2%	27		15	27	
3	0				3%	16		16	36	
4	0				4%	34		34	51	
5	0				5%	38		29	56	
6	0				6%	53		50	69	
7	0				7%	77		55	95	
8	1				8%	89		64	93	
9	0				9%	100		82	101	
10	0				10%	99		89	110	
11	0									
12	1							**iterations on**		
13	0									
14	0									

Columns H and I serve as some kind of memory and keep track of the highest and lowest values reached so far. Each time you get a value in column F that is the same as the value for either the maximum or minimum, the max or min cell in column H or I gets marked. When the value in column F goes below the minimum or above the maximum, the corresponding values in column H and I get updated.

Each time you hit F9, the columns A and F will be recalculated. Whether the columns H and I change depends on the outcome in column F. The range from minimum to maximum can be pretty wide because we use only 1000 cases in column A

What you need to know

The formulas in columns H and I contain circular references as discussed in Simulation 62. So you need to turn iteration ON with some 1000 iterations or so.

The formulas in column E use the ROW function to increase the percentage by 1%.

The formulas in columns H and I use an IF function nested inside another IF function.

What you need to do

1. Place in cell A1: =IF(RAND()<=$C$1,1,0).

2. Copy the formula downwards to cell A1000 or so.

3. Place in cell F1: =COUNTIF(A:A,1).

4. Place in cell E2: =$C$1+ROW(A1)/100.

5. Copy this formula down to cell E10.

6. Select E1:F10 and implement a Data Table with only a column input for C1.

7. Turn iterations ON.

8. Place in cell H2: =IF(H2=0,F2,IF(F2<H2,F2,H2)), and copy downwards to cell H10.

9. Place in cell I2: =IF(I2=0,F2,IF(F2>I2,F2,I2)) and copy downwards to cell I10.

10. Implement Conditional Formatting for H2:I10: =$F2

11. When you want to reset the memory, select H2:H10, click in the formula bar, then hit Ctr + Enter.

12. Do the same for I2:I10. In the beginning the difference between min and max is small (below), but then gradually grows (above).

C	D	E	F	G	H	I
1%			11		Min	Max
		2%	28		19	28
		3%	35		35	36
		4%	74		65	74
		5%	107		99	107
		6%	150		150	155
		7%	237		206	237
		8%	278		277	278
		9%	345		345	355
		10%	453		453	466

82. Graph Manipulation

What the simulation does

Open file 82-FrequencyTables.xlsx. On this spreadsheet, we create in column A 1,000 random numbers with a normal distribution around a mean of 10.5 and a standard deviation of 1. Then we create a frequency table for means between 7 and 15, and plot them below the table. Upon hitting F9, the graph may change quite a bit because we are dealing only with a sample of 1,000 cases.

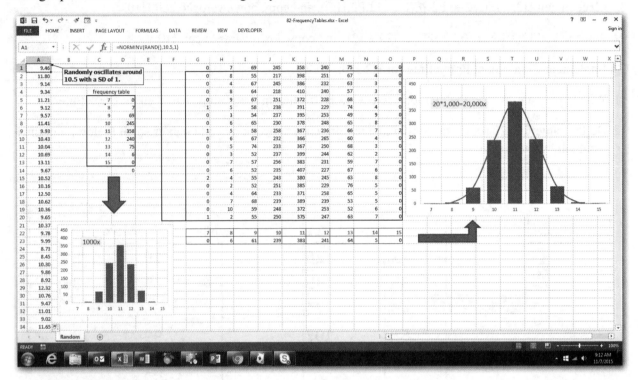

Next we repeat this entire process some 20 more times with a Data Table (G1:20) and calculate the average of the frequencies per frequency bin (G23:O23). This means we are actually working with 20 * 1,000 = 20,000 cases. As a consequence the graph for this frequency distribution (top right) hardly changes after repeatedly hitting F9.

What you need to know

We use again the function NORMINV with a nested RAND function to create randomly distributed numbers.

To calculate the frequencies for a set of bins, we use the array function FREQUENCY. We also need the array function TRANSPOSE.

What you need to do

1. Start in cell A1: =NORMINV(RAND(),10.5,1), and copy downwards to A1000.

2. Select the range D5:D13 at once for the following function: =FREQUENCY(A1:A1000,C5:C13). Don't forget to use Ctr+Shift+Enter.

3. Select range D1:O1: =TRANSPOSE(D5:D13). Use again Ctr+Shift+Enter.

4. Select range F1:O20, and implement a Data Table with only the column input of any empty cell outside the range.

5. Place in range G22:O22 at once: =TRANSPOSE(C5:C13), followed by Ctr+Shift+Enter.

6. Place in cell G23: =AVERAGE(G1:G18), and copy to O23.

7. Hitting F9 repeatedly shows you how the left graph (1,000 cases) changes more than the right graph (20,000 cases).

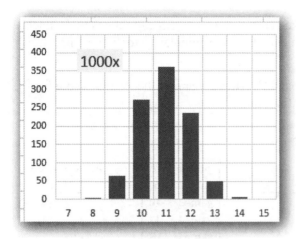
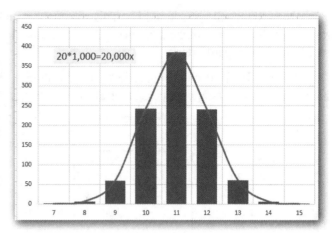

83. Simulation of a Slot Machine

What the simulation does

Open file 83-SlotMachine.xlsx. This spreadsheet makes 20 runs for each game (columns F:H). Each run creates 3 random numbers between -2 and +2, and then calculates the cumulative total in column J. After 20 run, a new game starts.

The results for each game are recorded in columns N and O. After 20 games, the average score features in cell R3. Then the process starts all over with run 1 for game 1.

	A	B	C	D	E	F	G	H	I	J	K	L	M	N	O	P	Q	R	S
1					**0**					cumulative									
2		**run**			1	-1	-1	-1		**-3**		**game**		game1	-2			average score	
3		14	20		2	2	0	2		1		13		game2	5			4	
4					3	1	-2	1		1				game3	-10				
5					4	-1	1	-1		0				game4	-11				
6					5	1	1	1		3				game5	16				
7					6	-1	1	-1		2				game6	4				
8					7	-1	2	-1		2				game7	10				
9					8	1	0	-2		1				game8	12				
10					9	-2	-1	1		-1				game9	14				
11					10	2	-1	2		2				game10	12				
12					11	2	2	0		6				game11	0				
13					12	0	1	0		7				game12	-2				
14					13	-2	2	0		7				game13					
15					14	0	-1	1		7									
16																			
17																			
18																			
19																			
20																			
21																			

What you need to know

The tables E2:H21 and N2:O21 automatically expand with a new row after hitting F9. Once we reach the last row, the process starts all over again. Holding the F9 key, makes you run through the game quite quickly.

To make all of this possible, we need nested IF functions, plus the ROW function. Instead of RAND-BETWEEN(-2,2), we used RAND here: -2+INT(RAND()*5). Take your pick.

Because most of these IF functions regulate the outcome in their very own cell, we need to avoid circular references by making sure iterations are ON, set to 1 iteration.

What you need to do

1. Turn iterations ON, set to 1 iteration.

2. Place in cell B3: =IF(L3=21,1,IF(B3>=C3,1,B3+1)).

3. Place in range E2:E21: =IF(ROW(A1)<=$B$3,ROW(A1),"").

4. Place in the next 3 columns (F2:H21): =IF($E2="","",IF(F2="",-2+INT(RAND()*5),F2)).

5. Place in cell J2: =IF(E2="","",SUM($F$2:H2)). Copy down.

6. Place in cell L3: =IF(L3=21,0,IF(B3=2,L3+1,L3)).

7. Place in N2: =IF(ROW(A1)<=$L$3,"game"&ROW(A1),"").

8. Place in O2: =IF(N2="","",IF(O2="",$J$21,O2)). Copy down.

9. Place in cell R3: =IFERROR(AVERAGE(O2:O21),0). Prior to Excel 2007, you had to use a longer formula: =IF(ISERROR(AVERAGE(O2:O21)),0,AVERAGE(O2:O21))

10. Below you see a possible outcome after 20 games with 20 runs each.

	A	B	C	D	E	F	G	H	I	J	K	L	M	N	O	P	Q	R	S
1					0					cumulative									
2		run			1	-1	-1	-1		-3		game		game1	-2			average score	
3		20	20		2	0	2	-2		-3		20		game2	5			1.26	
4					3	0	2	2		1				game3	-10				
5					4	-1	-1	-1		-2				game4	-11				
6					5	-1	0	-2		-5				game5	16				
7					6	2	2	1		0				game6	4				
8					7	2	-2	2		2				game7	10				
9					8	2	-2	-1		1				game8	12				
10					9	-1	-1	-2		-3				game9	14				
11					10	-2	1	0		-4				game10	12				
12					11	-2	-1	-1		-8				game11	0				
13					12	2	-1	0		-7				game12	-2				
14					13	0	-1	-2		-10				game13	-1				
15					14	-1	-2	1		-12				game14	14				
16					15	1	-2	-1		-14				game15	10				
17					16	-2	-1	1		-16				game16	-11				
18					17	2	2	0		-12				game17	-16				
19					18	2	2	2		-6				game18	-16				
20					19	-2	2	-2		-8				game19	-4				
21					20	-2	-2	1		-11				game20	-11				

84. Letter Game

What the simulation does

Open file 84-LetterGame.xlsx on sheet "Chars-Counted." On a "board" of 10 by 10, random letters appear each time we hit F9. If the word "NO"—or any other 2-letter word (see cell M2)—appears horizontally, the first letter gets marked. Besides, column P keeps track of how often each letter was used, equally distributed.

Switch to sheet "Chars-Weighted." Here we give each letter a different chance of being chosen, which is more natural in real languages. Column T shows what each letter is "worth." Notice now how column P has different hits for different characters. Column R calculates the cumulative totals of column T.

	A	B	C	D	E	F	G	H	I	J	K	L	M	N	O	P
1		Z	K	D	P	P	H	C	N	P	L		type 2 caps		A	501
2		O	V	X	Y	F	K	X	H	B	B		NO		B	498
3		I	L	D	R	U	H	Z	U	F	M				C	523
4		M	L	V	Y	M	G	J	P	F	G				D	463
5		N	O	T	K	D	M	K	A	T	F				E	531
6		X	L	L	F	W	Q	F	Y	R	Y				F	521
7		I	E	B	F	L	K	L	V	I	K				G	494
8		R	E	W	Z	V	O	N	R	I	G				H	496
9		N	B	S	Q	Y	L	R	Q	E	J				I	503
10		G	A	Q	J	H	S	Q	Y	A	P				J	520
11															K	526
12															L	462
13															M	473
14															N	495
15															O	536
16															P	460
17															Q	501
18															R	470
19															S	511
20															T	506
21															U	489
22															V	467
23															W	477
24															X	543
25															Y	517
26															Z	497

O	P	Q	R	S	T
A	981	0	A	4
B	690	4	B	3
C	567	7	C	2
D	722	9	D	3
E	1317	12	E	5
F	452	17	F	2
G	472	19	G	2
H	740	21	H	3
I	956	24	I	4
J	476	28	J	2
K	208	30	K	1
L	432	31	L	2
M	737	33	M	3
N	997	36	N	4
O	1249	40	O	5
P	744	45	P	3
Q	198	48	Q	1
R	1196	49	R	5
S	952	54	S	4
T	714	58	T	3
U	485	61	U	2
V	708	63	V	3
W	456	66	W	2
X	179	68	X	1
Y	178	69	Y	1
Z	188	70	Z	1

What you need to know

We need the function CHAR, like we did in Simulation 8. The capital letters A-Z run from asci numbers 65 to 90. We also use ROW, VLOOKUP, RANDBETWEEN (or RAND), and a cumulative SUM in column R. Since VLOOKUP can only search for exact values or for previous values in an ascending order, we need cell R1 to start at 0 (instead of 4).

As said before, there are various ways of replacing RANDBETWEEN with RAND. One is: =INT((high-low+1)*RAND()+low). Or for a random integer between 0 and 3: =INT(RAND()*4). Or for a random integer between 1 and 4: =1+INT(RAND()*4). The function INT always rounds a number down to the nearest integer. RAND runs from 0 to 0.9999.

What you need to do

1. Place in cell B1: =CHAR(RANDBETWEEN(65,90)). If you don't have RANDBETWEEN, use this formula instead: =CHAR(INT(90-65+1)*RAND()+65).

2. Copy this formula over the entire board.

3. Type in cell O1: =CHAR(ROW(A65)), copy down to row 26.

4. Turn iteration ON, set to 1 iteration.

5. Type in cell P1: =IF(COUNTIF($B$1:$K$10,O1)>1, P1+COUNTIF($B$1:$K$10,O1),P1).

6. Select the entire board and implement Conditional Formatting: =(B1&C1)=$M$2.

7. Go to the 2nd sheet. Fill the entire board with: =VLOOKUP(RANDBETWEEN(0,70),$R$1:$S$26,2).

8. The columns O, P, and S have the same formulas as sheet1.

9. Column T is handwork. Change whatever you want.

10. Column R starts with zero in cell R1.

11. Place in cell R2: =SUM($T$1:T1), and copy this downward. This is a cumulative summing operation.

12. To start column P from scratch again, select cells P1:P26, click in the formula bar, and hit Ctr + Enter.

	A	B	C	D	E	F	G	H	I	J	K	L	M	N	O	P	Q	R	S	T
1		I	F	M	O	I	G	B	A	T	E		type 2 caps		A	1197		0	A	4
2		O	U	U	J	Q	N	O	M	P	N		NO		B	873		4	B	3
3		G	H	S	N	L	J	V	A	O	I				C	683		7	C	2
4		O	P	J	E	B	D	O	L	S	E				D	912		9	D	3
5		A	W	S	C	H	T	Q	I	I	F				E	1617		12	E	5
6		D	Q	Q	B	N	E	S	X	F	A				F	554		17	F	2
7		C	J	R	G	N	D	E	R	H	R				G	557		19	G	2
8		P	E	V	S	O	N	P	Z	O	R				H	907		21	H	3
9		X	N	W	A	N	D	M	A	U	H				I	1193		24	I	4
10		S	B	G	A	S	R	T	N	T	B				J	563		28	J	2
11															K	273		30	K	1
12															L	536		31	L	2
13															M	916		33	M	3
14															N	1237		36	N	4
15															O	1550		40	O	5
16															P	934		45	P	3
17															Q	252		48	Q	1
18															R	1488		49	R	5
19															S	1201		54	S	4
20															T	864		58	T	3
21															U	604		61	U	2
22															V	898		63	V	3
23															W	577		66	W	2
24															X	214		68	X	1
25															Y	214		69	Y	1
26															Z	225		70	Z	1

85. A Hawk-Dove Simulation

What the simulation does

Open file 85-HawkDoveGame.xlsx. Game theory is the study of mathematical models of conflict and cooperation. The name "Hawk-Dove" refers to a situation in which there is a competition for a shared resource and the contestants can choose either conciliation or conflict; this terminology is most commonly used in biology and economics.

The traditional payoff matrix for the Hawk-Dove game includes the value of the contested resource, and the cost of an escalated fight. It is assumed that the value of the resource is less than the cost of a fight. Sometimes the players are assumed to split the payoff equally, other times the payoff is assumed to be zero.

A "mixed" evolutionary strategy (ESS) is where two strategies permanently coexist. For a given set of payoffs, there will be one set of frequencies where this mix is stable. A mixed ESS can be achieved if individuals either play one strategy all of the time in a population where the two strategies are at the equilibrium frequencies (for example, 60% of the individuals always call and 40% always act as satellites), or all individuals play a mixed strategy where each behavior in the mix is performed at the equilibrium frequency.

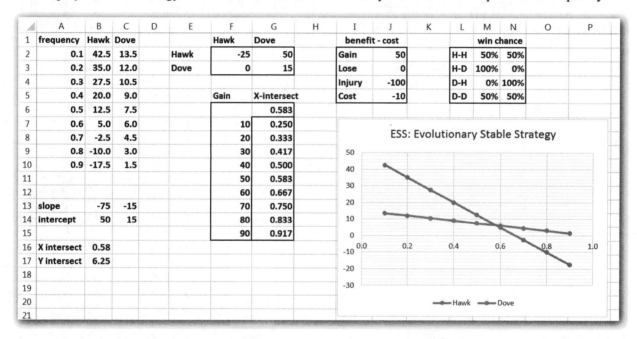

Every ESS is a so-called Nash equilibrium, called after the game theorist, mathematician, and Nobel Laureate John Nash whose life story was turned into the biopic *A Beautiful Mind* starring Russell Crowe.

What you need to know

We need at least two sets of assumptions. One set is regarding benefits and costs in a fight (I2:J5). Another set (M2:N5) determines the chances of winning for hawks (H) and doves (D).

We also need the functions SLOPE and INTERCEPT. In a linear regression equation, Y= slope * X + intercept. For hawks (in column B): = slope1*X + interc1. For doves (in column C): = slope2*X + interc2.

Besides, we need to know where X and Y intersect. The intersect on the X-axis: = (interc2 - interc1)/(slope1-slope2); on the Y-axis: = slope1 * intersectX + interc1.

We also use a Data Table (F6:G15) to see which effect any changes in the "Gain" factor would have, but you could do this also for any of the other factors, of course.

What you need to do

1. Place in cell F2: =($M$2*$J$2)+(($N$2*$J$4)).

2. Place in cell F3: =$M$4*$J$2+$N$4*$J$3.

3. Place in cell G2: =$M$3*$J$2-0.

4. Place in cell G3: =$M$5*($J$2+$J$5)-$N$5*-$J$5.

5. Place in cell B2: =A2*$F$2+(1-A2)*$G$2, and copy down.

6. Place in cell C2: =A2*$F$3+(1-A2)*$G$3, and copy down.

7. Place in cell B13: =SLOPE(B2:B10,$A$2:$A$10), and copy one cell to the right. I named these cells *slope1* and *slope2*.

8. Place in cell B14: =INTERCEPT(B2:B10,$A$2:$A$10), and copy to next cell. They are named *inter1* and *inter2*.

9. Place in cell B16: =(inter2-inter1)/(slope1-slope2).

10. Place in cell B17: =slope1*B16+inter1.

11. For the Data Table, place in G6: =B16.

12. Select range F6:G15, implement a Data Table with only a column input from cell J2 (the gain factor).

13. Check the effect of changing any given factor.

86. Flock Behavior

What the simulation does

Open file 86-FlockBehavior.xlsx. Flocking behavior is the behavior exhibited when a group of birds, called a flock, are foraging or in flight. There are clear parallels with the shoaling behavior of fish, the swarming behavior of insects, and herd behavior of land animals. It is considered the emergence of collective behavior arising from simple rules that are followed by individuals and does not involve any central coordination

Scientists have demonstrated a similar behavior in humans. In their studies, people exhibited the behavioral pattern of a "flock": If a certain percentage of the flock changes direction, the others would follow suit. When one person was designated as a predator and everyone else was supposed to avoid him or her, the human flock behaved very much like a school of fish.

	chance	direction	count	majority	preference
	0%	↖	23	-	
	25%	↗	25	-	
	50%	↘	32	-	
	75%	↙	24	-	

(Range B2:K11 contains a 10×10 grid of randomly-oriented directional arrows.)

What you need to know

We assume that all animals (100) start randomly in one of four different directions (M2:N5). Once animals with a certain direction happen to gain the majority (say, 35%), all the other animals follow suit.

What you need to do

1. Make sure iteration is ON and set for only 1 iteration.

2. Place in cell O2: =COUNTIF($B$2:$K$11,N2). Copy down.

3. Place in cell P2: =IF(O2>=35,"+","-"). Copy downwards.

4. Place in cell Q2: =IF(P2="+",OFFSET(P2,,-2),""). Copy.

5. The formula for range B2:K11 is a very long-winding one, so I split it in pieces to understand better what it really does:
   =IF(COUNTIF($O$2:$O$5,100),
   VLOOKUP(RAND(),$M$2:$N$5,2),
   IF(COUNTIF($B$2:$K$11,$N$2)>=35,$N$2,
   IF(COUNTIF($B$2:$K$11,$N$3)>=35,$N$3,
   IF(COUNTIF($B$2:$K$11,$N$4)>=35,$N$4,
   IF(COUNTIF($B$2:$K$11,$N$5)>=35,$N$5,
   VLOOKUP(RAND(),$M$2:$N$5,2))))))

6. Because iterations have to be limited to one, the system sometimes lags one step behind when pressing F9.

| B2 | | ▼ | : | ✕ | ✓ | f_x | =IF(COUNTIF($O$2:$O$5,100),VLOOKUP(RAND(),$M$2:$N$5,2),IF(COUNTIF($B$2:$K$11,$N$2)>=35,$N$2,IF(COUNTIF($B$2:$K$11,$N$3)>=35,$N$3,IF(COUNTIF($B$2:$K$11,$N$4)>=35,$N$$ |
| | | | | | | | $N$5)>=35,$N$5,VLOOKUP(RAND(),$M$2:$N$5,2)))))) |

	A	B	C	D	E	F	G	H	I	J	K	L	M	N	O	P	Q
1													chance	direction	count	majority	preference
2		↖	↖	↖	↖	↖	↖	↖	↖	↖	↖		0%	↖	73	+	↖
3		↖	↖	↖	↖	↖	↖	↖	↖	↖	↖		25%	↗	3	-	
4		↖	↖	↖	↖	↖	↖	↖	↖	↖	↖		50%	↘	6	-	
5		↖	↖	↖	↖	↖	↖	↖	↖	↖	↖		75%	↙	2	-	
6		↖	↖	↖	↖	↖	↖	↖	↖	↖	↖						
7		↖	↖	↖	↖	↖	↖	↖	↖	↖	↖						
8		↖	↖	↖	↖	↖	↖	↖	↖	↖	↖						
9		↖	↖	↖	↖	↖	↖	↖	↖	↖	↖						
10		↖	↖	↖	↖	↖	↖	↖	↖	↖	↖						
11		↖	↖	↖	↖	↖	↖	↖	↖	↖	↖						
12																	

87. Simulation of Sick Cases

What the simulation does

Open file 87-SickCases.xlsx. If a certain percentage of people is sick in the population (column A), we can find out with a 95% confidence how many in a sample of 100 persons will be sick, as a minimum (column B) or as a maximum (column C).

We can vary the sample size as well as the confidence level by manually typing values in cells B1 and B2, or by using the corresponding scrollbar controls.

We can also calculate what the probability is of finding up to a certain number of sick cases (G1), given a certain sample size (B1). Again, the number of sick cases is a variable that can be changed in this what-if analysis.

	A	B	C	D	E	F	G	H	I	J
1	Sample Size	100	◄ ⃞		►	Sick Cases	23	◄ ⃞		►
2	Confidence	95%	◄		⃞ ►					
3										
4	sick in popul.	Min sick of 100	Max sick of 100			sick in popul.	Prob. of finding up to 23 cases			
5	5%	2	9			5%	0.00%			
6	10%	5	15			10%	0.00%			
7	15%	9	21			15%	1.19%			
8	20%	14	27			20%	18.91%			
9	25%	18	32			25%	62.89%			
10	30%	23	38			30%	92.45%			
11	35%	27	43			35%	99.34%			
12	40%	32	48			40%	99.97%			
13	45%	37	53			45%	100.00%			
14	50%	42	58			50%	100.00%			
15	55%	47	63			55%	100.00%			
16										

What you need to know

One of the functions we need in column G is NORMDIST (or NORM.DIST). It returns a binomial distribution probability for problems with a fixed number of tests or trials, when the outcomes of any trial are either success or failure, when trials are independent, and when the probability of success is constant throughout the experiment.

The other crucial function is NORM.INV (which replaces CRITBINOM in earlier versions, as we discussed in Simulations 19 and 20). It has 3 arguments: the number of trials, the probability of a success on each trial, and the criterion value (alpha).

What you need to do

1. Place in cell B5: =BINOM.INV($B$1,$A5,1-$B$2), and copy downwards. You may need CRITBINOM instead.

2. Place in cell C5: =BINOM.INV($B$1,$A5,$B$2), and copy downwards. You may need CRITBINOM instead.

3. Place in cell G5 the following formula: =IFERROR(1-BINOMDIST(G$1,$B$1,$F5,TRUE),""""), and copy the formula downwards.

4. If you want, add three scrollbars controls (see Appendix 5 for more details).

5. Place a scroll-bar control next to cell B1. Set Min to 20, Max to 1000, and LinkedCell to cell B1.

6. Place a scroll-bar control next to cell B2. Set Min to 50, Max to 99, and LinkedCell to cell H1 (or any other cell hidden behind a control). And put in cell B2: =H1/100.

7. Place a scroll-bar control next to cell G1. Set Min to 0, Max to 1000, and LinkedCell to cell G1.

8. In cells B4, C4, and G4, you could place something like this: =”Min sick of “ & $B$1.

	A	B	C	D	E	F	G	H	I	J
1	Sample Size	200				Sick Cases	50			
2	Confidence	95%								
3										
4	sick in popul.	Min sick of 200	Max sick of 200			sick in popul.	Prob. of finding up to 50 cases			
5	5%	5	15			5%	0.00%			
6	10%	13	27			10%	0.00%			
7	15%	22	38			15%	0.01%			
8	20%	31	49			20%	3.45%			
9	25%	40	60			25%	46.21%			
10	30%	49	71			30%	93.05%			
11	35%	59	81			35%	99.85%			
12	40%	69	91			40%	100.00%			
13	45%	78	102			45%	100.00%			
14	50%	88	112			50%	100.00%			
15	55%	98	122			55%	100.00%			
16										

88. Ehrenfest's Urn Simulation

What the simulation does

Consider two urns A and B. Urn A contains N marbles and urn B contains none. The marbles are labelled 1,2,...N. In each step of the algorithm, a number between 1 and N is chosen randomly, with all values having equal probability. The marble corresponding to that value is moved to the opposite urn. Hence the first step of the algorithm will always involve moving a marble from A to B.

What will the two urns look like after k steps? If k is sufficiently large, we may expect the urns to have equal populations, as the probabilities of drawing a marble from A or from B become increasingly similar. States in which one urn has many more marbles than the other may be said to be unstable, as there is an overwhelming tendency to move marbles to the urn that contains fewer.

Ehrenfest sometimes used the image of two dogs; the one with fleas gradually infects the other one. In the long-time run, the mean number of fleas on both dogs converges to the equilibrium value.

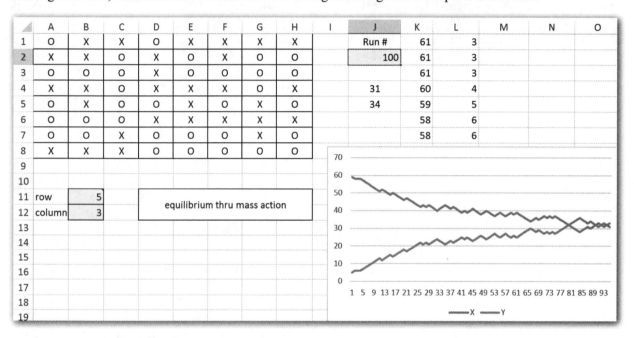

What you need to know

Instead of using two urns, we use a "board" that has X's at all positions. Each time, at a random row and column position (cells B11 and B12), an X is replaced by an O, or vice-versa. Gradually, we reach an equilibrium where the number of X's and O's have become very similar, with some oscillations of course.

All of this can be done with simple, but long formulas based on the functions IF, RAND or RANDBETWEEN, ROW, COLUMN, and COUNTIF.

What you need to do

1. First you need to turn iteration ON, with only 1 iteration.

2. Place in cell B11 and B12: =RANDBETWEEN(1,8). If you don't have RANDBETWEEN, use =INT(RAND()*8+1).

3. Place in range A1:H8 a formula that populates each cell: =IF(AND(ROW(A1)=$B$11,-COLUMN(A1)=$B$12),IF(A1="X","O","X"),IF(A1=0,"X",A1)). Be aware: O is not 0.

4. Place in cell J2: =J2+1. This counts the number of runs.

5. Place in cell J4: =COUNTIF($A$1:$H$8,"X"). Counts X's.

6. Place in cell J5: =COUNTIF($A$1:$H$8,"O"). Counts O's.

7. Place in cell K1, and as far down as you want: =IF(ROW(A1)=$J$2,COUNTIF($A$1:$H$8,"X"),K1).

8. Place in cell L1, and as far down as in column K: =IF(ROW(B1)=$J$2,COUN-TIF($A$1:$H$8,"O"),L1).

9. The chart is based on columns K and L.

10. To reset the ranges A1:H8, J2, columns K and L: Select that range, click in the formula bar, and hit Ctr + Enter.

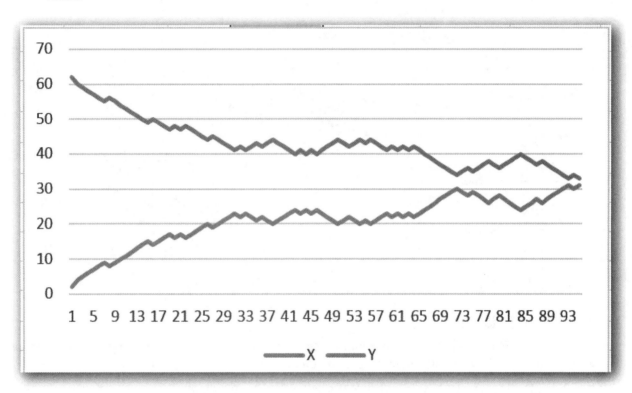

89. Two Monte Carlo Integrations

What the simulation does

Open file 89-MonteCarloIntegration.xlsx. If you don't feel comfortable with integration equations, you may want to consider Monte Carlo simulations to calculate the area under a curve. We did a case in Simulation 61, but by using an integration formula.

This time, we discuss only two equations as an example: Y=X (on the 1st sheet) and Y=X^2 (on the 2nd sheet), and without using any integration formula. That will probably help you to tackle similar situations. The range we want to cover for X and Y is set in the cells B4:C5.

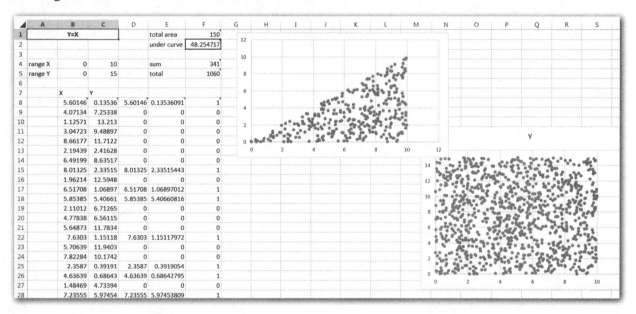

What you need to know

First we generate random X-values in column B between B4 and C4, plus random Y-values in column C between B5 and C5. They are plotted in the bottom graph.

In column D, we place the X-value when Y is smaller than X. In column E, we place the corresponding Y-value when there is an X-value in the previous column. Both columns are plotted in the top graph. In column F, we assign 1's when the two previous columns have X- and Y-values in it, so we can calculate the area under the curve with the cells F2, F6, and F7.

What you need to do

1. Place in cell B8: =$B$4+($C$4-$B$4)*RAND(). Copy downwards to cell B1067 or so.

2. Place in cell C8: =$B$4+($C$4-$B$4)*RAND(). Copy down.

3. Place in cell D8: =IF(C8<B8,B8,0). Copy downwards.

4. Place in cell E8: =IF(D8=0,0,C8). Copy downwards.

5. Place in cell F8: =IF(E8=0,0,1). Copy downwards.

6. Sum in cell F4 all 1's in column F below: =SUM(F8:F1067).

7. Count in F5 the number of values: =COUNT(F8:F1067).

8. Calculate in cell F1 the total area: =(C4-B4)*(C5-B5).

9. Determine what is under the curve in F2: =(C4-B4)*(C5-B5).

10. Switch to the 2nd sheet for equation Y=X^2. Everything is the same as on the 1st sheet except for the marked cells (below).

11. Cell B5: =B4^2. Cell C5: =C4^2.

12. Place in cell D8: =IF(C8<B8^2,B8,0), and copy downwards.

13. Cell G3 has the integration formula so we can compare with the simulation result in cell G2: =(C4^3/3)-(B4^3/3).

14. To improve the Monte Carlo results, we use a Data Table.

15. The start cell of the Data Table in J20 has: =G5

16. Select range I20:J29, implement a Data Table with only column input of any empty cell outside the range.

17. Cell J31 has the mean of all 10 runs.

18. Cell J16 uses the result of 10 runs: =G1*J31/G6.

19. Very often the Data Table gives better results (see below). But not always, of course, as results may vary!

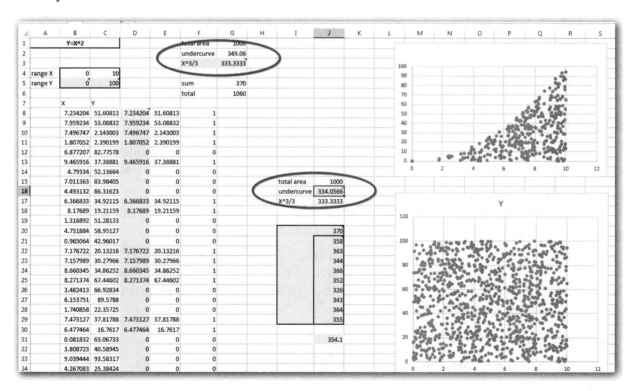

90. Randomness in Gene Pools

What the simulation does

Open file 90-RandomSelection.xlsx. This file uses the gene pool model to simulate how randomness can change in the gene pool generation after generation. Without randomness, the gene pool would keep the same composition every next generation.

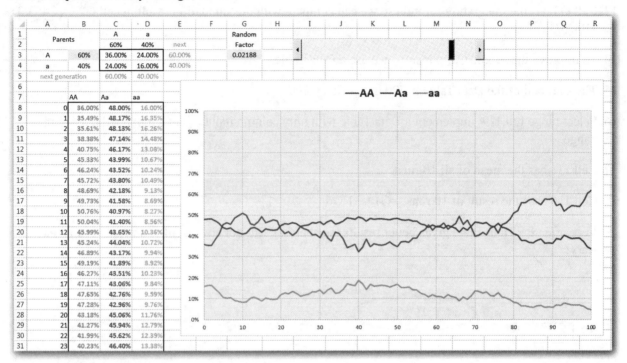

What you need to know

We assume the gene pool consists only of one gene with two alleles (*A* and *a*). Given a certain percentage (*p*) of allele *A* (in cell B3), we can calculate the percentage of each genotype in the start-up population (in cells A3:D4).

The frequency of the homozygotes *AA* would be p^2, q^2 for the homozygotes *aa*, and *2pq* for the heterozygotes *Aa*. These frequencies would remain stable without randomness.

Then we simulate what happens after each generation, up to 100 generations, given the impact of a specific random factor (in cell G3, regulated by a scrollbar control; see Appendix 5). When this randomize factor is very low, there is hardly any randomness involved, so the three curves are practically flat, but higher factors would cause more or less "genetic drift."

What you need to do

1. Whereas cell B3 is manually regulated, cell B4 can be calculated from this: =1-B3.

2. The cells C3:D4 have this formula in them: =$B3*C$2.

3. The cells bordering this matrix use SUM functions to show that the frequencies remain stable if there is no randomness or any other interfering factors (the Hardy-Weinberg law; see Simulation 24).

4. Cell B8: =C3. Cell C8: =C4+D3. Cell D8: =D4.

5. Cell B9: =NORMINV(RAND(),B8,$G$3). Copy to B108.

6. Cell C9: =IFERROR(2*SQRT(B9)*(1-SQRT(B9)),NA()).

7. Cell D9: =IFERROR((1-SQRT(B9))^2,NA()). Copy down.

8. Place a scrollbar next to cell G4. Set its properties: Max to 25000, Min to 10, LinkedCell to I3 (or another cell).

9. Place in cell G3: =I3/1000000.

10. Work with the scrollbar and/or manually change cell B3 to see the effect of random changes. For extremely low random impact, the curves are practically flat (see below).

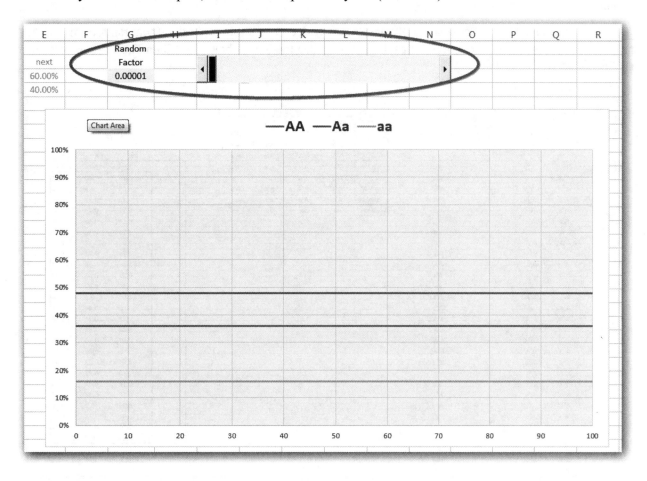

91. Random Mating

What the simulation does

Open file 91-OffspringSimulation.xlsx. In this file we simulate what happens when different genotypes (cells C2:C5) randomly mate (columns B and C). On the 1st sheet, they produce an offspring of 1 individual (column F), and on the 2nd sheet an offspring of 1 to 4 individuals (columns F:I) with an average of 2 individuals (columns K and L).

Then we repeat this process some 20 more times with a Data Table, to find out that random mating has hardly any impact on the frequencies of each genotype (see the means below the Data Table). This is known as the Hardy-Weinberg law.

	A	B	C	D	E	F	G	H	I	J	K	L	M	N	O	P	Q	R
1		cumul.	type	%				parents		offspring								
2		0%	aa	10%				A'A'A'A'	A'A'	A'A'	A'A'	A'A'						
3		10%	A'a	43%				A'A'A'a	A'A'	A'A'	A'a	A'a						
4		53%	A'A'	47%				A'A'aa	A'a	A'a	A'a	A'a						
5								A'aA'A'	A'A'	A'A'	A'a	A'a			aa	A'a	A'A'	
6			A'A'	A'a		A'a		A'aA'a	A'A'	A'a	A'a	aa			12%	44%	44%	
7			A'A'	A'a		A'a		A'aaa	A'a	A'a	aa	aa			0.16	0.44	0.4	
8			A'A'	A'a		A'A'		aaA'A'	A'a	A'a	A'a	A'a			0.04	0.6	0.36	
9			A'a	A'A'		A'A'		aaA'a	A'a	A'a	aa	aa			0.12	0.24	0.64	
10			A'a	A'a		A'A'		aaaa	aa	aa	aa	aa			0.12	0.32	0.56	
11			A'a	A'a		A'a									0.16	0.36	0.48	
12			A'A'	A'A'		A'A'									0.16	0.32	0.52	
13			A'A'	A'A'		A'A'									0.04	0.32	0.64	
14			aa	aa		aa									0.12	0.52	0.36	
15			A'a	A'A'		A'A'									0.16	0.36	0.48	
16			A'A'	A'a		A'a									0.12	0.56	0.32	
17			A'a	A'a		aa									0.16	0.32	0.52	
18			A'a	A'A'		A'a									0.04	0.6	0.36	
19			A'a	aa		A'a									0	0.44	0.56	
20			A'a	A'a		A'A'									0.2	0.24	0.56	
21			A'a	A'a		A'A'									0.08	0.44	0.48	
22			A'a	A'a		A'A'									0.12	0.36	0.52	
23			A'A'	A'A'		A'A'									0	0.44	0.56	
24			A'a	A'A'		A'a									0.04	0.52	0.44	
25			A'A'	A'A'		A'A'									0	0.36	0.64	
26			A'A'	A'a		A'a									0.16	0.44	0.4	
27			A'A'	A'a		A'a									0.16	0.32	0.52	
28			A'A'	aa		A'a									0.04	0.2	0.76	
29			A'a	A'a		aa									0.04	0.28	0.68	
30			A'a	A'A'		A'a									0.04	0.44	0.52	
31															0.08	0.4	0.52	
32		aa	4%	12%		12%												
33		A'a	48%	52%		44%									10%	40%	51%	
34		A'A'	48%	36%		44%												

What you need to know

Mendel's laws determine what the offspring is of two specific genotypes (H1:L10).

All the gray cells on the sheet have formulas in it. One of the functions we need is VLOOKUP, which can only search for exact values or for previous values in an ascending order. So we need to start cell B2 at 0 (instead of at 10%).

You also should know that formulas cannot distinguish between lower and uppercase, so instead of using the notation *A* and *a*, I decided to use *A'* and *a*.

We assume both alleles have the same fitness. If that is not the case, we would have to deal with Simulation 92.

	A	B	C	D	E	F	G	H	I	J	K	L	M	N	O	P	Q	R	S	T
1		cumul.	type	%										parents	offspring					
2		0%	aa	10%										A'A'A'A'	A'A'	A'A'	A'A'	A'A'		
3		10%	A'a	43%										A'A'A'a	A'A'	A'A'	A'a	A'a		
4		53%	A'A'	47%										A'A'aa	A'a	A'a	A'a	A'a		
5														A'aA'A'	A'A'	A'A'	A'a	A'a		
6		A'A'	A'A'						A'A'		1			A'aA'a	A'A'	A'a	A'a	aa		
7		A'a	A'a			A'a	A'A'				2			A'aaa	A'a	A'a	aa	aa		
8		aa	A'a			A'a	A'a	A'a	aa		4			aaA'A'	A'a	A'a	A'a	A'a		
9		A'A'	A'A'			A'A'					1			aaA'a	A'a	A'a	aa	aa		
10		A'A'	A'a			A'a			A'A'		2			aaaa	aa	aa	aa	aa		
11		A'A'	A'a			A'a					1									
12		A'a	A'a			aa	A'a	A'a			3						aa	A'a	A'A'	
13		A'A'	A'a			A'a					1						16%	43%	40%	
14		A'a	A'a			A'a		aa	aa		3						10%	37%	53%	
15		A'a	A'A'			A'a			A'A'		2						7%	32%	61%	
16		A'a	A'a			A'A'					1						5%	70%	25%	
17		A'a	A'a			A'a	A'a	A'A'			3						20%	43%	36%	
18		aa	aa			aa		aa			2	2.08					17%	51%	32%	
19		A'a	A'A'			A'a	A'A'	A'a			3						10%	46%	44%	
20		A'a	A'a			A'a	A'a		A'A'		3						9%	45%	46%	
21		A'A'	A'a			A'a			A'a		2						13%	41%	47%	
22		A'A'	A'A'			A'A'	A'A'				2						9%	52%	39%	
23		A'a	A'A'				A'a	A'A'	A'a		3						7%	44%	48%	
24		aa	A'A'			A'a	A'a				2						13%	54%	33%	
25		A'A'	A'A'			A'A'	A'A'	A'A'			3						7%	46%	46%	
26		A'A'	A'A'				A'A'		A'A'		2						8%	66%	26%	
27		A'a	aa			A'a	A'a				2						13%	45%	42%	
28		A'a	A'a			aa	A'A'				2						4%	47%	49%	
29		A'a	A'a			A'a					1						4%	43%	53%	
30		aa	A'a			aa					1						12%	53%	35%	
31																	6%	44%	50%	
32	aa	16%	8%			18%	0%	25%	22%				16%				21%	40%	39%	
33	A'a	48%	52%			59%	54%	38%	22%				43%	100%			0%	39%	61%	
34	A'A'	36%	40%			23%	46%	38%	56%				40%				10%	47%	43%	

What you need to do

1. Place on sheet1 in cell D3: =2*SQRT(D2)*SQRT(D4).

2. Place in cell D4: =(1-SQRT(D2))^2.

3. Place in cell B3: =SUM($D$2:D2), and copy one cell down.

4. Place in B6:C30: =VLOOKUP(RAND(),$B$2:$C$4,2,1).

5. Place in the range F6:F30 the following formula: =VLOOKUP(B6&C6,$H$2:$L$10,RANDBE-TWEEN(2,5),FALSE). This finds the offspring of two specific parents and randomly chooses one of the four possible genotypes.

6. Place in the cells B32:C34 and F32:F34 the same: =COUNTIF(B$6:B$30,$A32)/COUN-TA($B$6:$B$30).

7. Link O6 to F32, P6 to F33, and Q6 to F34.

8. Select range N6:Q31, start a Data Table with only column input set to any empty cell outside the range.

9. In O33: =AVERAGE(O6:O31), and copy 2 cells to the right.

10. The only differences on the 2nd sheet are in columns F:L.

11. In the range F6:I30 is the following formula: =IF(RANDBETWEEN(0,6)>COLUMN(A1),VLOOK-UP($B6&$C6,$N$2:$R$10,RANDBETWEEN(2,5),FALSE),"").

12. In K6:K30: =4-COUNTBLANK(F6:I6).

13. Place in cell L18: =AVERAGE(K6:K30).

14. Notice how the frequencies after 1 generation remain stable.

92. Differences in Fitness

What the simulation does

Open file 92-GenePoolChanges.xlsx. This simulation is similar to the previous simulation, but this time we also assign relative fitness factors—for instance, genotype AS (cell U4: 1) is more "fit" than genotype SS (cell U2: 0.4). So gradually, up to a certain point, the frequency of AS will increase, while the frequency of genotype SS (sickle cell anemia, for instance) will decrease in later generations.

	A	B	C	D	E	F	G	H	I	J	K	L	M	N	O	P	Q	R	S	T	U	V	W	X	Y	Z	AA	AB
1		cumul.	type	%										parents							fit		parents					
2		0%	SS	10%										AAAA	AA	AA	AA	AA		SS	0.4		AAAA	AA		AA		
3		10%	AA	47%										AAAS	AA	AA	AS	AS		AA	0.7		AAAS	AA	AS	AS		
4		57%	AS	43%										AASS	AS	AS	AS	AS		AS	1		AASS	AS	AS	AS	AS	
5				100%										ASAA	AA	AA	AS	AS					ASAA	AA	AA	AS	AS	
6														ASAS	AA	AS	AS	SS					ASAS		AS	AS		
7	SS	16%	8%			4%	0%	6%	10%		5%			ASSS	AS	AS	SS	SS					ASSS	AS	AS	SS		
8	AA	46%	58%			33%	32%	28%	20%		28%	100%		SSAA	AS	AS	AS	AS					SSAA	AS	AS	AS	AS	
9	AS	38%	34%			63%	68%	67%	70%		67%			SSAS	AS	AS	SS	SS					SSAS	AS	AS		SS	
10														SSSS	SS	SS	SS	SS					SSSS	SS				
11		AA	AA			AA																						
12		AS	AS					AS								5%	28%	67%										
13		AA	AS					AS								3%	37%	60%										
14		SS	AA			AS			AS							7%	24%	69%										
15		AA	AA				AA									2%	44%	55%										
16		AS	AS			AS	AS									5%	31%	63%										
17		AA	AA			AA										10%	41%	49%										
18		AS	SS													8%	43%	49%										
19		AA	AS					AS								12%	23%	64%										
20		AS	AS			AS		AS	AS							13%	32%	56%										
21		AA	AS			AS	AS		AS							5%	41%	54%										
22		SS	SS													1%	34%	65%										
23		AS	AA			AS										5%	42%	53%										
24		AS	AA			AA	AS		AS							7%	40%	53%										
25		AA	AA													1%	47%	51%										
26		AA	AA					AA	AA							0%	42%	58%										
27		AS	AA				AS	AA	AS							3%	34%	63%										
28		AS	AA			AS	AS	AS								6%	25%	69%										
29		AA	AA													5%	45%	50%										
30		AA	AA													7%	37%	56%										
31		AA	SS			AS		AS	AS							0%	48%	52%										
32		AS	AA			AA										8%	41%	51%										
33		AA	AA																									
34		SS	AA			AS	AS	AS						average		5%	37%	57%										

What you need to know

All the gray cells on the sheet have formulas in it. We assume that parents have up to 4 children each generation (columns F:I). Most formulas are identical to the ones used in Simulation 91.

The main difference is that the range X2:AA10 is based on the different fitness factors for each genotype. The offspring is not only determined by Mendel's laws but also by the fitness of that specific genotype. That's why certain cells remain empty.

This will obviously affect frequencies in the next generation. Key is the range O34:Q34, which shows the average frequencies based on 50 couples with up to 4 children after 20 runs. We will also see the effect after two more generations on the 2nd and 3rd sheet.

What you need to do

1. Offspring varies, so place in range X2:AA10: =IF(RAND()<VLOOKUP(O2,$T$2:$U$4,2,0),O2,"").

2. Place in the entire range F11:I60 this formula: =IF(RANDBETWEEN(0,6)>COLUMN(A1),VLOOKUP($B11&$C11,$W$2:$AA$10,RANDBETWEEN(2,5),FALSE),"").

3. All the other formulas are the same as the ones used in Simulation 91.

4. On the 2nd sheet, for the second generation, we changed range D2:D4 by replacing it with links to the frequencies after 1 generation on the 1st sheet in range O34:Q34.

5. On the 3rd sheet, for the third generation (see below), we changed range D2:D4 again, but now by replacing it with links to the frequencies after 2 generations in range O34:Q34 on the 2nd sheet.

6. You will probably find that the SS frequency has declined—in this particular case, from 10% to 3%, and then back to 4%.

	A	B	C	D	E	F	G	H	I	J	K	L	M	N	O	P	Q	R	S	T	U	V	W	X	Y	Z	AA	AB
1		cumul.	type	%						original				parents							fit			parents				
2		0%	SS	3%						10%				AAAA	AA	AA	AA	AA		SS	0.4		AAAA	AA		AA	AA
3		3%	AA	44%						47%				AAAS	AA	AA	AS	AS		AA	0.7		AAAS	AA	AA	AS	AS
4		47%	AS	53%						43%				AASS	AS	AS	AS	AS		AS	1		AASS	AS	AS	AS	AS
5				100%										ASAA	AA	AA	AS	AS					ASAA	AA	AA	AS	AS
6														ASAS	AA	AS	AS	SS					ASAS	AA	AS	AS	
7	SS	0%	6%			0%	0%	0%	0%		0%			ASSS	AS	AS	SS	SS					ASSS	AS	AS		
8	AA	40%	46%			52%	61%	45%	67%		56%	100%		SSAA	AS	AS	AS	AS					SSAA	AS	AS	AS	AS
9	AS	60%	48%			48%	39%	55%	33%		44%			SSAS	AS	AS	SS	SS					SSAS	AS	AS		
10														SSSS	SS	SS	SS	SS					SSSS			SS	
11		AS	AA			AS	AS	AA																				
12		AS	AS													0%	56%	44%										
13		AS	AS						AS							0%	45%	55%										
14		AA	AS				AA		AS							9%	47%	44%										
15		AS	AS					AA								0%	43%	57%										
16		AS	AA			AS	AA	AS								5%	11%	84%										
17		AS	AS					AS								2%	52%	46%										
18		AA	AA						AA							8%	41%	51%										
19		AA	AS			AS	AA	AA								10%	36%	54%										
20		AS	AA				AA	AA								4%	47%	49%										
21		AS	AA			AA	AA	AS								0%	34%	66%										
22		AS	AS			AS	AS	AS	AA							9%	51%	39%										
23		AS	AA													9%	44%	47%										
24		AA	AA			AA										6%	53%	42%										
25		AS	AA			AS	AA		AA							1%	52%	47%										
26		AS	AS			AS	AS	AA								3%	51%	46%										
27		AS	AS			AA										1%	32%	67%										
28		AS	AS					AS	AA							0%	42%	58%										
29		AS	AS				AS	AS								1%	51%	48%										
30		AS	AA					AA								0%	44%	56%										
31		AA	AS				AA	AA	AA							0%	41%	59%										
32		AS	AA			AA	AA									13%	28%	58%										
33		AS	AA			AA																						
34		AA	AA			AA	AA							average		4%	43%	53%										

◄ ► Offspring Offspring (2) **Offspring (3)** ⊕

93. Loan Simulation

What the simulation does

Open file 93-LoanSimulation.xlsx. This is basically a simple simulation. We enter estimates for loan amount, term of the loan, and annual percentage rate—either manually of through scroll-bar controls. If you decide on controls, you can no longer enter values manually. Then we calculate the monthly payments, the total of payments, and the total of interest.

With the help of 4 Data Tables, we can find out what the effect is of changes in monthly payment and/or any of the manually chosen or entered data. Since there are not too many iterations in each Data Table, the use of these tables is right.

We can use Conditional Formatting to highlight all the rows in each table that are below the monthly payment shown in cell B9.

	A	B
1	Loan Amount	$ 100,000
2	◄ ☐ ►	
3	Term (years)	25
4	◄ ☐ ►	
5	APR	4.56%
6	◄ ☐ ►	
7		
8		
9	Monthly Payment	$ 559.24
10	Total Paid	$ 167,773.07
11	Total Interest	$ 67,773.07
12		

What you need to know

We need the Excel function PMT. Its syntax is: PMT(rate, nper, pv, [fv], [type]). It calculates the payment for a loan (*pv* or present value) based on constant monthly payments and a constant interest rate (*rate* per month) for a certain period of time (*nper* in months). The last two arguments we can ignore here. PMT returns a negative value (a value that is owed), unless you enter the present value as a negative amount.

Since there is not much "uncertainty" involved—all variables are fixed—don't expect any volatility here.

What you need to do

1. If you want so, implement 3 scroll-bar controls (see Appendix 5 for more details).

2. Set the 1st control: Linkedcell A2; Min 600; Max 2200; SmallChange 50; LargeChange 100. In B2: =A2*100.

3. Set the 2nd control: Linkedcell B3; Min 5; Max 30; SmallChange 5; LargeChange 10.

4. Set the 3rd control: Linkedcell A6; Min 200; Max 1000; SmallChange 25; LargeChange 50. In B5: =A6/10000.

5. Place in cell B9: =IFERROR(PMT(B5/12, B3*12,-B1),0).

6. Place in cell B10: =IFERROR(B9*B3*12,0).

7. Place in cell B11: =IFERROR(B10-B1,0).

8. In the 2nd row of each table (under the headers), place links to the corresponding cells in column B.

9. Select in each table the 2nd row through the last row and start a Data Table with only column input: from B5, B9, B1, and B3 in the last table.

10. The Conditional Formatting formulas are: =$E3<$B$9, =$I3<$B$9, =$N3<$B$9, and =$S3<$B$9 respectively.

11. If you use scroll-bar controls, you may want to lock all cells.

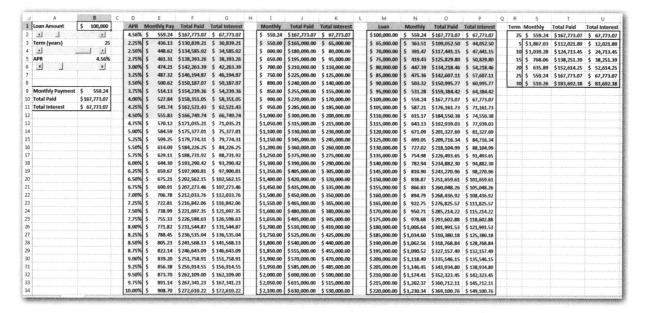

94. Stock Volatility

What the simulation does

Open file 94-StockVolatility.xlsx. There is much uncertainty on the stock market. Monte Carlo simulations are a great tool to get a bit more certainty in the midst of many uncertainties.

We run in column B the changes in stock value for 250 trading days. To harness our uncertainty a little better, we run these values 10 times more, so we can calculate the average outcome for a sequence of 20-day periods. The end results are shown in row 32. The chart only shows the first run, based on column B.

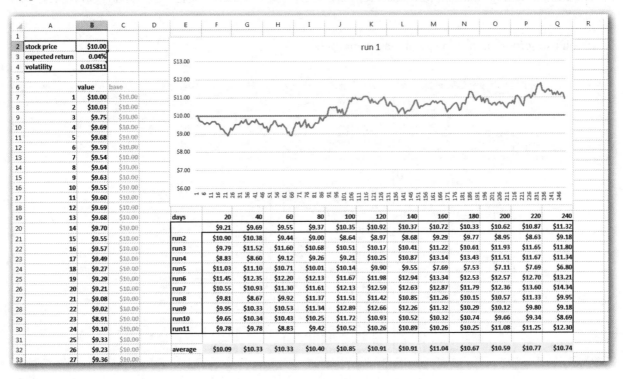

What you need to know

The information needed is in the left top corner. The expected return in cell B3 is based on history: an expected return of 10% divided by 250 trading days. The volatility in cell B4 is also based on past performance: an annualized volatility of 25% divided by the square root of trading days per year.

In general, you should always run at least 1,000 iterations of Monte Carlo models. This is to ensure that you have a statistical chance of getting sufficient outliers (extreme values) to make the variance analysis meaningful. I do not always follow that rule in this book since Data Tables do come with overhead costs.

What you need to do

1. Place in cell B3: =10%/250 (or replace 10% with a reference to a cell where you can enter that percentage).

2. Place in cell B4: =25%/SQRT(250) (or reference 25%).

3. Place in cell B7 a link to cell B2.

4. Place in the range B8:B256 the following formula: =B7+B7*($B$3+$B$4*NORMINV(RAND(),0,1)).

5. Column C has in every row the stock price from B2, so it can create a "base line" in the chart.

6. In range F20:Q20 we find values after each 20 days: =VLOOKUP(F19,$A$7:$B$256,2,FALSE).

7. Select range E20:Q30 for a Data Table with only column input from any empty cell outside the range.

8. Row 20 calculates the averages after each 20-day period.

9. On the sheet below, we plotted the averages for 10 runs.

10. Since there is still an enormous uncertainty in these "predictions," you may want to go for many, many more runs to capture some rare extreme values. But as to be expected, results keep varying!

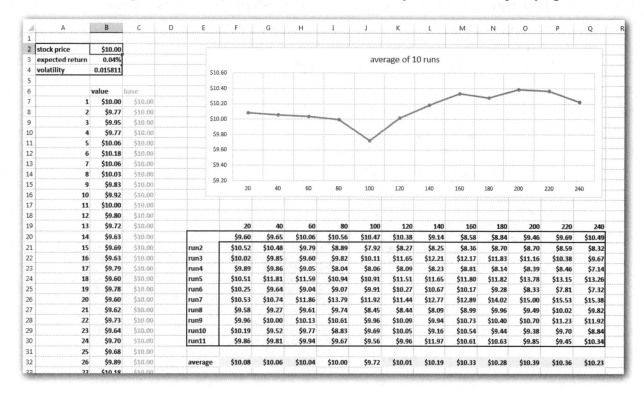

95. S&P 500 Performance

What the simulation does

Open file 95-SP500Performance.xlsx. Based on data from 1950 to 2012, we have an average daily return value (in cell B2) and a daily standard deviation value (in cell B3) for S&P500 performance. This information we use to calculate what the percentage would be at the end of a week (in cell F6).

Then we repeat this volatile calculation some 10,000 times with a Data Table. The graph shows quite some volatility, but because we have a reasonable size sample now, we can find a more reliable average (in cell C8) and SD (in cell C9). That may give is some more certainty in the midst of uncertainties.

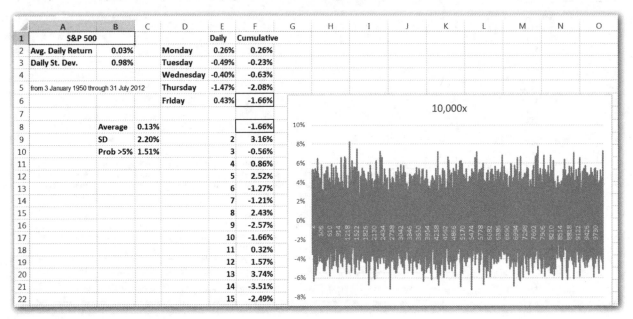

What you need to know

In range E2:E6, we calculate a normally distributed daily performance with the function NORMINV. In cell F6, we calculate the cumulative end-of-week result: (daily % +1) * (previous cumulative % + 1) – 1. In cell C10, we count how often the end-week percentage was greater than 5% in this run of 10,000 cases.

What you need to do

1. Place in range E2:E6: =NORMINV(RAND(),$B$2,$B$3).

2. Place in cell F2: =E2.

3. Place in cell F3: =(E3+1)*(F2+1)-1, and copy to F6.

4. Cell F8 is linked to F6.

5. Cell E9 has either the number 2 in it or a formula: =ROW(A2) which you can then copy down to E10009 or so.

6. Select range E8:F10009 for a Data Table with only column input to any empty cell outside the range.

7. Place in cell C8: =AVERAGE(F8:F10009).

8. Place in cell C9: =STDEV(F8:F10009), or use STDEV.S.

9. Place in cell C10: =COUNTIF(F8:F10009,">0.05")/10000. Do not forget the double quotes for criteria if you type.

10. Recalculations of 10,000 runs may take some time depending on your machine's speed.

11. As always, results may (or should) vary, but less and less so!

	A	B	C	D	E	F
1	S&P 500				Daily	Cumulative
2	Avg. Daily Return	0.03%		Monday	-1.10%	-1.10%
3	Daily St. Dev.	0.98%		Tuesday	0.83%	-0.28%
4				Wednesday	-0.32%	-0.60%
5	from 3 January 1950 through 31 July 2012			Thursday	-1.12%	-1.71%
6				Friday	-1.04%	-2.73%
7						
8		Average	0.15%			-2.73%
9		SD	2.19%		2	0.77%
10		Prob >5%	1.35%		3	-0.02%

	A	B	C	D	E	F
1	S&P 500				Daily	Cumulative
2	Avg. Daily Return	0.03%		Monday	-0.61%	-0.61%
3	Daily St. Dev.	0.98%		Tuesday	-1.21%	-1.82%
4				Wednesday	0.94%	-0.90%
5	from 3 January 1950 through 31 July 2012			Thursday	-0.16%	-1.06%
6				Friday	2.04%	0.95%
7						
8		Average	0.17%			0.95%
9		SD	2.20%		2	-1.68%
10		Prob >5%	1.53%		3	0.15%

96. Scenario Risks

What the simulation does

Open file 96-ScenarioRisks.xlsx. When you have a likely, best, and worst scenario for your costs, benefits, and growth rate (in A1:D4), you probably want a random outcome between the extremes of best and worst. Then ultimately you want to calculate the net present value (NPV) of your cash flows (in cell K10).

Here is some terminology. Having projected a company's free cash flow for the next five years, we want to figure out what these cash flows are worth today. That means coming up with an appropriate discount rate which we can use to calculate the net present value (NPV) of the cash flows. A discount rate of 5% is used in column I.

The most widely used method of discounting is exponential discounting, which values future cash flows as "how much money would have to be invested currently, at a given rate of return, to yield the cash flow in the future."

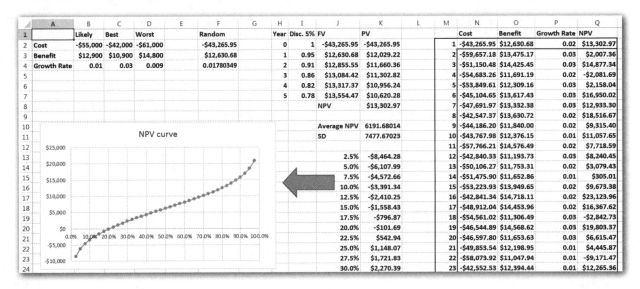

What you need to know

After running our 5 year projection (H1:K8), we repeat this with some 10,000 runs (columns M:Q). Notice the big differences in column Q, so we calculate the average NPV and its standard deviation in cell K10 and K11.

Based on this information, we may want to find out what the distribution of NPV values would be given the average of K10 and the standard deviation of K11. This is done below them in cells J17:K51, ranging from 2.5% to 97.5%. The graph shows the results, with the "average" featuring at 50%.

What you need to do

1. Place in cell F2: =RAND()*(D2-C2)+C2. Copy to cell F4.

2. Place in cell I2: =1/1.05^H2. Copy down to cell I7.

3. Cell J2: =F2. Cell J3: =F3. Cell J4: =J3*(1+$F$4) to J7.

4. Place in cell K2: =I2*J2. Copy down to cell K7.

5. Place in cell K8: =SUM(K2:K7).

6. In N2: =F2. In O2: =F3. In P2: =F4. In Q2: =K8 (not F5).

7. Select range M2:Q10001 for a Data Table with only column input for any empty cell outside the range.

8. Place in cell K10: =AVERAGE(Q2:Q10001).

9. Place in cell K11: =STDEV(Q2:Q10001) (or STDEV.S).

10. Place in cell K13: =NORMINV(J13,$K$10,$K$11). Copy downward to cell K51.

11. The Monte Carlo calculations are extensive, so the system may need its time when you hit F9 or change input.

12. New results should hardly affect the curve because we used 10,000 runs at some overhead costs.

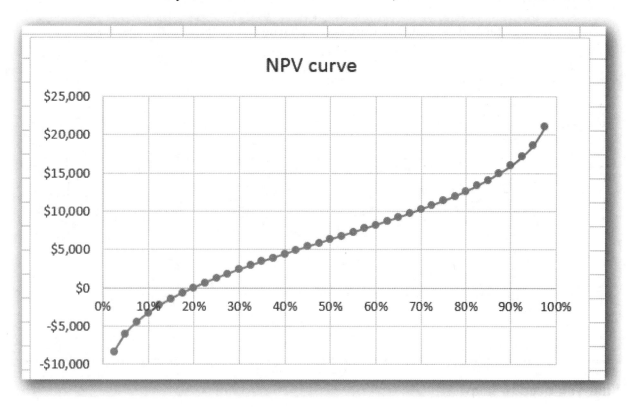

97. Temperature Fluctuations

What the simulation does

Open file 97-TempSimulation.xlsx. As they say, nothing is as volatile as the weather. We will simulate this for temperature, having it oscillate around a mean of 65° Fahrenheit and a standard deviation of 10 during a period of 65 years.

As to be expected, there will be some relatively extreme values below the 5% percentile mark (column D) or above the 95% percentile mark (column C) by mere randomness. Sometimes we might hit more "peaks" than usual.

A Data Table might help us capture an extremely high temperature (an outlier) more easily.

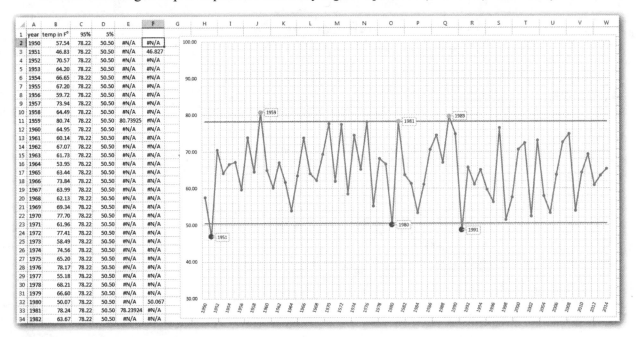

What you need to know

To create a random distribution of temperatures in column B, we need the function NORMINV again.

To mark the 5% and 95% percentiles with a line in the chart, we need columns C and D with the function PERCENTILE (replaced in later versions of Excel with PERCENTILE.INC).

In columns E and F, we use the IF function in combination with the NA function for situations where values are not extreme. The NA function prevents the chart from showing zeros.

What you need to do

1. Place in cell B2: =NORMINV(RAND(),65,10). Copy to B66.

2. Place in cell C2: =PERCENTILE($B$2:$B$66,$C$1). Copy.

3. Place in cell D2: =PERCENTILE($B$2:$B$66,$D$1). Copy.

4. Place in cell E2: =IF(B2>C2,B2,NA()). Copy downwards.

5. Place in cell F2: =IF(B2<D2,B2,NA()). Copy downwards.

6. Results are unpredictable, of course. Sometimes, for instance, we have hot years long ago but not recently (see below).

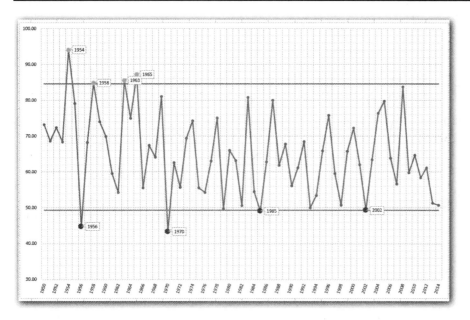

7. On a copy of the 1st sheet, put in cell I1: =MAX(B2:B66).

8. Start a Data Table with column input from an empty cell.

9. I happened to hit 104o F in cell I28: =MAX(I2:I26).

	A	B	C	D	E	F	G	H	I	J
1	year	temp in F°	95%	5%					84.61	
2	1950	67.18	78.44	46.86	#N/A	#N/A		1	89.42	
3	1951	73.46	78.44	46.86	#N/A	#N/A		2	85.79	
4	1952	83.49	78.44	46.86	83.49424	#N/A		3	103.63	
5	1953	55.57	78.44	46.86	#N/A	#N/A		4	86.83	
6	1954	66.30	78.44	46.86	#N/A	#N/A		5	80.61	
7	1955	62.46	78.44	46.86	#N/A	#N/A		6	92.63	
8	1956	52.38	78.44	46.86	#N/A	#N/A		7	93.38	
9	1957	48.85	78.44	46.86	#N/A	#N/A		8	83.69	
10	1958	67.04	78.44	46.86	#N/A	#N/A		9	82.69	
11	1959	68.47	78.44	46.86	#N/A	#N/A		10	91.32	
12	1960	38.90	78.44	46.86	#N/A	38.903		11	104.24	
13	1961	62.87	78.44	46.86	#N/A	#N/A		12	84.87	
14	1962	55.12	78.44	46.86	#N/A	#N/A		13	89.54	
15	1963	77.92	78.44	46.86	#N/A	#N/A		14	89.98	
16	1964	84.61	78.44	46.86	84.61157	#N/A		15	85.60	
17	1965	71.72	78.44	46.86	#N/A	#N/A		16	92.65	
18	1966	54.50	78.44	46.86	#N/A	#N/A		17	99.20	
19	1967	52.07	78.44	46.86	#N/A	#N/A		18	86.99	
20	1968	64.88	78.44	46.86	#N/A	#N/A		19	82.98	
21	1969	61.29	78.44	46.86	#N/A	#N/A		20	91.09	
22	1970	46.45	78.44	46.86	#N/A	46.45		21	96.40	
23	1971	69.86	78.44	46.86	#N/A	#N/A		22	93.84	
24	1972	61.67	78.44	46.86	#N/A	#N/A		23	90.99	
25	1973	58.00	78.44	46.86	#N/A	#N/A		24	81.39	
26	1974	57.18	78.44	46.86	#N/A	#N/A		25	91.53	
27	1975	71.19	78.44	46.86	#N/A	#N/A				
28	1976	69.01	78.44	46.86	#N/A	#N/A			104.24	
29	1977	62.31	78.44	46.86	#N/A	#N/A				

98. Juror Selection

What the simulation does

Open file 98-JurorSelection.xlsx. Countries with a juror system in court have to face the fact that they must choose 12+12 jurors from a larger pool of candidates after checking each candidate for certain criteria.

We assume we need 24 jurors (cell I1) from a pool of 100 (cell B1). We also use the following criteria: #1 they have no opinion yet whether the defendant is guilty (column B); #2 they were not witness to the crime (column C); #3 they accept the possibility of the death penalty (column D). These criteria have a probability as shown in range B4:D4. Column E decides whether all three conditions have been met. Cell F4 counts how many in the pool of candidates actually qualified to be a juror in the case.

Finally we run this setup 10 more times (H:I), but for different pool sizes (from 100 to 1000). We mark sufficient pool sizes.

	A	B	C	D	E	F	G	H	I	J
1	**Candidates**	100						**Needed**	24	
2										
3		No opinion	No witness	Yes death		qualified				
4		0.4	0.3	0.6	Juror?	8		Pool	8	
5	Juror 1	+	+	+	1			100	3	
6	Juror 2				0			200	13	
7	Juror 3	+		+	0			300	18	
8	Juror 4				0			400	30	
9	Juror 5		+	+	0			500	43	
10	Juror 6			+	0			600	46	
11	Juror 7	+			0			700	54	
12	Juror 8	+			0			800	54	
13	Juror 9		+	+	0			900	54	
14	Juror 10		+	+	0			1000	75	
15	Juror 11				0					
16	Juror 12		+	+	0					
17	Juror 13	+		+	0					
18	Juror 14	+	+		0					
19	Juror 15				0					
20	Juror 16				0					
21	Juror 17			+	0					
22	Juror 18		+	+	0					
23	Juror 19			+	0					
24	Juror 20				0					
25	Juror 21			+	0					
26	Juror 22				0					
27	Juror 23		+	+	0					
28	Juror 24		+		0					

What you need to know

One of the problems in this simulation is that we may need more than 100 candidates to reach our quorum. So the Data Table will change cell B1, so we may need more candidate records. We tackle this problem with formulas in column A that determine whether there should be a next candidate. If so, we need to check whether these new ones meet the conditions as well.

What you need to do

1. All cells with a formula have a gray background.

2. Place in cell A5: =IF(ROW(A1)<=$B$1,TEXT(ROW(A1), "Juror 0"),""). Copy downwards to cell A1005.

3. Place in range B5:B1005 the following formula: =IF(ROW(A1)<=$B$1,IF(RAND()<B$4,"+",""),"").

4. Place in range C5:C1005 the following formula: =IF(ROW(B1)<=$B$1,IF(RAND()<C$4,"+",""),"").

5. Place in range D5:D1005 the following formula: =IF(ROW(C1)<=$B$1,IF(RAND()<D$4,"+",""),"").

6. Place in range E5:E1005 the following formula: =IF(COUNTIF(B5:D5,"+")=3,1,0).

7. Place in cell F4: =SUM(E5:E1006).

8. Place in cell I4: =F4.

9. Select range H4:I14 for a Data Table with only column input from cell B1 (the pool size of candidates).

10. Use Conditional Formatting for range H5:I14: =$I5>=$I$1.

11. Sometimes, we may need a larger pool by mere chance.

	A	B	C	D	E	F	G	H	I	J
1	Candidates	100						Needed	24	
2										
3		No opinion	No witness	Yes death		qualified				
4		0.4	0.3	0.6	Juror?	9		Pool	9	
5	Juror 1		+		0			100	11	
6	Juror 2			+	0			200	20	
7	Juror 3	+		+	0			300	18	
8	Juror 4				0			400	18	
9	Juror 5	+	+	+	1			500	32	
10	Juror 6	+	+		0			600	42	
11	Juror 7	+			0			700	50	
12	Juror 8	+	+	+	1			800	63	
13	Juror 9		+		0			900	63	
14	Juror 10		+	+	0			1000	83	
15	Juror 11				0					

99. Waiting Time Simulation

What the simulation does

Open file 99-WaitingTime.xlsx. We simulate here the flow of patients in something like a walk-in clinic. Based on experience, we know the probabilities of patients coming in with 5, 10, or 15 minutes between arrivals (B2:C4). We also know the probabilities that the treatment takes 5, 10, or 15 minutes (F2:G4). Let's assume there are usually 10 patients in the AM (which we won't simulate, though). And there is only one nurse or doctor in the clinic.

Now we can simulate the flow of patients through the system (A7:G16). The chart shows how visit times can vary randomly. Since there is much volatility involved, we repeat this process some 1,000 times (F19:G1018), so we can calculate what the average maximum visit time is, based on waiting time and treatment time (cell C18) after 1,000 runs.

What you need to know

To randomly assign arrival times and treatment times, we need an extra column in front of the two probability tables shown on top of the sheet. These two columns must start at 0 and then cumulatively increase, so we can use VLOOKUP to assign these times in a random fashion.

What you need to do

1. Place in cell A3: =SUM($C$2:C2), and copy 1 cell down.

2. Place in cell E3: =SUM($G$2:G2), and copy 1 cell down.

3. Place in B7: =VLOOKUP(RAND(),$A$2:$B$4,2,TRUE), and copy downwards to B16.

4. Place in range C7:C16: =SUM($B$7:B7).

5. In D7: =C7. In D8:D16: =IF(C8<F7,F7,F7+(C8-F7)).

6. In E7:E16: =VLOOKUP(RAND(),$E$2:$F$4,2,TRUE).

7. In F7:F16: =D7+E7.

8. In G7:G16: =F7-C7.

9. Place in cell G18: =MAX(G7:G16).

10. Select range F18:G1018 for a Data Table with only column input from any empty cell outside the range.

11. Place in cell C18: =AVERAGE(G18:G1018).

12. The average time in the clinic appears to oscillate around 27 minutes, but the time per patient may vary quite a bit (compare the two charts shown here).

	A	B	C	D	E	F	G
1	scale	min. b/t arrival	probability		scale	treatment	probability
2	0	5	0.5		0	5	0.4
3	0.5	10	0.3		0.4	10	0.35
4	0.8	15	0.2		0.75	15	0.25
5							
6		next arrival	arrival time	start time	treatment	finish time	total time
7	Customer1	5	5	5	10	15	10
8	Customer2	5	10	15	15	30	20
9	Customer3	5	15	30	15	45	30
10	Customer4	5	20	45	10	55	35
11	Customer5	15	35	55	5	60	25
12	Customer6	15	50	60	10	70	20
13	Customer7	15	65	70	10	80	15
14	Customer8	10	75	80	10	90	15
15	Customer9	5	80	90	5	95	15
16	Customer10	5	85	95	15	110	25

total visit time per customer (first run)

100. Project Delays

What the simulation does

Open file 100-ProjectDelays.xlsx. Here we have a sequence of tasks that start at a certain day, have a certain duration, and then end, to be followed by the next task. So the entire project is supposed to be finished on the date shown in cell E11.

Usually, however, there are random changes in the duration (column F)—say, up to 2 days shorter or longer. Such random changes would obviously affect the end date of the total project. In cell H11, we calculate what the actual end date of the project would be.

We run this project some 100 times in total, so we can calculate what on average the "real" end date of the project would be (in cell E15) after random changes in duration per task. We then calculate how the final end dates for each run are distributed in a frequency chart (in the right lower corner).

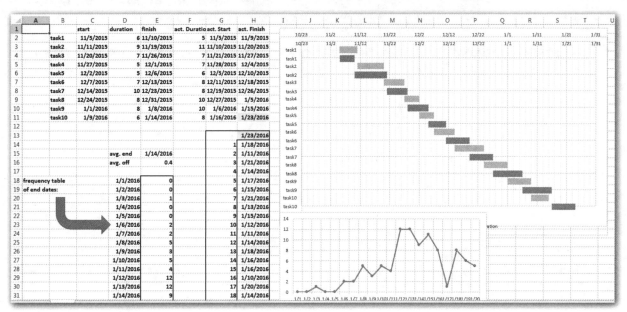

What you need to know

The chart in the upper right is a so-called Gantt chart. In Excel, it is a *stacked* bar chart with two series of values, of which the first series has no fill color or line color, so it is actually invisible. We have actually 2 charts here. One is based on B1:B11 (invisible) and E1:E11. The other one is plotted from B1:B11 and H1:H11. The second one has a plot area with no fill, so you can lay it over the first one with a slight offset down.

What you need to do

1. Place in cell C3 (not C2): =E2+1, and copy down to cell C11.

2. Place in cell E2: =C2+D2-1, and copy down to cell E11.

3. Place in cell F1: =D2+RANDBETWEEN(-2,2). If you don't have RANDBETWEEN, use: =D2+(-2+INT(RAND()*5)).

4. Place in cell G2: =C2.

5. Place in cell H2: =G2+F2-1 and copy down.

6. Place in cell G3: =H2+1, and copy down.

7. Link cell H13 to cell H11.

8. Select the range G13:H114 for a Data Table with only column input from any empty cell outside the range.

9. Place in cell E15: =AVERAGE($H$13:$H$114).

10. Place in cell E16: =$E$15-$E$11.

11. Select range E18:E37 at once for this formula: =FREQUENCY($H$13:$H$114,$D$18:$D$37). Accept this array formula with Ctr+Shift+Enter.

12. As always, results may vary!

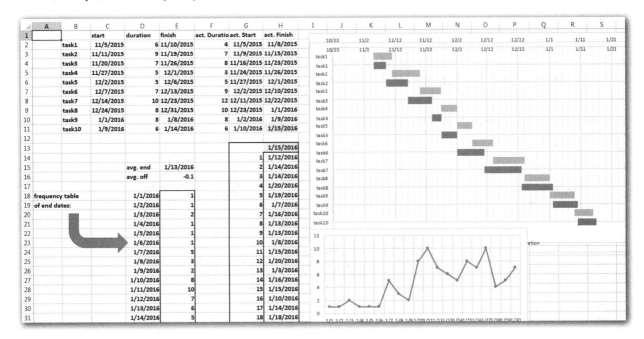

Appendices

1. Locking Cell References

Most formulas in Excel contain references to one or more cells. When you copy such formulas to another location, the cell references automatically adjust to their new location. These references are called *relative*—they adjust when moved or copied.

Usually that is good news, but sometimes you want certain references to keep referring to the same cell, or at least to the same row or the same column. Such references are called *absolute*—they remain "locked" when moved or copied.

Unlocked, or relative, references look like this, =A1, whereas locked, or absolute, references look like =$A$1 or =A$1 or =$A1. The $-sign locks one part of the reference. It is not really a dollar-sign but a string-sign. You can type that sign by hand, but it is usually much easier and faster to hit the key *F4*. The F4-key is a cycle key—it cycles from A1 to $A$1 to A$1 to $A1 and then starts all over again.

	A	B	C	D	E	F	G	H	I	J	K	L
1	A1	B1										
2	A2	B2			APR	4%	5%	6%	7%			
3					$ 5,000.00	$ 200.00	$ 250.00	$ 300.00	$ 350.00			
4	A1	B1			$10,000.00	$ 400.00	$ 500.00	$ 600.00	$ 700.00			
5	A2	B2			$15,000.00	$ 600.00	$ 750.00	$ 900.00	$1,050.00			
6					$20,000.00	$ 800.00	$1,000.00	$1,200.00	$1,400.00			
7	A1	A1			$25,000.00	$1,000.00	$1,250.00	$1,500.00	$1,750.00			
8	A1	A1			$30,000.00	$1,200.00	$1,500.00	$1,800.00	$2,100.00			
9					$35,000.00	$1,400.00	$1,750.00	$2,100.00	$2,450.00			
10	A1	B1			$40,000.00	$1,600.00	$2,000.00	$2,400.00	$2,800.00			
11	A1	B1			$45,000.00	$1,800.00	$2,250.00	$2,700.00	$3,150.00			
12					$50,000.00	$2,000.00	$2,500.00	$3,000.00	$3,500.00			
13	A1	A1										
14	A2	A2										
15												
16												
17			key F4: Cycles between relative and (partially) absolute cell references									
18												
19	=A1	=B1	=$A$1	=$A$1		=A$1	=B$1			=$A1	=$A1	
20	=A2	=B2	=$A$1	=$A$1		=A$1	=B$1			=$A2	=$A2	
21												
22	A1	B1	A1	A1		A1	B1			A1	A1	
23	A2	B2	A1	A1		A1	B1			A2	A2	
24												

I explained this behavior in the figure above (file 9-Appendices.xlsx on sheet "Locking"). Cell F4 has the following formula in it: =$E3*F$2. Notice that column E is locked, so it stays that way when we copy the formula to the right, whereas row 3 is unlocked and will change into 4 in the next cell down. Notice also that row 2 is locked, so it keeps referring to row 2 when copied down, whereas column F will change to G when copied to the right (or to E when copied to the left). As a consequence of these "locks," the formula can be copied over the entire range F3:I12.

Sometimes it is nice, handy, or even necessary to see all the formulas on your sheet at once—for instance, to make sure your formulas remained correct after you moved or copied them. If you want to get a formula-view of your sheet, just hit (this is called a tilde, which can be found under the *Esc* key). *Ctr ~* is a toggle shortcut, switching back and forth between value-view and formula-view per sheet.

	E	F	G	H	I
	APR	0.04	0.05	0.06	0.07
	5000	=$E3*F$2	=$E3*G$2	=$E3*H$2	=$E3*I$2
	10000	=$E4*F$2	=$E4*G$2	=$E4*H$2	=$E4*I$2
	15000	=$E5*F$2	=$E5*G$2	=$E5*H$2	=$E5*I$2
	20000	=$E6*F$2	=$E6*G$2	=$E6*H$2	=$E6*I$2
	25000	=$E7*F$2	=$E7*G$2	=$E7*H$2	=$E7*I$2
	30000	=$E8*F$2	=$E8*G$2	=$E8*H$2	=$E8*I$2
	35000	=$E9*F$2	=$E9*G$2	=$E9*H$2	=$E9*I$2
	40000	=$E10*F$2	=$E10*G$2	=$E10*H$2	=$E10*I$2
	45000	=$E11*F$2	=$E11*G$2	=$E11*H$2	=$E11*I$2
	50000	=$E12*F$2	=$E12*G$2	=$E12*H$2	=$E12*I$2

Locking cells can also be very important when you work with conditional formatting. Say we have the following situation: We want to compare an old value with a new value by marking the new value if it went up by more than 5, 10, 15, or 20 units. In this case (shown below), the values I used are systolic blood pressure (BSP) units in mmHg.

The amount of units up is chosen in cell G1 on sheet "ValueUp" shown below. After selecting the cells that we want to mark conditionally, D2:D19, we implement conditional formatting with the following formula: =($D2-$C2)>$G$1.

Make sure that the references to columns D and C are locked, but not to their rows. The reference to cell G1 has to be completely locked, as every cell in column D has to "listen" to that one cell G1. If you do not follow these rules, conditional formatting will not work the way you want it to work.

	A	B	C	D	E	F	G	H
1	Date	Patient	Old SBP	New SBP		Up by more than	10	
2	5/5/2006	Bush	120	127			5	
3	5/8/2006	Carter	139	152			10	
4	5/9/2006	Clinton	160	165			15	
5	5/10/2006	Eisenhower	148	180			20	
6	5/11/2006	Ford	167	158				
7	5/12/2006	Johnson	145	160				
8	5/15/2006	Kennedy	137	142				
9	5/16/2006	Nixon	155	190				
10	5/17/2006	Reagan	137	125				
11	5/18/2006	Bush	120	141				
12	5/19/2006	Carter	139	155				
13	5/22/2006	Clinton	160	155				
14	5/23/2006	Eisenhower	148	160				
15	5/24/2006	Ford	167	141				
16	5/25/2006	Johnson	145	132				
17	5/26/2006	Kennedy	137	139				
18	5/29/2006	Nixon	155	147				
19	5/30/2006	Reagan	137	151				
20								

2. Nested functions

Nested functions are functions "nested" within other functions. They are quite common in Excel—and in this book—but you may not be familiar with them yet.

If you are a "pro," you probably type functions, including nested functions. But if you are new to this, it is probably wise to create your functions by clicking the *fx* button in front of the formula bar. This makes a dialog screen pop up, which gives you usually much more detailed information as to what to do (and besides, it has a *Help* option in the lower left corner).

To show you the technique of creating nested functions, I use an example shown below on sheet "Nested." This sheet creates a formatted version (in column C) of an unformatted phone number (in column B).

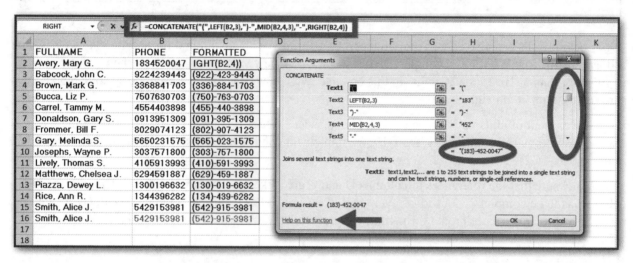

The function to start with is CONCATENATE. This function "strings" a series of components together. It begins with an opening parenthesis in the 1st argument, *Text1*. Click in the 2nd argument, *Text2*, where we want a nested LEFT function.

To do so, while in *Text2*, click on the dropdown box way in front of the formula bar (top left in the figure above) and locate the function LEFT. Now the CONCATENATE dialog box gets replaced with the LEFT dialog box. Enter B2 for its 1st argument and 3 for its 2nd argument.

The question is now how we can get back to CONCATENATE in order to finish our work in the main function. We do so—not by clicking OK—but by clicking on CONCATENATE in the formula bar. Notice now how the LEFT function has been nested in the 2nd argument of CONCATENATE.

Click in the 3rd argument, *Text3*, and enter "literally" a closing parenthesis plus a dash: ")-". In the 4th argument, *Text4*, we need a nested MID function with three arguments (B2, 4, 3). Go back to CONCATENATE by clicking on its name in the formula bar and enter a dash in its 5th argument, *Text5* (if you think there are no more arguments available, use its vertical scroll bar to the right). Finally, call the RIGHT function in *Text6*, and set its two arguments to B2 and 4.

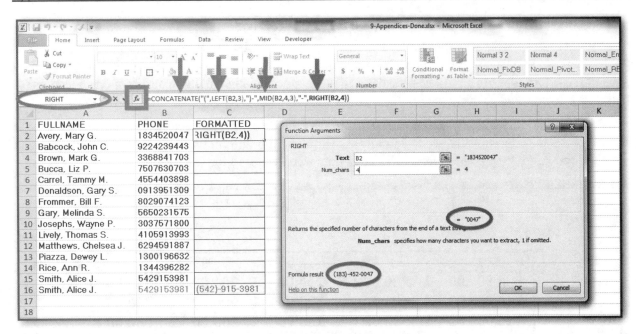

Notice, when you are in a nested argument, how the first formula result (in our picture, "0047") is the result of the nested function (in our case, RIGHT), whereas the final formula result (in our case (183)-452-0047) comes from the entire formula.

Once you are finished and you want to check the outcome of a particular nested function, highlight that nested function in the formula bar and hit *F9*. This gives you the result for that particular part of the total function. Do not forget to hit *Esc*, otherwise you would replace that function with a numeric value.

By the way, instead of using CONCATENATE, you could also "hook" the parts that were inside CONCATENATE together by using the ampersand (&)—like this: ="(" & LEFT(B2,3) & ")-" & MID(B2,4,3) & "-" & RIGHT(B2,4).

3. What-If Tables

What I like to call a "What-If Table" is called a "Data Table" by Microsoft (what's in a word). A Data Table is a range of cells that shows how changing one or two variables in your formulas will affect the results of those formulas. A Data Table provides a shortcut for calculating multiple results in one operation and a way to view and compare the results of all the different variations together on your worksheet.

On sheet "DataTable," I used the same example as I did earlier in Appendix 1, but this time by using a Data Table. Data Tables usually need a formula at their point of origin (in this case cell B3, which contains a simple formula: =B1*B2). The cells C4:F13 are empty when you start the Data Table.

	A	B	C	D	E	F	G
1	AMOUNT	$ 5,000.00					
2	APR	4%					
3		$200.00	4%	5%	6%	7%	APR
4		$ 5,000.00	$ 200.00	$ 250.00	$ 300.00	$ 350.00	
5		$10,000.00	$ 400.00	$ 500.00	$ 600.00	$ 700.00	
6		$15,000.00	$ 600.00	$ 750.00	$ 900.00	$1,050.00	
7		$20,000.00	$ 800.00	$1,000.00	$1,200.00	$1,400.00	
8		$25,000.00	$1,000.00	$1,250.00	$1,500.00	$1,750.00	
9		$30,000.00	$1,200.00	$1,500.00	$1,800.00	$2,100.00	
10		$35,000.00	$1,400.00	$1,750.00	$2,100.00	$2,450.00	
11		$40,000.00	$1,600.00	$2,000.00	$2,400.00	$2,800.00	
12		$45,000.00	$1,800.00	$2,250.00	$2,700.00	$3,150.00	
13		$50,000.00	$2,000.00	$2,500.00	$3,000.00	$3,500.00	
14		AMOUNT					

To implement a Data Table, you select the entire range, including its point of origin with a formula in it—so that is B3:F13. Then go through the following menus: Data | What-If Analysis | Data Table. In the dialog box, set the row input to cell B2 and the column input to cell B1.

Once you click OK, Excel replaces all empty cells with an array formula like this: {TABLE(B2,B1)}. Or more in general, {TABLE(row-input-cell, column-input-cell)}. Sometimes, one or both of the two arguments are missing. Do not type the braces—Excel creates them automatically when you hit the Data Table button. And do not type the formula!

The results of this particular Data Table should be the same as if we had used the formula =C$3*$B4, which we did in Appendix 1. Why use Data Tables then? There are several reasons. First, it might be easier to implement them than working with locked and unlocked cell references. Second, no part of the array can inadvertently be deleted or changed, because the array acts as one entire unit. Third, Data Tables have much more potential, as you can see in many of the simulations we use in this book.

However, there is one drawback. Because there may be many operations involved in a Data Table, Excel can run into speed problems. There are two ways to get around this speed issue.

Method #1 is to stop automatic recalculation—at least for Data Tables. Do the following: File | Options | Formulas | ⊙ Automatic Except for Data Tables (you can even set all calculations to manual). If you ever need to recalculate a Data Table, just use *Sh F9*, and that will recalculate only the particular sheet you are on (whereas *F9* alone would recalculate the entire file).

Method #2 is that, after you run a specific what-if analysis, you copy the Data Table Area—that is, the area between the top row and the left column—and then paste it as values over itself. Move on to the next Data Table, run it, and paste values again. Whenever you need to run a pasted table again, quickly re-implement the Data Table.

One more limitation: A Data Table cannot accommodate more than two variables. So they are at best two-dimensional but never three-dimensional. There are ways to get around this limitation as you will see in several simulations (e.g. 28 and 35).

4. Monte Carlo Simulations

Why are they called *Monte Carlo* simulations? The name came up in the 1940s when Los Alamos physicists John von Neumann, Stanislaw Ulam, and Nicholas Metropolis were working on nuclear weapon projects during the Manhattan Project in the Los Alamos National Laboratory. They were unable to solve their problems using conventional, deterministic mathematical methods. Then one of them, Stanisław Ulam, had the idea of using random simulations based on random numbers.

Being secret, the work of von Neumann and Ulam required a code name. Von Neumann chose the name Monte Carlo. The name refers to the Monte Carlo Casino in Monaco where Ulam's uncle often gambled away his money. The Monte Carlo simulations required for the Manhattan Project were severely limited by the computational tools at the time. Nowadays we have Excel!

Monte Carlo simulations are computerized mathematical techniques that allow people to account for risks in quantitative analysis and decision making. Nowadays, the technique is used by professionals in such widely disparate fields as finance, project management, energy, manufacturing, engineering, research and development, insurance, and transportation. Monte Carlo simulation furnishes you as a decision-maker with a range of possible outcomes and the probabilities they will occur for any choice of action.

How do they work? Instead of using a fixed value for input variables, we can model an input variable with a probability distribution and then run the model a number of times and see what impact the randomized variation has on the output. Always run at least 1,000 iterations of Monte Carlo models. This is to ensure that you have a statistical chance of getting sufficient outliers (extreme values) to make the variance analysis meaningful. This is important because as the number of iterations increases, the variance of the average output decreases.

In life most distributions are *normal* in nature indicating that the distribution is bell-shaped around a mean with a known method of describing the variability around this. However, the functions RAND and RANDBETWEEN both have a *uniform* or *equal* distribution—that is, any value between the minimum and maximum values will have the same probability of occurring.

Luckily, we can convert a uniform distribution into a normal distribution with the simple function NORMINV, which has the following syntax: *=NORMINV(RAND(), mean, SD)*. For instance, =NORMINV(rand(),100,10) will generate a distribution of random numbers centered on 100 with a spread having a bell shaped curve with a standard deviation of 10. This means that the function will produce a number with a 99.7% probability of being between 70 and 130 and, on average, will have a mean of 100. (See also Simulation 13.)

This really illustrates how we can tame the uncertainty of the future with ranges and probabilities, but it also shows how impossible it is to be extremely precise. The amazing accomplishment of probability calculus is to put a meaningful numerical value on things we admit we do not know exactly.

Because Monte Carlo simulation is a method of analysis based on artificially recreating a chance process (usually with a computer), running it many times, and directly observing the results, Excel should be a great tool to perform such simulations. However, since there are many operations involved, Excel may run into speed problems again. So we have the same two ways again to get around this speed issue, as we discussed in Appendix 3. Either you stop automatic recalculation or copy the Data Table Area, and then paste it as values over itself.

Be prepared that a file using several Monte Carlo Simulations with more than 1,000 iterations will save and open slowly because of its numerous calculations. So be patient or change your Excel settings.

5. Simulation Controls

Controls such as spin buttons and scroll bars are great tools for many kinds of what-if analysis. They quickly reset specific hard-coded values and then show you the impact of such operations.

In order to create such controls, you need the *Developer* tab in your menu, which may not be present on your machine. To add it to the ribbon, you do the following, depending on your Excel version. Pre-2010: File | Options | General | ☑ Enable the Developer Tab. In 2010 and 2013: File | Options | Customize Ribbon | in the far right list þ Developer. From now on, the tab can be found in the menu on top.

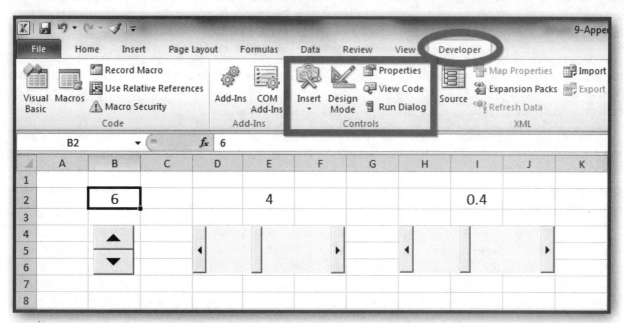

On sheet "Controls" (see above), we place three controls. You do so by clicking on the *Insert* button and then on one of the options in the lower section of the list (Active-X Controls). Draw the control you have chosen on your sheet.

Then click on the *Properties* menu (make sure the control you want to set the properties for is still selected, or select it). Set at least the properties Min, Max, and LinkedCell (that is, the cell where you want the control's value to appear).

Once you are done, do not forget to click the *Design Mode* menu OFF, so you can go back to your sheet!!! Be aware, though, that when you change a control and calculation is not automatic, you need to activate the sheet first before you can hit the "run" keys *Sh F9*.

You probably noticed already that the properties Min and Max can only hold integers. So if you want to regulate decimals with your control (like in the scroll bar to the far right), you need an intermediate cell. I happened to choose a LinkedCell reference located behind the control (e.g. cell I5). In the cell where you want the decimal number visibly displayed, you need to place a formula like =I5/10 (or I5/100, etc.).

Controls like these are fantastic. I used them for several simulations in this book. They are not only fun, but also very informative and revealing. I think you will love them more and more, if you did not already.

About the Author

Dr. Gerard M. Verschuuren is a human geneticist who also earned a doctorate in the philosophy of science. He studied and worked at universities in Europe and the United States and wrote several biology textbooks in Dutch. During this time, he also used and programmed computer software, including Excel, to simulate scientific problems.

Currently, he is semi-retired and spends most of his time as a writer, speaker, and consultant on the interface of science and computer programming.

His most recent computer-related books are:

1. Excel 2007 for Scientists (Holy Macro! Books, 2008).

2. From VBA to VSTO (Holy Macro! Books, 2006).

3. Visual Learning Series (MrExcel.com).

4. Excel 2013 for Scientists (Holy Macro! Books, 4/2014).

For more info see: http://en.wikipedia.org/wiki/Gerard_Verschuuren
He can be contacted at www.genesispc.com

Index

Symbols

$ in cell references 202
:east squared residuals 135
#N/A
  explained 50
  generated by =NA() 50
  hiding chart points 74
#VALUE! error 130

A

ABS
  to highlight lowest value 59
  to remove minus sign 33
Absolute cell references 202
Allele
  dominant vs. recessive 46
Alpha error
  explained 32
  from CONFIDENCE 30
Amortization table 186
Ampersand operator (&) 16
Amplitude 92
Analysis Toolpak
  for CONVERT function 102
  for Moving average 75
  for Normal distribution 24
  for QUOTIENT function 154
  for RANDBETWEEN 2
AND for multiple conditions 37
Annuity 79
APR 64
  raise to (1+APR)^Years 65
Area under the curve 178
Array functions
  as result of Data Table 206
  can not delete part of array 31
  compared to SUMPRODUCT 130
  for Least squares 137
  FREQUENCY 6
  multi-cell 29, 44, 88
  require Ctr+Shift+Enter 45
  single-cell 130, 132, 137
  TABLE 30
  TREND for extrapolation 88
  TREND for interpolation 44
Asian options 82
Auto numbering records 154
AVERAGE
  for calculating mean 7
  for moving averages 75
  inside NORMDIST 25
  with circular reference 128

B

Bayesian probability 151
Bayes Theorem 148
Beautiful Mind, A 170
Bell-shaped curve
  defined 27
  with BINOMDIST 19
Beta error 32
BINOMDIST
  for bell-shaped curve 19
  with BINOM.INV 40
  with "successes" 41
BINOM.INV
  for chromosomes 40
  for quality control 38
Birds in flight 172
Black-Scholes model 84
Brownian motion 110
Brown, Robert 110

C

Calculation
  for data tables 206
  manual 9, 206
Cell references
  Locking 202
CHAR
  for lower case 16
  for upper case 168
Chromosomes
  for sex determination 42
  from grandparent 40
  recessive allele 46
Circular references
  for iteration 124
  for memory 162
Clinic
  waiting time 198
CODE 16
Coin flip 19
Collective behavior 172
Combination 154
Compounding 65
CONCATENATE
  formatting phone numbers 204
  vs & operator 16
Conditional Formatting 7
Conditional probability 148
Confidence
  defined 27
  margin 30
  with exchange rates 117
CONFIDENCE 30
Conflict and cooperation 170
Confounding factor 144
CONVERT 102
Converting metric 102

COUNT 25
  versus COUNTA 158
COUNTA 158
COUNTIF
  for data management 133
  for uncertainty 114
  with ROW 153
  with SMALL 139
COUNTIFS 13
CRITBINOM 38
  versus BINOMDIST 40, 174
Crowe, Russell 170
Ctr Sh Enter
  braces in formula bar 7
  for array formulas 6
  versus SUMPRODUCT 130
  with squared residuals 137
  with TREND 44
Ctr ~ to show formulas 3, 141, 202
Cumulative summing 169

D

Data Table
  as What-If Table 206
  for chromosmes 41
  for iterations of RAND 11
  for random walk 13
  genetic drift 50
  how to use 30
  no row, empty column 111
  Overhead 188
  reduced vitality 54
  sampling sizes 37
  to detect repeats 29
  with DGET 142
  with only row input 67
Data Validation
  from formula 157
  from list 33
Death penalty 196
Delays, project 200
Denaturation 62
Developer tab 208
DGET 142
Discounting cash flows 192
Discrete distribution 14
DNA
  sequencing 62
Dogs with fleas 176
DSUM 70

E

EC50 100
Ehrenfest's urn 176
Einstein, Albert 110
Employee stock 78
Epidemic 106
Equations 134

Excel 2013 for Scientists CD-ROM

Complete Excel Course for the Sciences

Finally - visual training written for scientists by a scientist. Are you tired of trying to learn Excel with examples from accounting? With over 1900 slides, this self-paced training package is loaded with informative samples from the world of science plus frequent self-tests to enhance your learning. Learn the pitfalls of Excel for scientists and how to work around them.

Author: Dr. Gerard Verschuuren
ISBN: 978-1-61547-024-2
Over 1900 Slides on CD-ROM
$99 US

Module 1: Data Analysis
Summaries
Lookups and Trends
Filtering Tools
Getting the Right Numbers
Complex Formulas

Module 2: Plotting Data
Chart Basics
Axis Issues
Bars and Error Bars
Interpolation
Graph Formulas

Module 3: Curve Fitting
Linear & Non-Linear
Sigmoid/Logistics Curves
The Best Fit Test
Correlations
Solving Equations

Module 4: Statistical Analysis
Types of Distributions
Sampling Techniques
Estimating Margins
Testing for Significance
ANOVA and Chi-Squared

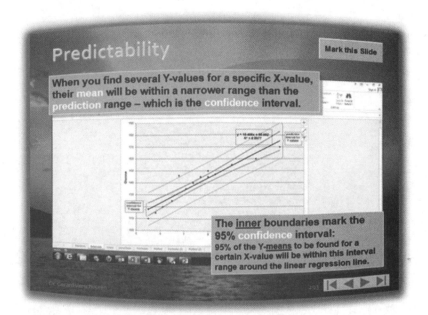

Types of Distributions

Mark this Slide

There are actually 3 (or 4) different versions of T.DIST:
- **T.DIST.2T** returns the <u>two</u>-tailed t-distribution
- **T.DIST.RT** returns the <u>right</u>-tailed t-distribution
- **T.DIST** returns the <u>left</u>-tailed t-distribution (cumulative and non-)

T.DIST.2T — 2-tailed
T.DIST.RT — right-tailed
T.DIST — left-tailed / T.DIST cumul
T.DIST non-cum — left-tailed

5% 2-tailed is the same as 2.5% 1-tailed. More on tails later.

Trends

Mark this Slide

This sheet has many features that we won't discuss here:
- Controls are part of Module Curve Fitting
- Graphs or charts are part of Module Plotting Data

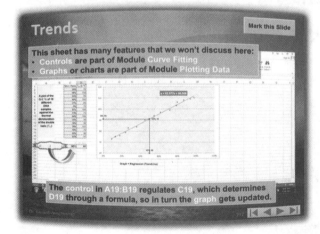

The control in A19:B19 regulates C19, which determines D19 through a formula, so in turn the graph gets updated.

Chi-Squared and Box-Cox

Mark this Slide

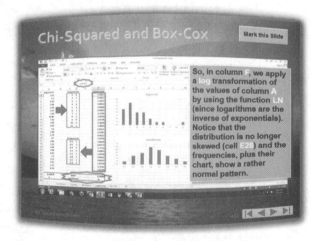

So, in column F, we apply a log transformation of the values of column A by using the function LN (since logarithms are the inverse of exponentials). Notice that the distribution is no longer skewed (cell E28) and the frequencies, plus their chart, show a rather normal pattern.

Excel 2013 VBA
A Complete Course in Excel VBA

The "Excel 2013 VBA" CD-ROM is not only an excellent learning tool to master VBA, but also a gold mine for very powerful and useful macros. The CD-ROM has more than 1200 PowerPoint slides that guide you through the learning process. In addition, it comes with Excel files for you to work on as well as files that have the VBA code all done.

Author: Dr. Gerard Verschuuren
ISBN: 978-1-61547-031-0
Over 1200 Slides on CD-ROM
$99 US

Part 1: Basic Essentials
1. Object Oriented
2. Recording Macros
3. Branch Statements
4. Interaction
5. Variables (Value Type)
6. Variables (Object Type)
7. Collections
8. Loop Statements
9. Variables as Arguments
10. Pivot Tables and Charts

Part 2: Formulas and Arrays
11. Dates and Calendars
12. The Current-Region
13. Property WorksheetFunction
14. Property Formula
15. Property FormulaR1C1
16. Custom Functions
17. Array Functions
18. 1D- and 2D-Arrays
19. Customized Arrays
20. Variant Arrays

Part 3: Buttons, Forms, and more
21. Importing and Exporting
22. Buttons, Bars, Menus
23. Application Events
24. User Forms
25. Data Entry + Mail Merge
26. Custom Classes
27. Class Collections
28. Error Handling
29. Distributing VBA code
30. VBA Monitoring VBA

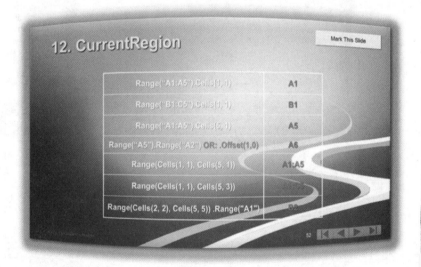

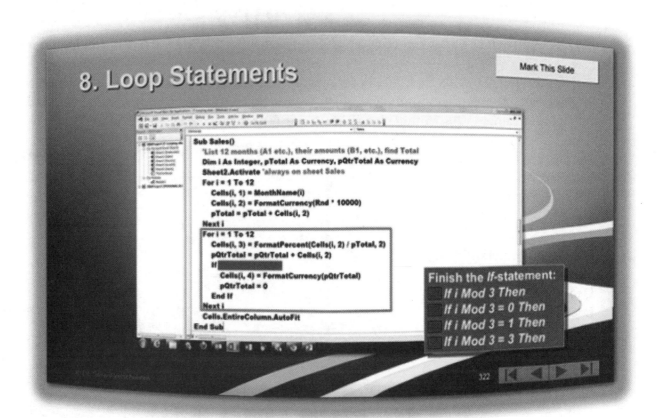

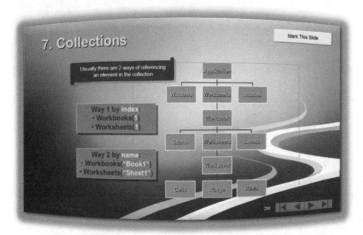

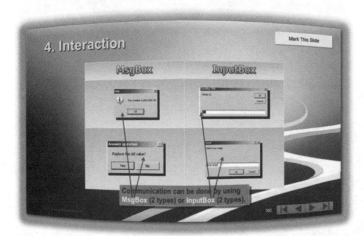

217

VBSCRIPT

A Lightweight Language With a Fast Interpreter For a Wide Variety of Environments.

A definitive guide to VBScript. Tired of trying to learn VBScript without a guide, or by reverse engineering existing programming? With 367 slides, this self-paced training package is loaded with informative sample VBScripting plus frequent self-tests to enhance your learning.

Author: Dr. Gerard Verschuuren
ISBN: 978-1-61547-018-1
367 Slides on CD-ROM
$99 US

What is VBScript?
Variables
Decision Structures
Loops
Arrays
Custom Subs and Functions
File Management
Interacting with Excel
Data Validation
Tapping into Access and ADO
Dictionary
Error Handling
Web Pages (HTML)
Mobilizing MS Outlook
Shell Services

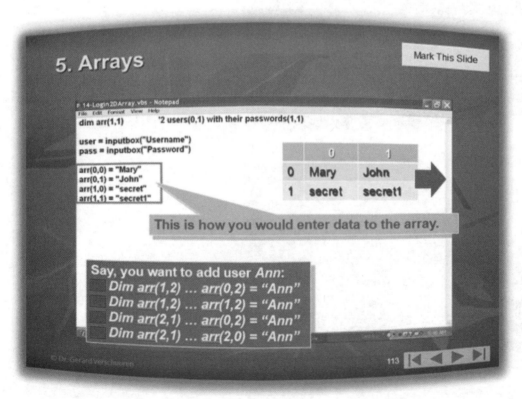

Excel 2013 For Scientists
Revised & Expanded 3rd Edition

This book will cover the topics truly important to science professionals. Learn about sampling distributions and regressions and graphing. With examples from the world of science, this reference teaches scientists how to create graphs, analyze statistics and regressions, and plot and organize scientific data.

Author: Dr. Gerard Verschuuren
ISBN: 978-1-61547-025-9
314 Pages $19.95 US
Kindle & ePub editions available

Excel Video Medley
71 Excel Video Tutorials

Author: Dr. Gerard Verschuuren
ISBN: 978-1-61547-046-4
71 videos on DVD-ROM
$39.95 US

Each video runs from 4 to 14 minutes.
Learn at your own pace on your computer.
Sections include:
General Excel Operations, Excel Formulas,
Charts & Graphs, Tables, Pivot Tables,
Science & Statistics,
Simulations

Full list of the 71 tutorials are below:

Dr. Gerard Verschuuren

Excel Video Medley

71 Excel Video Tutorials

MREXCEL.COM

1. Manipulating Date and Time in Excel
2. Dropdown Boxes for a Variety of Lists
3. Dropdown Boxes with Unique Entries in Excel
4. Trouble When Numbers Are Not Numbers
5. Autonumbering of Records in an Excel Spreadsheet
6. Creating Advanced and Calculated Filters in Excel
7. Allowing Others to Change Your Excel Spreadsheets
8. How to Use the FREQUENCY Function in Excel
9. Nested Functions in Excel
10. VLOOKUP on Multiple Columns or Tables
11. INDEX beats VLOOKUP in Excel
12. INDEX and MATCH with Wildcards
13. Streamlining Data Entry in Excel
14. The Power of SUMIFS in Excel Reports
15. SUMIFS and AVERAGEIFS
16. SUMIF, SUMIFS, COUNTIF, COUNTIFS
17. An Array Formula for STDEV-IFS
18. Mean, Median, and SD for Grouped Data
19. Solving 3 Equations with 3 Unknown X's
20. Subtotals with OFFSET, ROWS, ROW, and MOD
21. The Power of Range Names in Excel Formulas
22. Make Range Names in Your Excel Formulas Dynamic
23. Conditional Formatting with Formulas
24. Creating Charts in Excel
25. Creating Markers in Your Excel Charts-Graphs
26. Percentile Markers in an Excel Chart
27. How Do I Create Error Bars in Excel Charts
28. Does Excel Have a Broken Axis
29. 3D Charts and Graphs in Excel
30. A Comparative Histogram in Excel
31. Extrapolation and Forecast
32. Excel Tricks- Automatic change of chart data
33. Pie Charts with Automatic Data Changes
34. The Perfect Bell Shape Curve
35. What-If Analysis with a Data Table
36. Table of Frequency Distributions in Excel
37. Tricks to Create Totals and Filter Them
38. Creating a Summary Based on Several Spreadsheets
39. Compare a New List with an Old List in Excel
40. Pivot Table Secrets
41. Pivot Table Secrets in Excel
42. How to Tackle Some Pivot Table Hurdles
43. Pivot Table Calculations- Manually or with VBA
44. Table Structure and Calculations
45. Sampling Sizes and Sampling Tools
46. Statistical Testing for Normality in Excel
47. How to Deal with Skewed Data
48. Outliers in Research
49. Trends, interpolation, and extrapolation
50. Curve Fitting in Excel
51. Curve Fitting for a Hyperbolic Curve
52. LINEST Can Do What TREND Cannot Do
53. Multiple Regression with Excel's LINEST
54. Correlation, Range Names, and INDIRECT
55. Confidence Intervals vs. Prediction Intervals
56. EC50 and IC50 Determination in Excel
57. Confidence and Prediction Limits for EC50 and IC50
58. Testing for Statistical Significance in Excel
59. The Chi-Squared Significance Test
60. ANOVA or Analysis of Variance in Excel
61. Temperature Fluctuations- Results May Vary
62. A Data Table Simulation with Memory
63. Frequency Simulations with Memory
64. Monte Carlo Simulations in Excel
65. Simulation of Binomial Samples from Populations
66. Simulating Genetic Drift in Excel
67. Monte Carlo Simulation of Random Walk in Evolution
68. Monte Carlo Simulation of Mendel's Laws in Excel
69. Monte Carlo Simulation of Natural Selection
70. Monte VCarlo Simulation of Juror Selection in USA
71. Monte Carlo Simulation of DNA Sequencing in Excel